AF378462

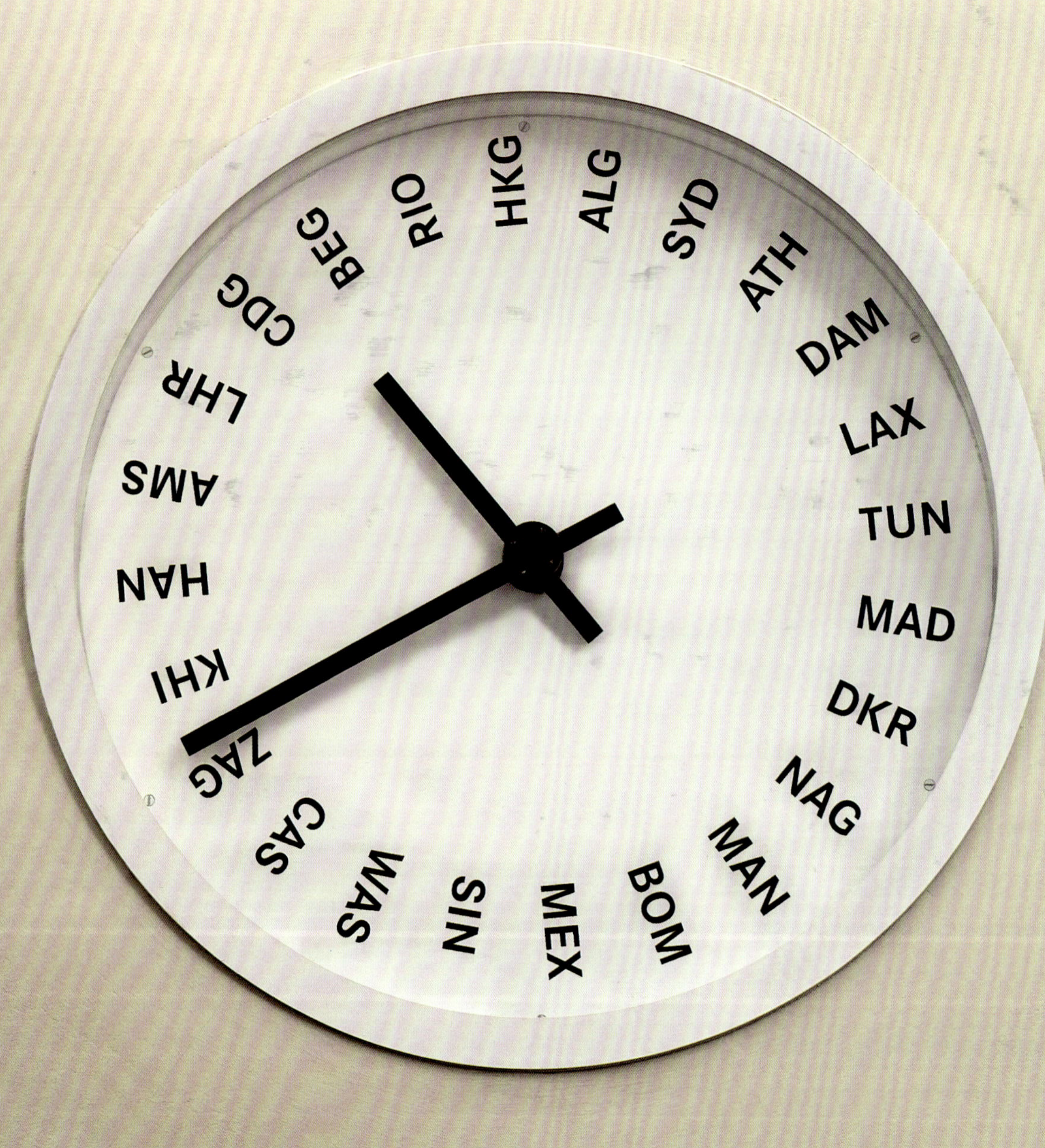

HKG
RIO
BEG
CDG
LHR
AMS
HAN
KHI
ZAG
CAS
WAS
SIN
MEX
BOM
MAN
NAG
DKR
MAD
TUN
LAX
DAM
ATH
SYD
ALG

ECLECTIC

The Julie and Robert Breckman Collections at the Victoria and Albert Museum

Gill Saunders

with contributions from

Annemarie Bilclough   Stephen Calloway   Catherine Flood

Sarah Grant   Robin Hildyard   Liz Miller   Frances Rankine

Margaret Timmers   Tim Travis   Rebecca Wallis

V&A Publishing

First published by V&A Publishing, 2016
Victoria and Albert Museum
South Kensington
London SW7 2RL
www.vandapublishing.com

ISBN: 978 1 85177 888 1

10 9 8 7 6 5 4 3 2 1
2020 2019 2018 2017 2016

A catalogue record for this book is available from
the British Library.

Project manager: Linda Schofield
Designer: Clifford Richards
Copy-editor: Mandy Greenfield
Indexer: Christine Shuttleworth
New V&A photography by Richard Davies and
Paul Robins, V&A Photographic Studio
Origination by DL Imaging Ltd, London
Printed and bound in China

Cover: details of: top left: Sickboy, *Love Supreme*
(see p.83); top right: José Bardasano Baos,
Spanish Civil War poster (see pl.21); centre
left: Staffordshire figure, *The Death of Munrow*
(see p.157); centre right: lapel badge (see
p.137); bottom: Bartolozzi after Albani, *Cupid's
Manufactory* (see pl.1)

Frontispiece and p.1: Clock by Langlands & Bell,
2004, Prints & Drawings Study Room;
RIBA Study Room

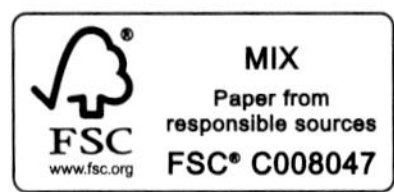

V&A Publishing
Supporting the world's leading
museum of art and design,
the Victoria and Albert
Museum, London

CONTENTS

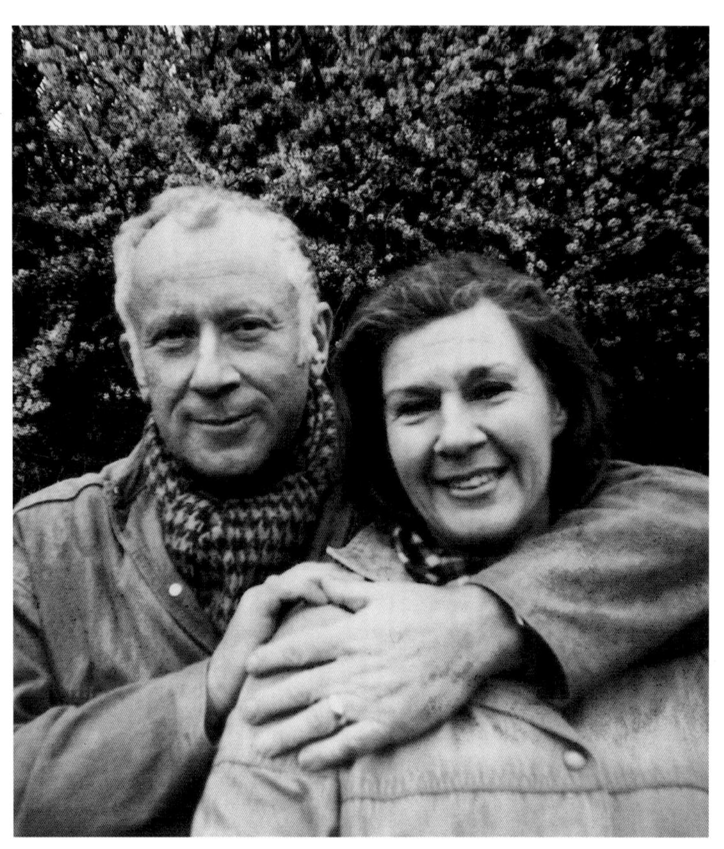

FOREWORD

Trousseaux come in all forms!

When I met Julie in 1977, hers came in the form of a large collection of Staffordshire china and an eclectic selection of paintings. She had been an actress and had cultivated an appreciation of the arts.

For my part, I had worked as a chartered accountant in the theatre and then expanded into general practice, specializing in the arts.

We were a match made in heaven...

Sadly, Julie died from Alzheimer's in 2003. But, during our all-too-brief relationship, we expanded our collection to become a cornucopia, an Aladdin's cave. She continued with her Staffordshire collection, and I found Conta and Boehme tobacco jars and prints and a myriad collection of theatrical memorabilia.

Our first joint purchase was a David Hockney print, purchased in Betty's tea rooms in Harrogate on a day trip. We were allowed to take the print back to London with us, and paid for it over the course of a year. We obviously had honest faces!

As Julie succumbed to Alzheimer's, we decided to leave our collection of artefacts to the Victoria and Albert Museum, which we used to visit on a regular basis.

When Julie died, I set up a fund in her memory, from which the seeds of this book were sown. The first purchase was a sheet of English wallpaper in the Chinese style, *c.*1780–1800 (see p.111). I well remember the first viewing! Two V&A curators, Liz Miller and Sue Lambert, arrived at our house and displayed this marvellous piece of ephemera on the kitchen table. And so started the 'spree' that resulted in more than a thousand purchases, some of which are displayed in this book.

This volume is in memory of dear Julie, 'without whose help...', in theatrical parlance. I miss her a lot. She will never be replaced, and her like will never be seen again.

Robert Breckman, 2016

Introduction

Gill Saunders

The V&A's collections are the product of the efforts and enthusiasms of successive donors, benefactors and curators over the lifetime of the institution, stretching back to the middle of the nineteenth century. Many of the V&A's most important collections – of prints, paintings, sculpture, furniture, ceramics, metalwork, textiles and fashion – were inaugurated, or significantly enhanced, by major gifts and bequests from private collectors. In the field of prints, drawings and paintings, these generous donors are remembered in the names that still attach to their collections: the Sheepshanks Gift, the Dyce and Forster Bequests, the Ionides Bequest, the Jones Bequest, the Seligman Gift, the Schreiber Gift. In each case these collections were shaped by the tastes, knowledge and passions of an individual.

Julie and Robert Breckman were likewise enthusiastic collectors, with particular interests in Staffordshire ceramic figures (see pl.2), and in prints, especially stipple engravings by Francesco Bartolozzi (1727–1815); and when Robert first approached the V&A in May 2000, at a time when Julie had sadly been diagnosed with Alzheimer's disease, it was with the intention of planning a gift or bequest of pieces from their collections especially in honour of Julie. But what has made the Julie and Robert Breckman Collections at the V&A truly exceptional is that they not only donated key pieces from their existing collections, but went on to support the V&A in making many new acquisitions, going far beyond their own established tastes and interests. As a result, the Julie and Robert Breckman Collections at the V&A are defined not by their specificity, but by their diversity. They reflect the institution's wider purposes and priorities; the specialisms of the curators; and, above all, Robert's open-minded

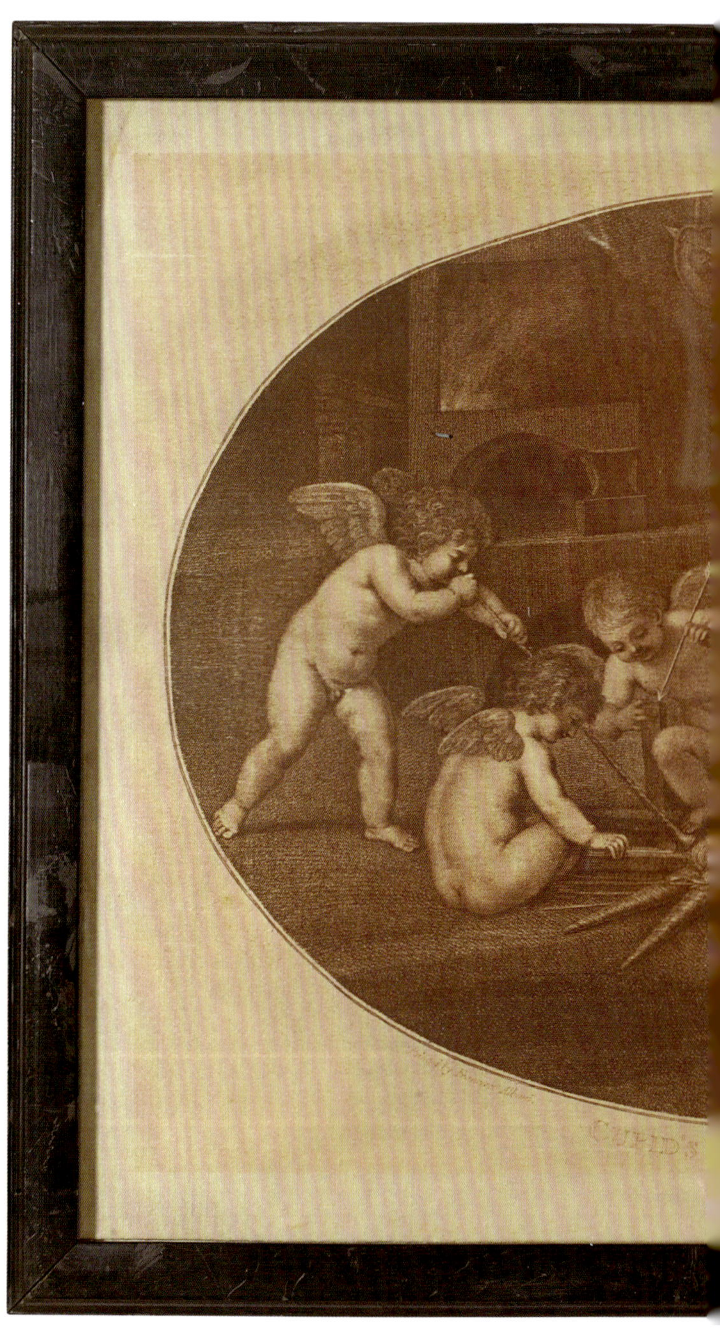

1. *Cupid's Manufactory*, 1800, by Francesco Bartolozzi after Francesco Albani
Stipple engraving on silk
V&A: E.932–2000
Given by Julie and Robert Breckman

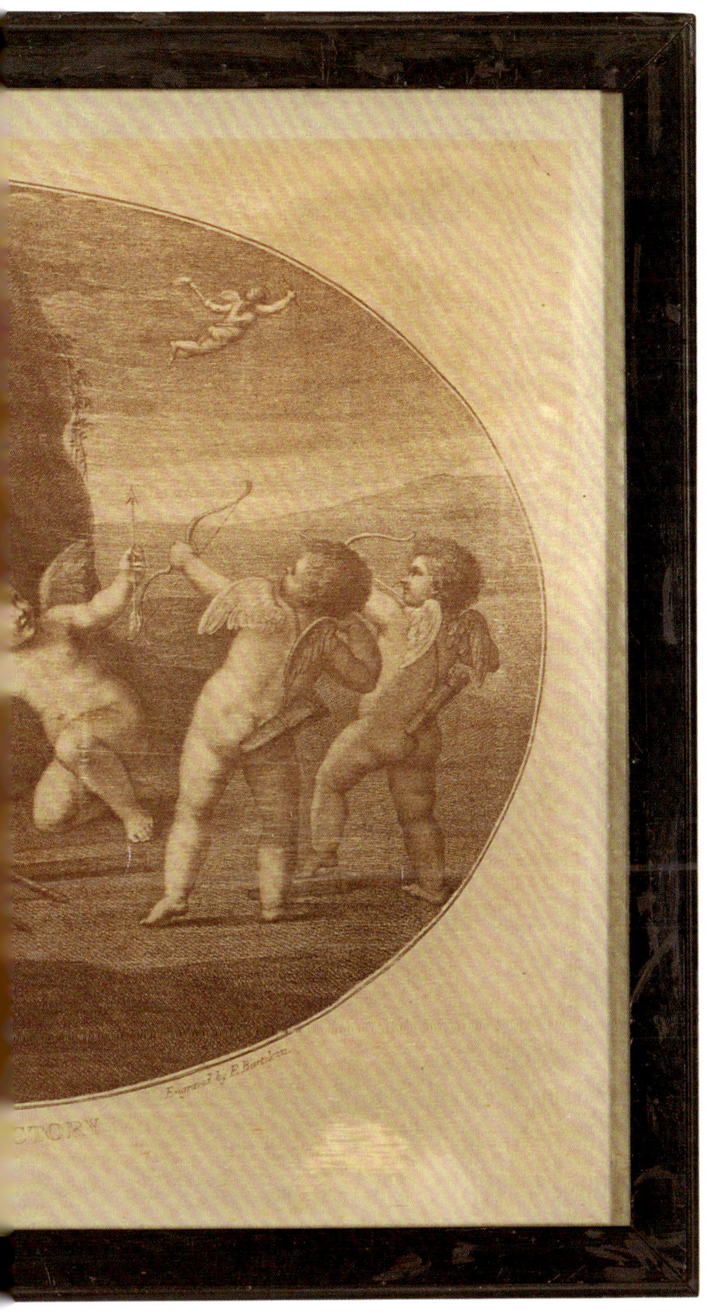

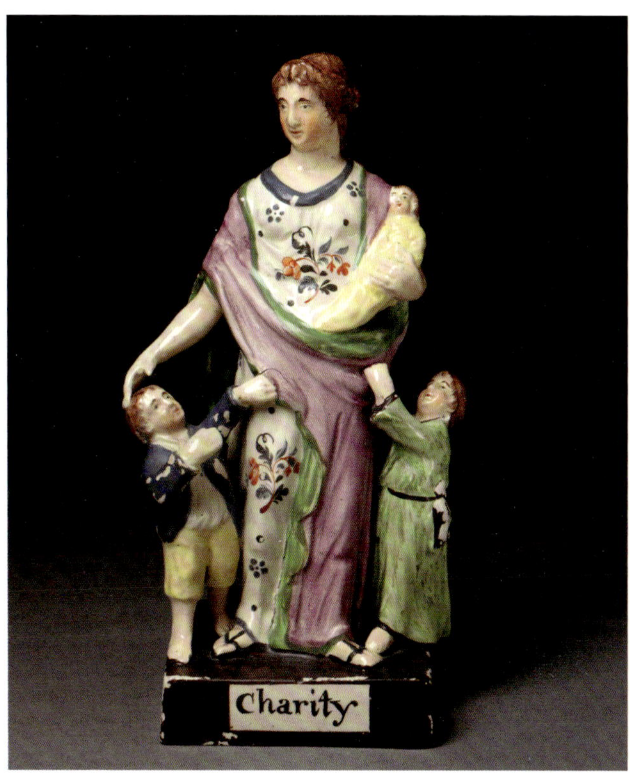

2. Figure group representing *Charity*, c.1795,
Staffordshire
Moulded lead-glazed earthenware
V&A: C.59–2001
Given by Julie and Robert Breckman

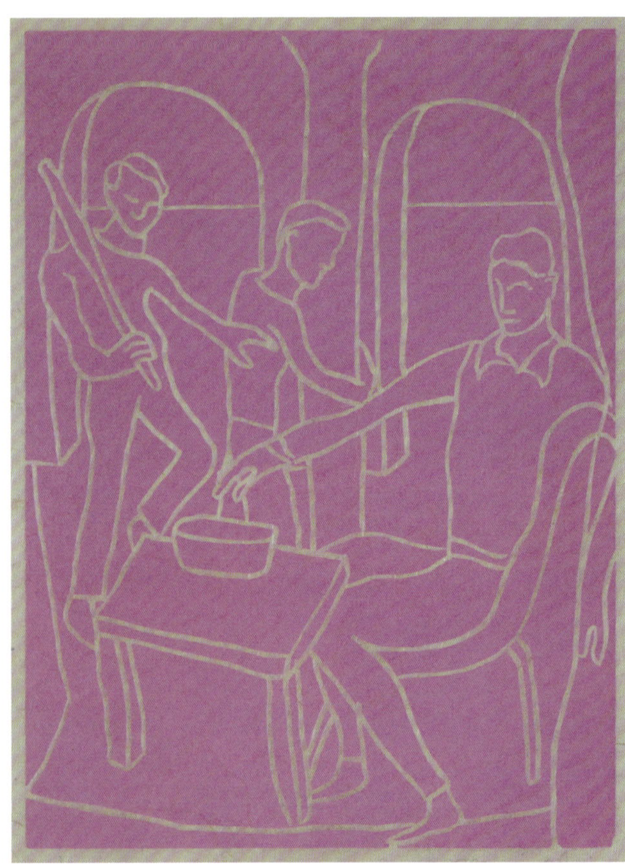

3. *Pontius Pilate* from the portfolio *Stations of the Cross*, 1999,
by Adrian Wiszniewski
Colour woodcut
V&A: E.522:1–2001
Purchased through the Julie and Robert Breckman Print Fund

generosity and his willingness to engage with everything from political posters and street-art prints to challenging conceptual text-pieces and innovative 3D multiples.

The original gifts from the Julie and Robert Breckman Collection included a number of Staffordshire figures and some fine stipple engravings by Bartolozzi, most notably *Cupid's Manufactory* (after Francesco Albani, 1578–1680), printed on silk (pl.1). Following swiftly from the initial gifts, in September 2000 Robert pledged monies to two dedicated funds to support new acquisitions at the V&A – one for Staffordshire, and the other more generally for prints. And so began a rewarding relationship, which has enriched the V&A's collections in many ways. For the print curators, it opened a new chapter in our collecting. No longer were we constrained by the shrinking resources allocated to acquisitions from the Museum's government grant. Instead, supported by the Julie and Robert Breckman Print Fund, we were able to respond promptly to opportunities as they arose, and to collect proactively, pursuing prints of all kinds as they were needed for new galleries and temporary exhibitions, or to fill gaps in otherwise very strong collections.

Our first purchase was exceptional in a number of ways. It was a late eighteenth-century hand-coloured etching, designed for use as wallpaper (see pl.5 and p.111), one of several unused sheets on offer from the print dealer Andrew Edmunds. The vivid, unfaded colours and the unusual design made it highly desirable, and we were delighted when Robert agreed that he would fund its purchase. It has since featured in the *V&A Magazine*, and in Gill Saunders' book *Wallpaper in Interior Decoration* (2002), where it exemplified the English chinoiserie style.

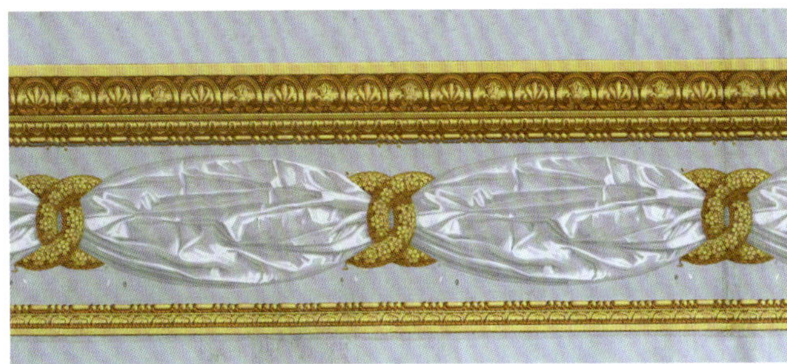

4. Drapery wallpaper border, French, *c.*1820, possibly by Dufour & Cie
Colour print from woodblocks
V&A: E.9–2006
Purchased through the Julie and Robert Breckman Print Fund

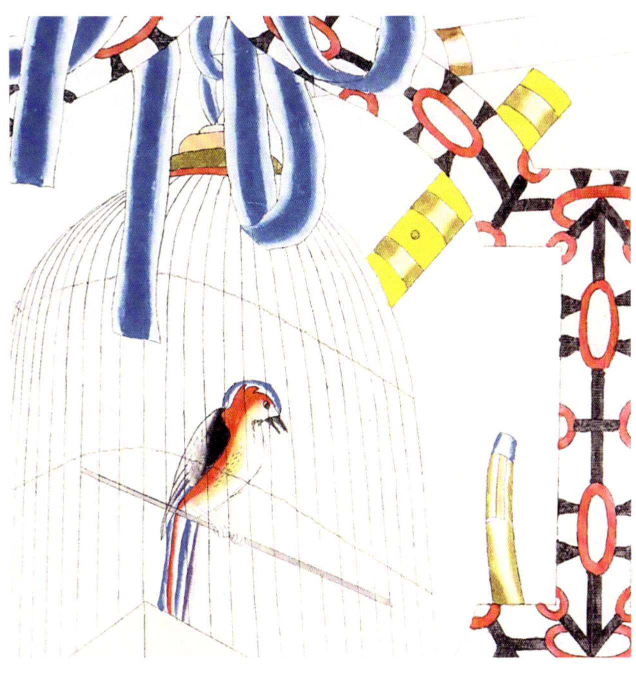

5. Detail from an unused sheet of wallpaper in the chinoiserie style,
English, *c.*1780–1800
Etching, coloured by hand
V&A: E.937–2000
Purchased through the Julie and Robert Breckman Print Fund

It is undoubtedly the finest, and the most intriguing, of such 'single-sheet' papers in the V&A's world-renowned collection of wallpapers. This was the first of several wallpapers to be acquired with the support of the Fund.

Although in due course the Print Fund supported the acquisition of several other wallpapers (pl.4), old and new, the accounts for the first year show in microcosm the extraordinary range of what was to become the 'Breckman Collection'. In addition to the sheet of wallpaper, the Fund enabled us to purchase the beautiful portfolio of colour linocuts by Adrian Wiszniewski (b.1958), *The Stations of the Cross* (pl.3, and see p.69), published in 1999 by Glasgow Print Studio; and supported the purchase of the so-called 'Ionides Album' (pl.6), an extraordinary collection of prints and drawings amassed by Alexander Constantine Ionides (1810–90), whose earlier bequest had so enriched the V&A's holdings of paintings, prints and drawings.

Acquisitions continued apace. We quickly established an effective modus operandi. Individual curators identified specific pieces they would like to acquire and, as soon as there

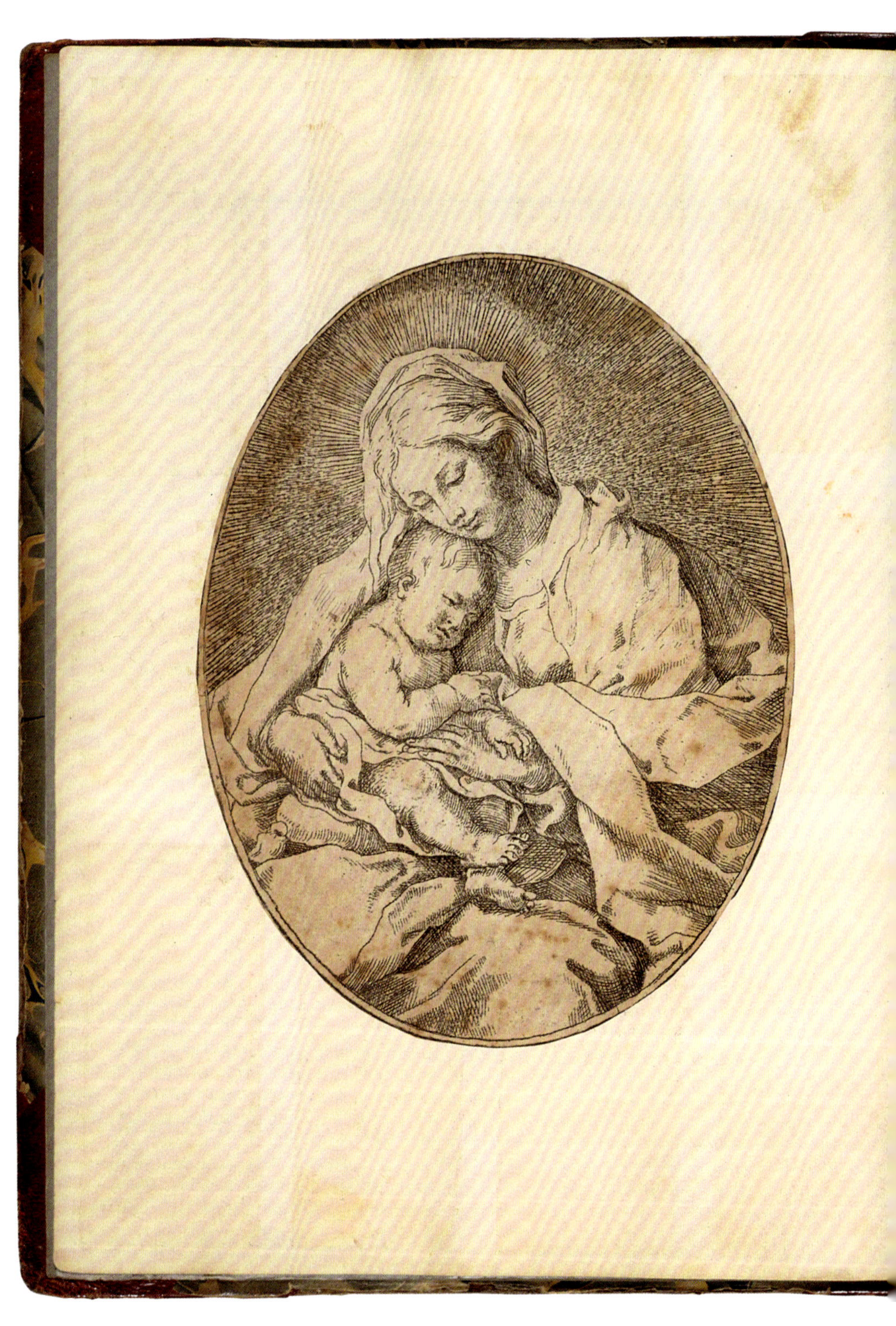

6. Album of prints and drawings compiled by
Alexander Constantine Ionides (1810–90)
V&A: E.1394:1 to 94–2001
Purchased with the assistance of The Art Fund, the Friends of the V&A,
the Julie and Robert Breckman Print Fund, and the Marks Trust

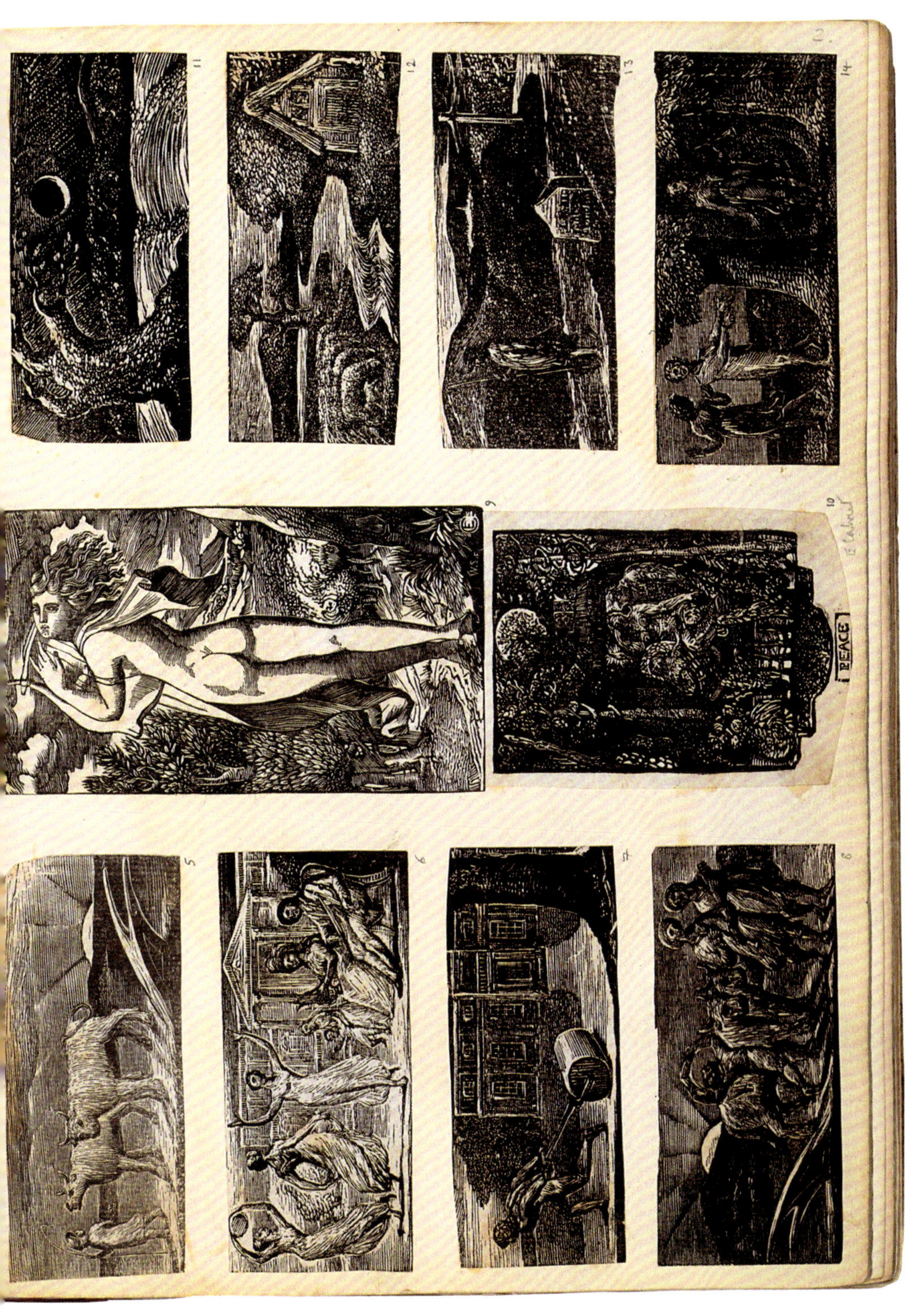

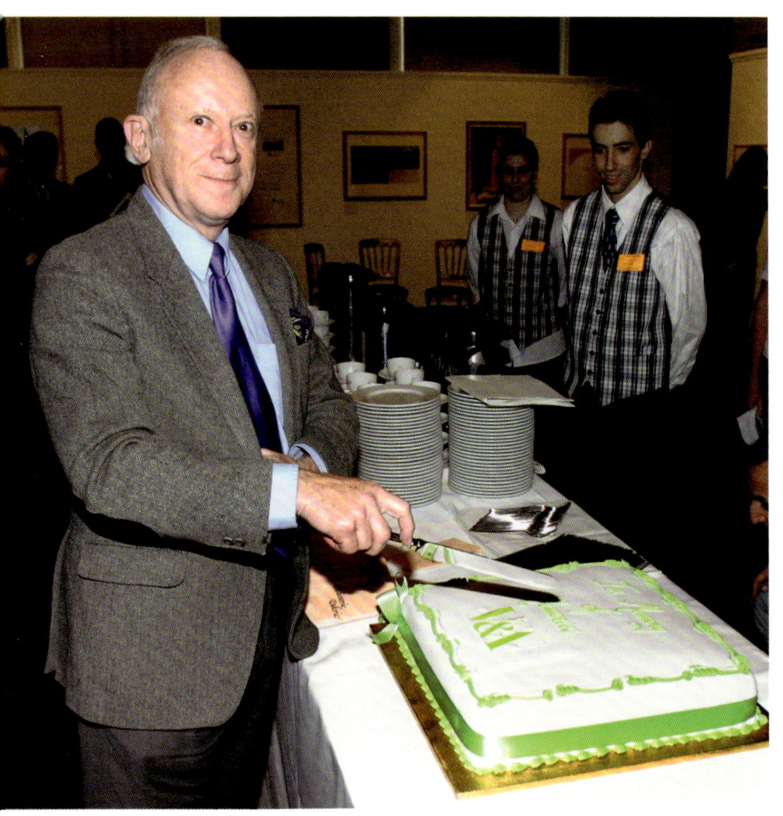

7. Robert Breckman cutting the cake at the tea party on
10 November 2003, after viewing an exhibition of works acquired
through the Julie and Robert Breckman Print Fund

were several pending, we would invite Robert to come and take a look. We would each take it in turns to present, arguing the case for 'our' objects, while Robert would ask questions and, most importantly, establish that we had used the opportunity to negotiate the best possible price from the vendor! Robert was not always wholly convinced by our arguments, but he respected our judgements and valued our expertise, and only rarely did he refuse his support. He baulked at Banksy (b.1974), for example, but by and large he was happy to say yes, and happier still to celebrate over tea and cake afterwards. Indeed, his annual tea party (pl.7) – with an extravagant iced cake supplied by Patisserie Valerie – became the defining event of these years. At regular intervals the acquisitions from the past year or so would be laid out in the Prints & Drawings Study Room, for viewing by a specially invited audience (pl.8) – which included Robert's family, friends and colleagues, the V&A Director and Trustees and fellow curators, as well as artists and gallerists.

Meanwhile, the curators in the Ceramics collection were able to buy long-desired Staffordshire pieces as they came onto the market. The magnificent group entitled *Polito's Royal Menagerie* (see p.159) was acquired in 2003, and in 2007 it was joined by another fine piece with a special resonance in the V&A: *The Death of Munrow* (see p.157). This was inspired by – perhaps even modelled on – the marvellous automaton/ mechanical organ known as *Tippoo's Tiger* (see p.156), made for the Indian ruler Tipu Sultan, and which has been in the V&A since the nineteenth century. Knowing how important this particular piece of Staffordshire was for the Museum, Robert chose to donate it in memory of Julie, who had died in 2003 after a long and very brave struggle with Alzheimer's disease.

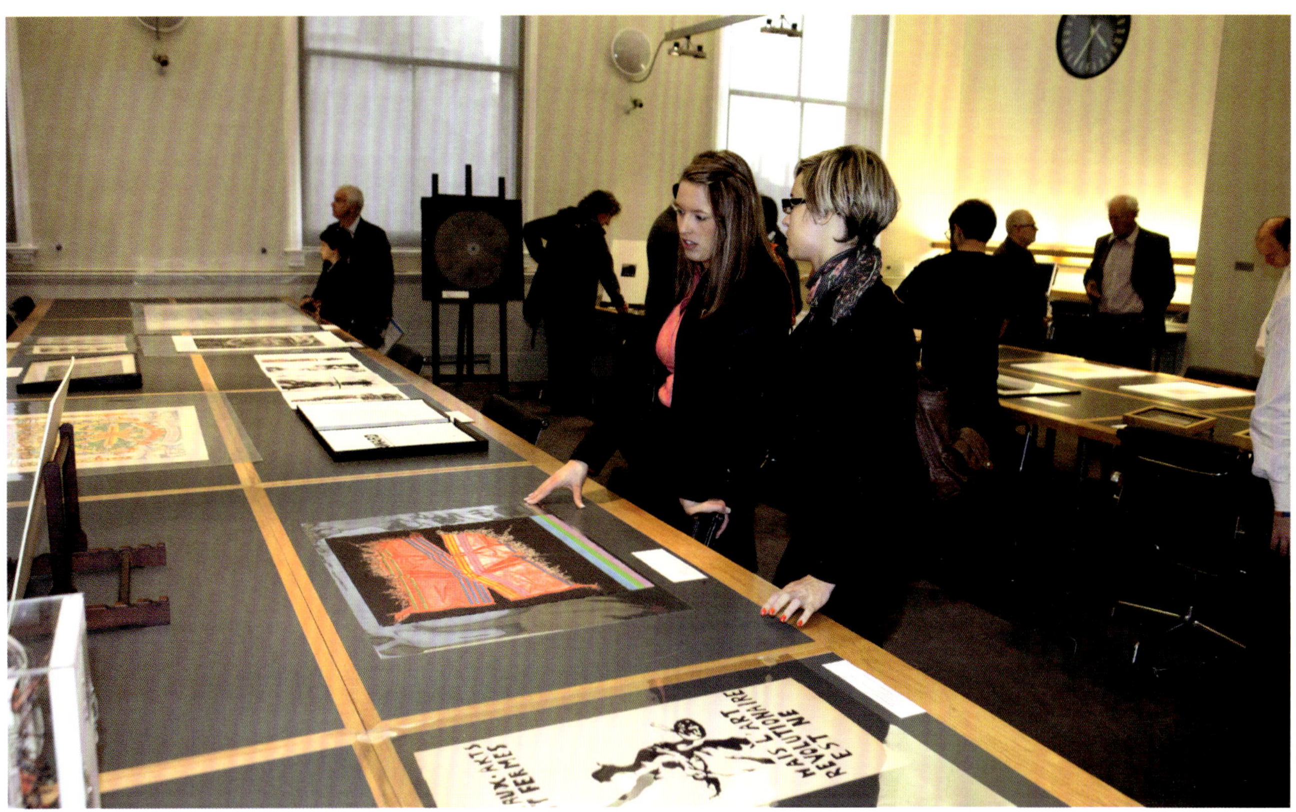

8. Guests in the Prints & Drawings Study Room looking at a selection of prints acquired through the Julie and Robert Breckman Print Fund, on the occasion of the installation of a new commission by Liz Collini, 24 October 2011

The Julie and Robert Breckman Collections are indeed eclectic; they encompass not only the Staffordshire figures and other ceramic pieces, such as spill jars and Conta and Boehme tobacco jars, but everything from topographical prints, fashion plates, wallpapers and caricatures, to posters (pl.9), packaging (pl.10) and playing cards, as well as fine-art prints by a number of leading contemporary artists from around the world. Nevertheless, all were chosen purposefully and with reference to the V&A's collecting policy and priorities and, as such, they reflect particular aims and ambitions of the Museum over the first decade of the new millennium.

The V&A's collecting policy is regularly reviewed and revised, but its basic principles are still largely shaped by the Museum's founding objectives: to demonstrate the best in design

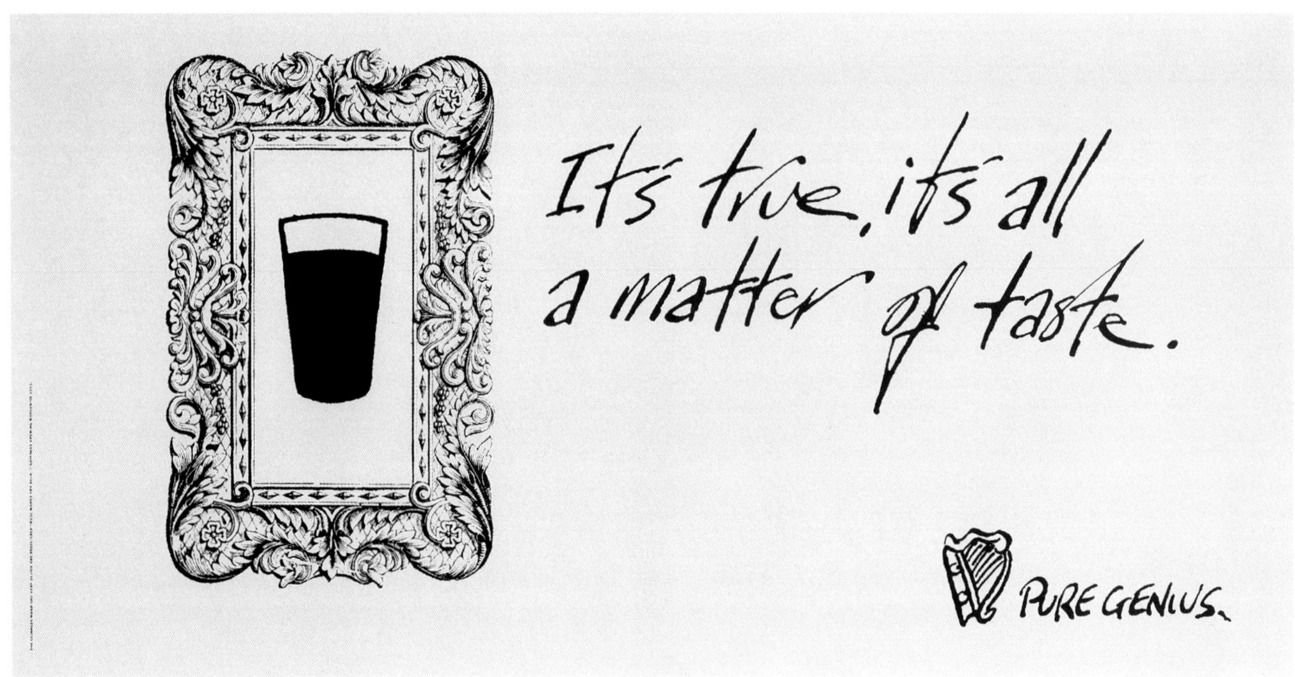

9. Poster advertising Guinness, c.1992
Offset lithograph
V&A: E.972–2002
Purchased through the Julie and Robert Breckman Print Fund

and manufacture, to explain processes and techniques, and to showcase the achievements of artistic and technical innovation. The V&A is also the only national museum in the UK to collect across the whole spectrum of 'print', from ephemera to fine art, and it has a particular interest in work that extends the definition of the term 'print'. From the beginning, our collecting policy has always placed a special emphasis on making, and on new technologies and media, as well as innovative applications of traditional media – a tradition that we are proud to continue.

Thanks to the V&A's mix of fine and applied art, we can show the relationships between one print medium and another, between commercial art and fine art, between the handmade and the digital, and so on. We also continue to build on the collection's established strengths and specialisms, focusing on particular themes and areas of practice, such as issues around cultural and personal identity and self-presentation, work that engages with political issues, with social life and with the arts of living. The V&A is also uniquely able to represent work in which the fine and applied arts intersect – wallpaper, for example, which in recent years has often been designed by artists for installation projects rather than for domestic decoration. We also collect examples of print applied to 3D formats such as dress, furnishings (pl.11) and even sculpture.

*

From the beginning, Robert was keen that the works acquired through the Staffordshire and the Print Funds should go on public display whenever possible (pl.12). As a consequence, the Breckman Funds have supplied key exhibits for new galleries and for temporary displays and exhibitions. The Staffordshire pieces were promptly

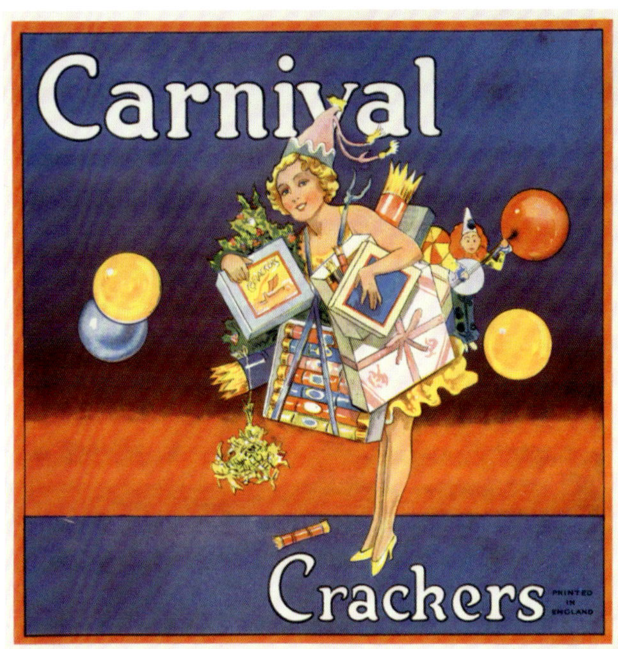

10. Label for a box of Christmas crackers, c.1920–30, Batger's & Co.
Lithograph
V&A: E.1042–2003
Purchased through the Julie and Robert Breckman Print Fund

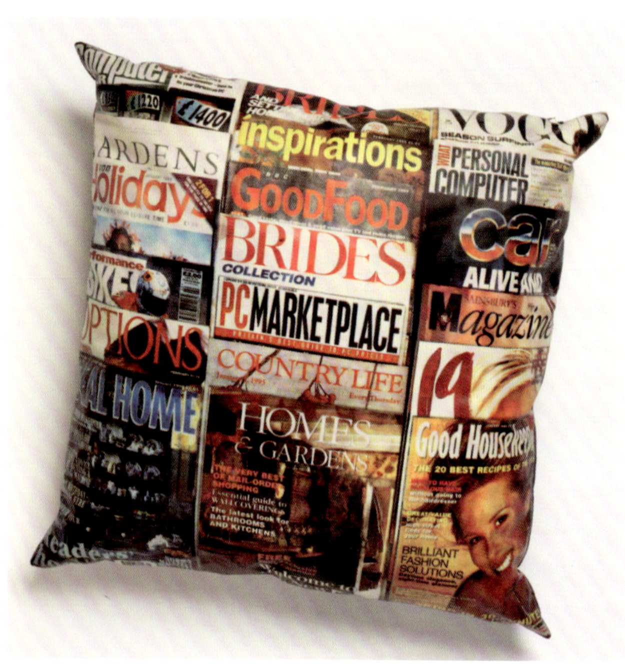

11. Cushion cover by Bill Woodrow, 1994, produced for the exhibition
Portable Fabric Shelters, London Printworks Trust
Screen print
V&A: E.22-2006
Purchased through the Julie and Robert Breckman Print Fund

installed in the Ceramics Galleries as they were acquired, and the most important works now have a prominent place in the suite of new galleries devoted to ceramics, which opened in 2009/10.

We marked the first three years of the Print Fund in 2003 with a display that showcased the highlights of our collecting and emphasized the marvellous diversity of the acquisitions (pl.13). The display took place in the prints and drawings gallery in the Henry Cole Wing, a space that was soon to be remodelled to become part of the Sackler Education Centre. Prompted by the loss of this display space, Robert quickly appreciated the importance of a dedicated space to show prints and drawings, and offered to fund a new gallery. The Julie and Robert Breckman Prints & Drawings Gallery was opened by HRH Princess Alexandra on 2 March 2005. The inaugural display, *The Spirit of Place: Landscape in British Printmaking*, curated by Stephen Calloway, spanned 100 years of British printmaking and included works by Paul Drury (1903–87), Lucian Freud (1922–2011), Julian Opie (b.1958) and Anya Gallaccio (b.1963), all recent acquisitions made possible by the Print Fund. The gallery itself was designed by Dinah Casson of Casson Mann, and is distinguished by the elegant fixtures that hold the labels for the exhibits, leaving the walls free of visual clutter. Dinah also designed a bench for the gallery, which was made by Luke Hughes and Company. This carries the dedication 'In Memory of Memories', with a motif inspired by the curly tail of Julie and Robert's much-loved pug dog, Brian.

Since that first event we have curated a succession of themed displays for the Julie and Robert Breckman Prints & Drawings Gallery (often running into the adjoining space, which is part of the suite of painting galleries). We frequently target our collecting to the theme

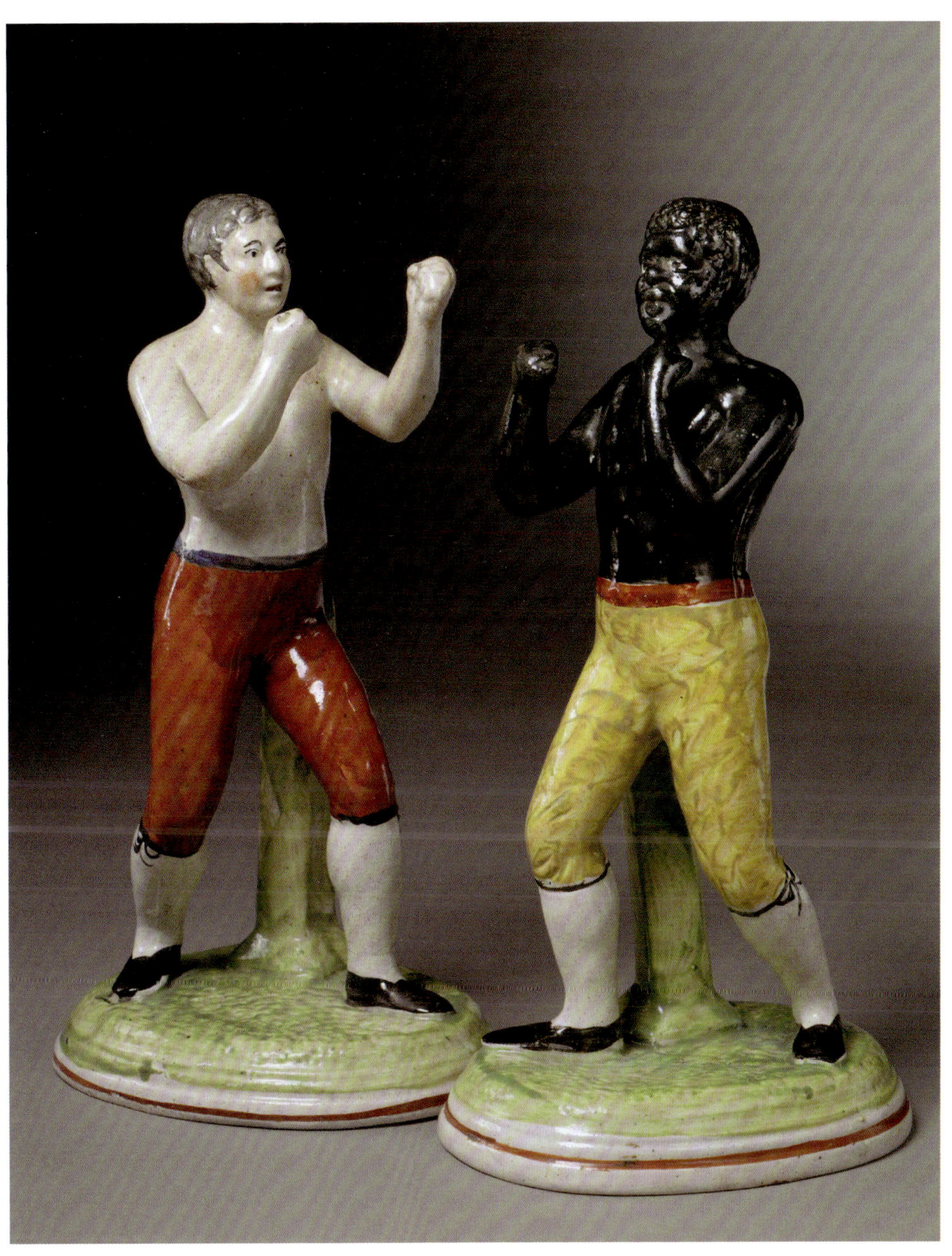

12. Figures of the boxers Tom Cribb and Tom Molineaux, c.1815,
Staffordshire
Moulded lead-glazed earthenware painted in enamel colours
V&A: C.130:1–2003 and C.130:2–2003
Purchased through the Julie and Robert Breckman Staffordshire Fund

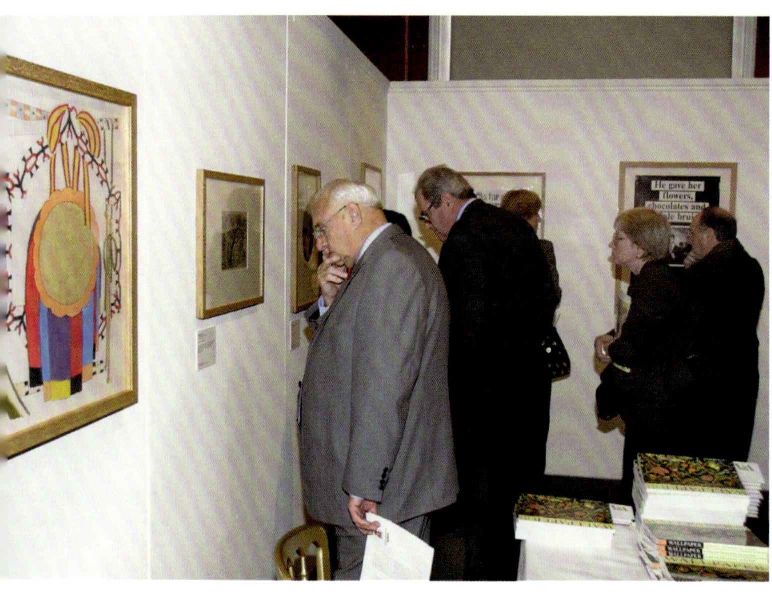

13. Guests at the tea party on 10 November 2003, viewing an exhibition of works acquired through the Julie and Robert Breckman Print Fund

of a planned temporary display, and it is here that Robert's support has been invaluable. For example, in 2006 *Prints Now* – an original survey show, curated by Rosie Miles and Gill Saunders – looked at the many innovative applications and new technologies in contemporary fine-art printmaking, and more than half of the exhibits were new or recent works that had been purchased through the Julie and Robert Breckman Print Fund. Digital prints, prints on metal and Perspex, stitched and folded and woven prints, prints in the form of coat-linings and umbrellas – all these featured alongside such equally diverse pieces as prints by Native American (pl.14) and Australian Aboriginal artists, Cornelia Parker's meteor-scorched atlas, Rachel Whiteread's 3D 'printed' multiple *Secondhand* and Julian Opie's striking lenticular 'striptease', *Sara Gets Undressed*. Robert also underwrote the production costs of the accompanying book. Both the show and the book were well received, with one reviewer writing, 'This handsome tome offers a fascinating take on today's print scene… its content reflects the eclecticism and open-minded erudition of the curators…this is a truly invaluable resource for collectors and students of the new.'[1]

Also acquired for *Prints Now* was Marilène Oliver's extraordinary *Self-Portrait*, which takes the form of screen-printed sheets of Perspex assembled to form a ghostly sculptural figure, which seems to materialize and then dissolve, depending on the angle from which it is viewed. Printed with bronze ink and protected by a Perspex cover, the piece is now on permanent display in the Prints & Drawings Study Room, where it never fails to beguile and intrigue new visitors.

Breckman Fund acquisitions also featured strongly in *Mapping the Imagination* (2008–9),

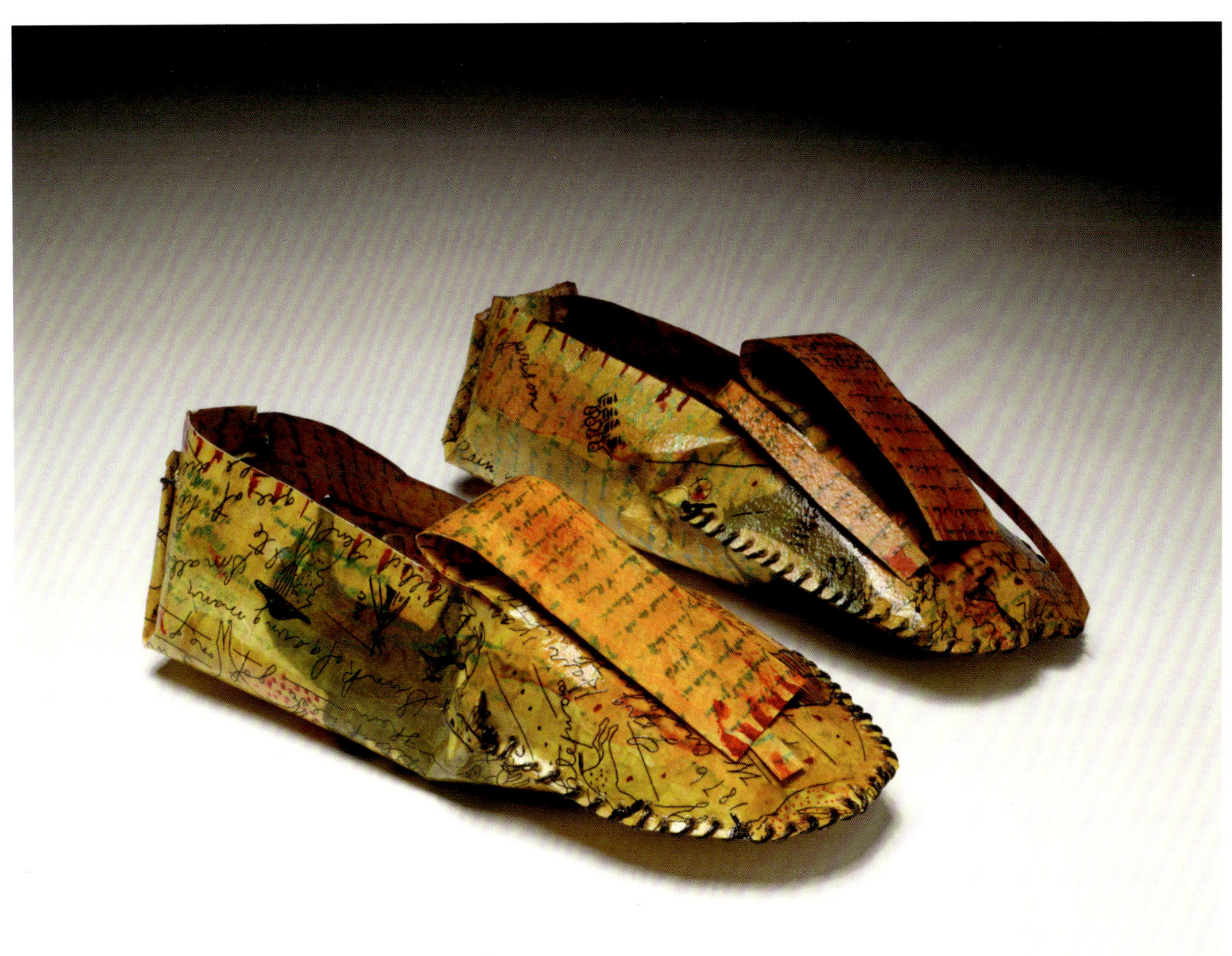

14. *Untitled*, pair of miniature paper moccasins, *c*.2000, by Lynne Allen.
Etching on handmade paper, cut and stitched with cotton thread and
varnished with shellac
V&A: E.3584:1 to 2–2004
Purchased through the Julie and Robert Breckman Print Fund

a display that addressed the graphic and
conceptual iconography of the map, as explored
by artists and designers as well as cartographers.
Star of the show was the pair of screen prints
Frozen Sky (Day) and *Frozen Sky (Night)* by
Langlands & Bell (Ben Langlands, b.1955, and
Nikki Bell, b.1959), beautiful black-and-white
images that 'map' the world by showing only
the major air routes as skeins of lines and dots
that evoke maps of the constellations (see p.79).
In *Druksland Physical and Social* (see p.61),
Israeli-born conceptual artist Michael Druks
(b.1940) used the visual vocabulary of mapping
to engage with his own personal and political
circumstances. *Archipelago II*, made by Russian
émigré Sergei Tsvetkov (b.1958) (pl.15) using
irregularly shaped geometric etched plates,
deeply bitten, has the appearance of an antique
map, with eroded coastlines, a mysterious
territory lacking the usual signs of settlement and
situation. As in the etching *Birth of a Thought*,
2007, by Susan Aldworth (b.1955) (pl.16), which
we bought especially for the show, every work on
view was characterized by multiple meanings, a
subtle allusiveness that connected and amplified
the idea of the map as metaphor.

More recently the display *In Black and White:
Prints from Africa and the Diaspora* (2014–15)
showcased major acquisitions of work by artists
from Africa, the USA, the UK and the Caribbean.
This was an important display for the V&A,
conceived as part of our efforts to raise the profile
of the Museum's rich and varied holdings of art
and design from Africa and the diaspora, and
designed to engage black audiences as part
of a larger programme in partnership with the
Black Cultural Archives. Established names such
as Willie Cole (b.1955), Faith Ringgold (b.1930),
Frank Bowling (b.1936) and Chris Ofili (b.1968)
(pl.17) were represented by important works

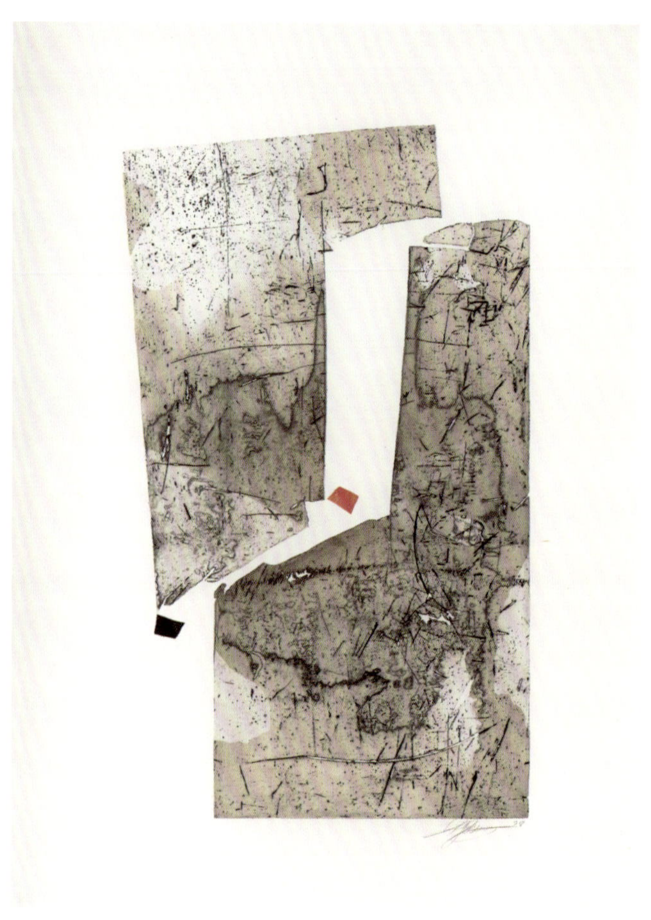

15. *Archipelago II*, 1998, by Sergei Tsvetkov
Open-bite etching from two irregular-shaped plates
V&A: E.3583–2004
Purchased through the Julie and Robert Breckman Print Fund

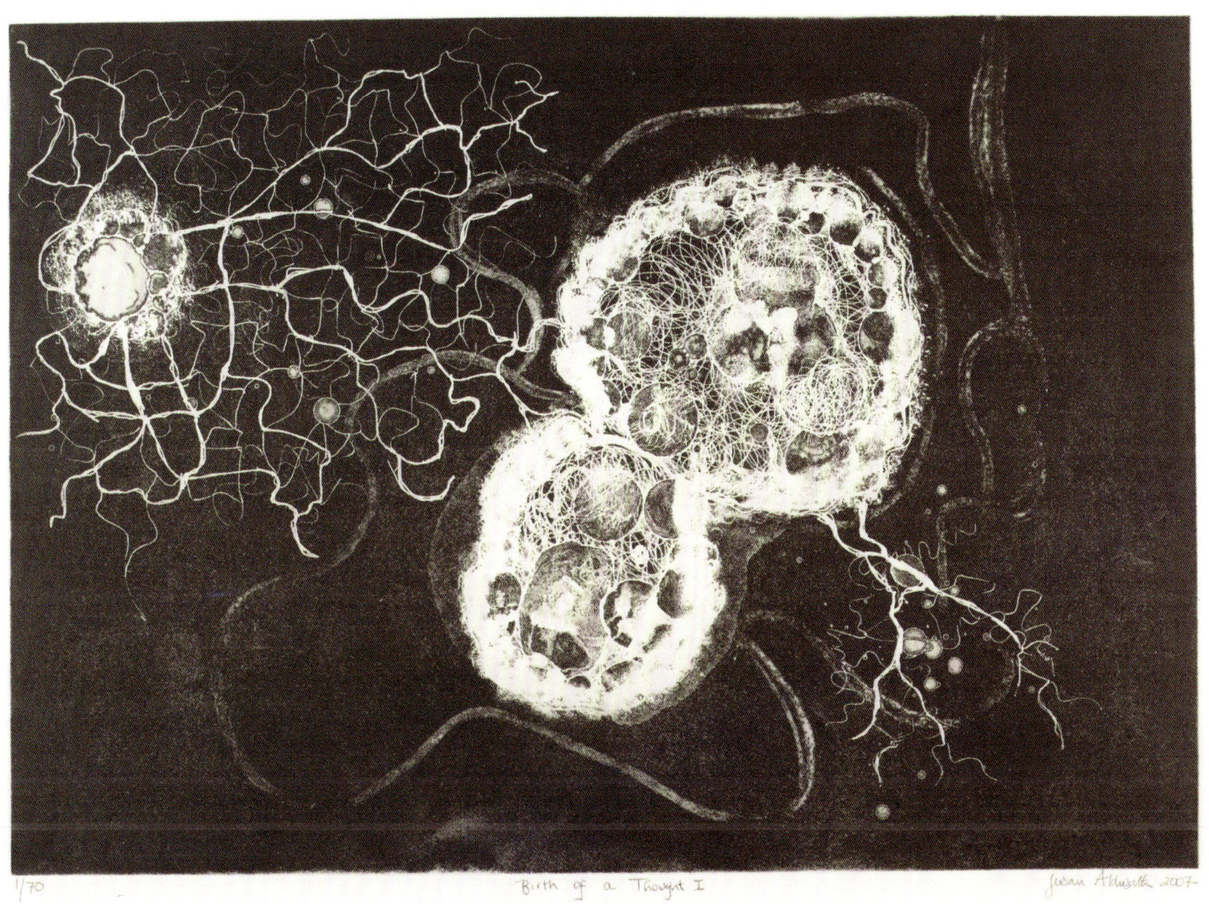

16. *Birth of a Thought 1*, 2007, by Susan Aldworth
Etching
V&A: E.2547–2007
Purchased through the Julie and Robert Breckman Print Fund

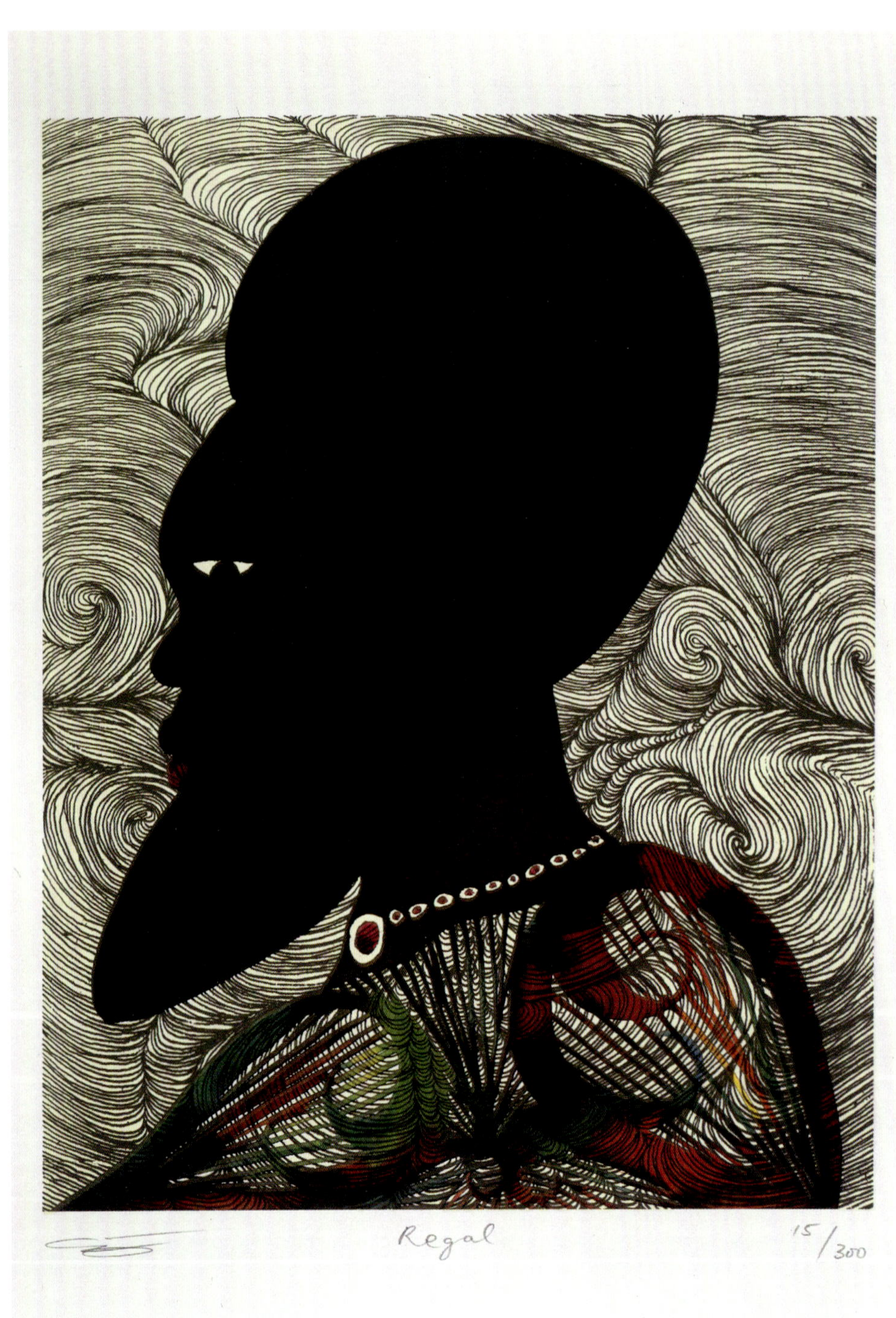

17. *Regal*, 2000, by Chris Ofili
Lithographic print in four colours on a silkscreened
glow-in-the-dark background
V&A: E.1570–2001
Purchased through the Julie and Robert Breckman Print Fund

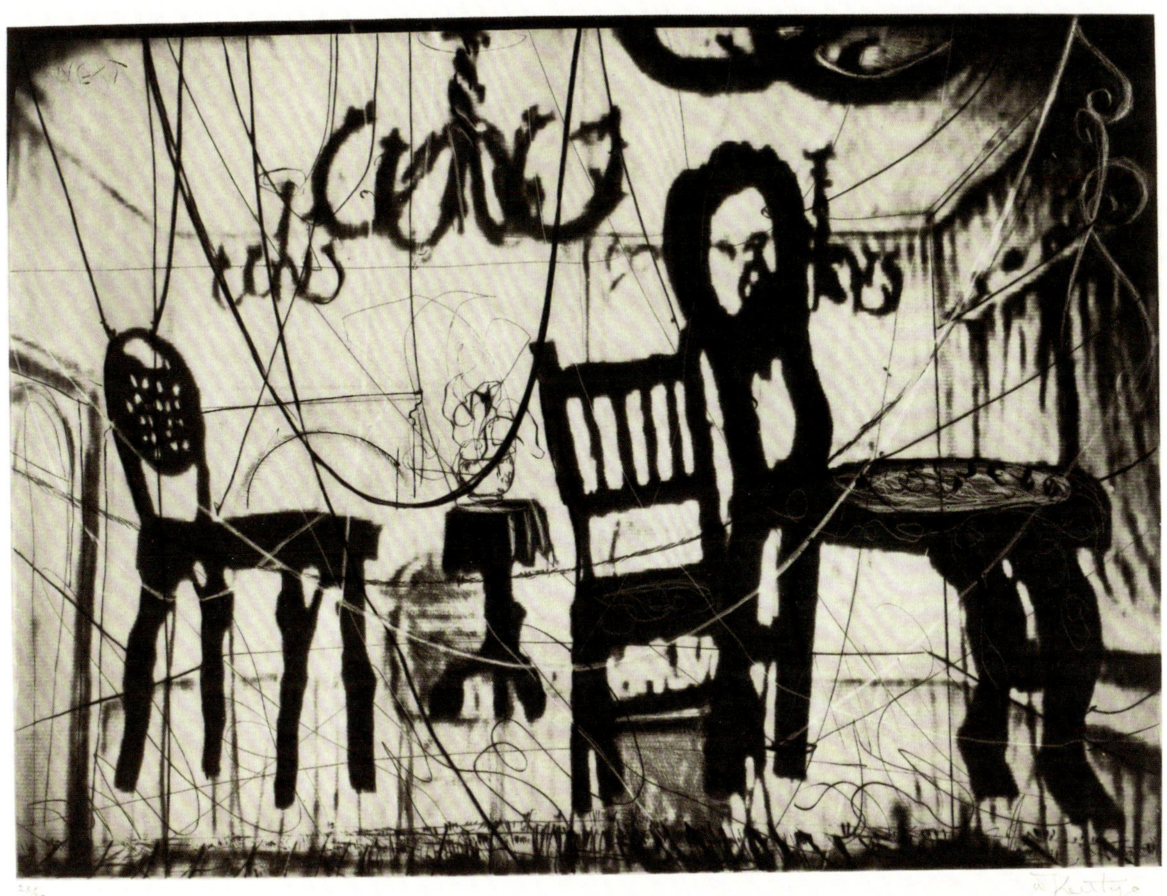

18. *Zeno Writing*, 2002, by William Kentridge
Photogravure, etching and drypoint
V&A: E.133–2005
Purchased through the Julie and Robert Breckman Print Fund

that engaged with a social, cultural and artistic heritage rooted in Africa. We also showed a compelling complex print by Cuban-born artist Maria Magdalena Campos-Pons (b.1959) (see p.67), addressing issues of history and memory and the experience of migration and exile. All were Breckman Fund acquisitions, as was the characteristically oblique but evocative print *Zeno Writing*, 2002, by South African William Kentridge (b.1955) (pl.18), thus far the only piece we have by this highly regarded artist.

The following show, *Facing History: Contemporary Portraiture* (2015–16) (pl.19), also had Breckman Fund acquisitions among its key exhibits. The display presented works by contemporary artists and photographers who have taken historical modes of portraiture as their inspiration. Portraiture is a strong and significant strand of the V&A's collections – and of the print collections

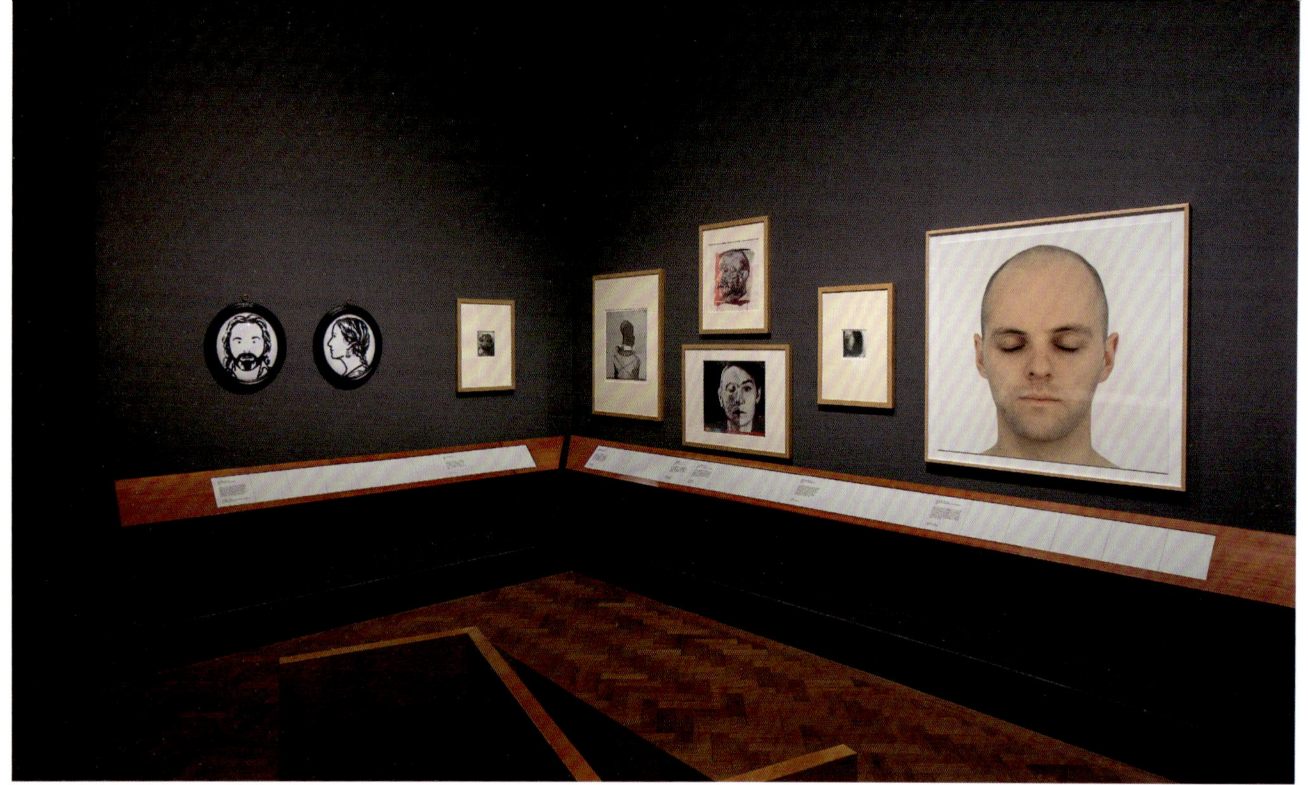

19. Installation view of the display *Facing History: Contemporary Portraiture*, 2015–16, in the Julie and Robert Breckman Prints & Drawings Gallery, with bench in the foreground, and *Luc and Ludivine Get Married, No. 7*, 2007, by Julian Opie, on the far wall

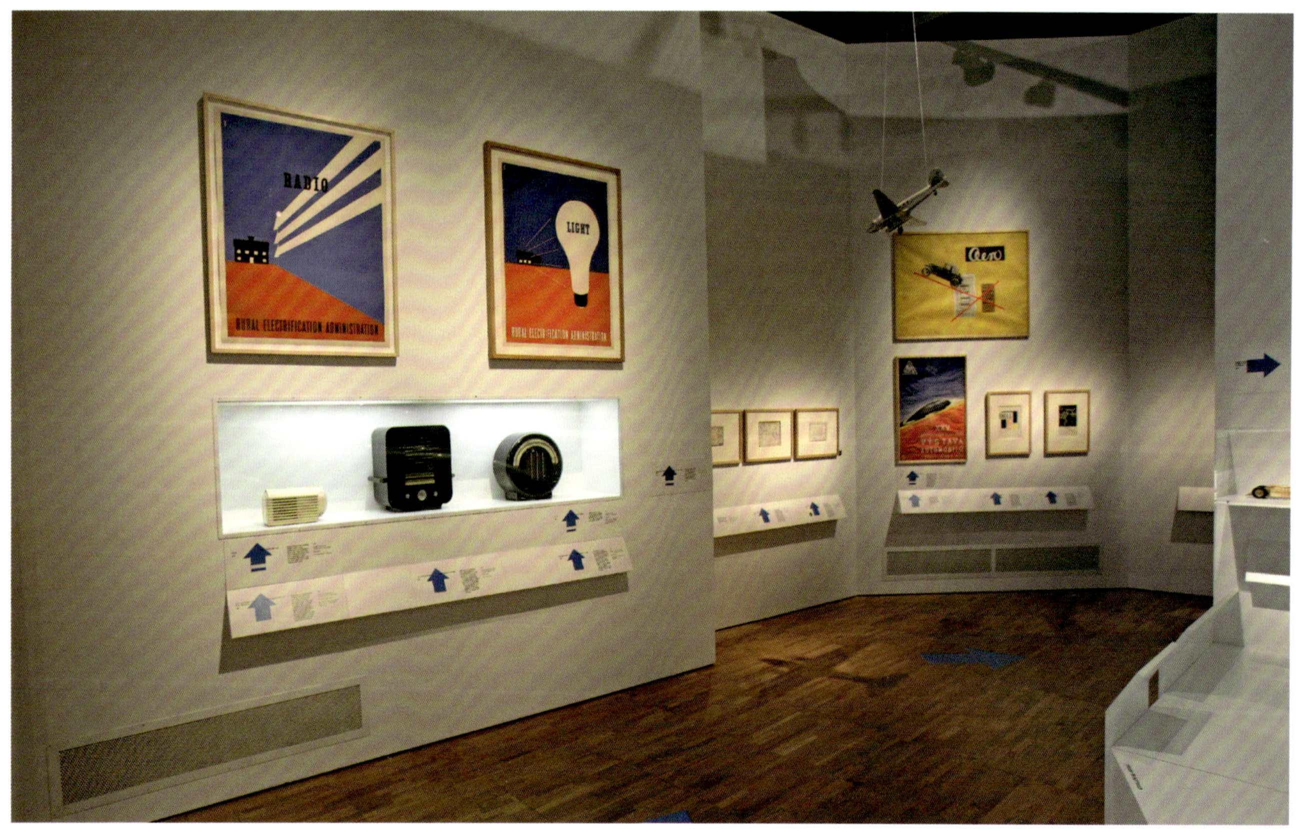

20. Installation view of the exhibition *Modernism: Designing a new world 1914–1939*, 2006, showing posters by Lester Beall

in particular, thanks to the 1958 Seligman Gift of 5,000 engraved portraits. This has been reflected in several of the prints we have acquired through the Print Fund – among them the charming pair of 'wedding portraits' by Julian Opie, *Luc and Ludivine Get Married, No. 7* (see pl.19), which draws on the tradition of silhouettes and keepsake miniatures, and the characteristically faux-naïve renderings of himself and his wife by Grayson Perry (b.1960) (see p.87), in the style of American folk-art paintings.

But fine-art printmaking is by no means the only area in which the Breckman Fund has enabled us to build and expand our collections. The V&A holds the National Collection of Posters, and some of the finest Print Fund purchases have been advertising posters and political graphics, ranging from masterpieces of Modernist graphic design, such as Willi Baumeister's *Die Wohnung* (see p.123), 1927, Ernst Mumenthaler's *Typenmöbel* (see p.125), 1929, and Lester Beall's *Light* (see p.127), 1937 – acquired for the V&A's *Modernism* exhibition in 2006 (pl.20) – to posters issued by the Communist Party during the Spanish Civil War (pl.21 and see p.129), and a rare and important screen-printed poster created by the Atelier Populaire (see p.135) as part of the student protests in Paris in 1968. Contemporary protest is represented by the blood-spattered *NO* of David Gentleman (b.1930) (see p.141), the emphatic logo of the 'Stop the War Coalition', which organized the marches against Britain's involvement in the Iraq war. This and the Atelier Populaire poster featured in *A World to Win: Posters of protest and revolution*, a popular V&A display curated by Catherine Flood, which later toured to several venues in the UK and Ireland.

The acquisitions of posters and popular graphics were complemented by purchases of printed

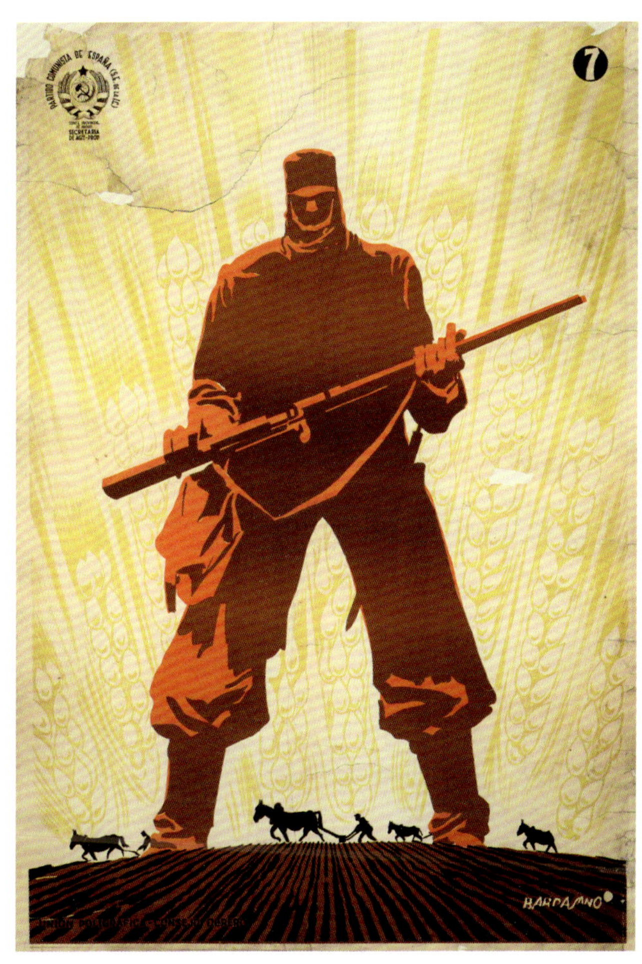

21. Propaganda poster, 1937, designed by José Bardasano Baos and issued by Partido Communista de España during the Spanish Civil War
Lithograph
V&A: E.360–2003
Purchased through the Julie and Robert Breckman Print Fund

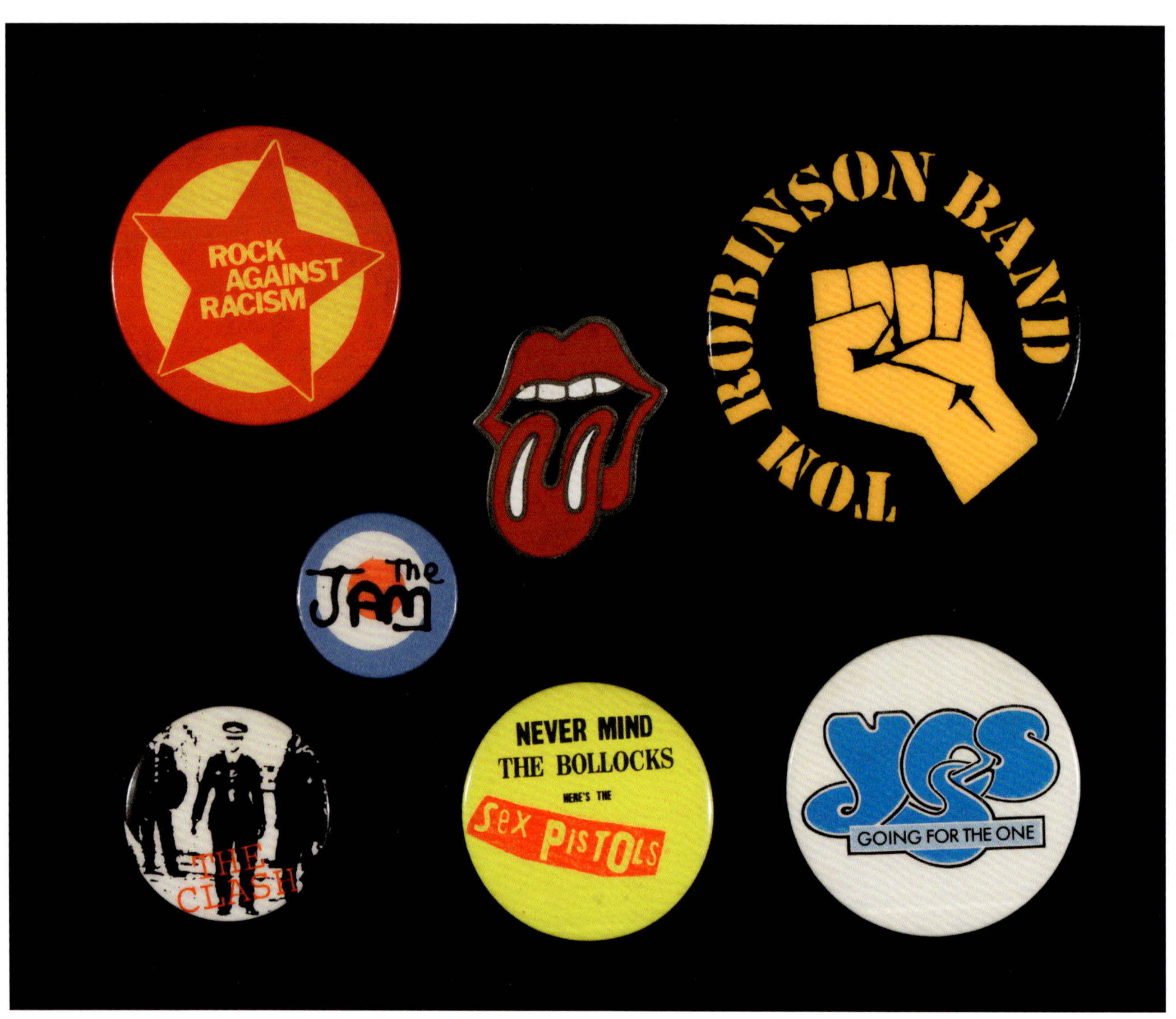

22. A selection of badges, from a collection of 482, 1960s–80s
V&A: E.300-782–2002
Purchased through the Julie and Robert Breckman Print Fund

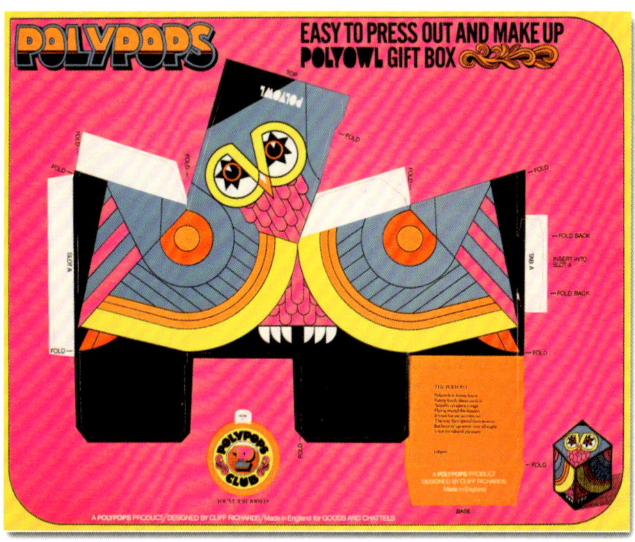

23. *The Polyowl, c.*1968, gift box from the 'Polypops' series
designed by Clifford Richards
Litho-printed on card, varnished and die-cut
V&A: E.3677:1 to 3–2004
Purchased through the Julie and Robert Breckman Print Fund

ephemera of all kinds, notably a wonderful collection of nearly 500 lapel badges (pl.22) amassed by Barry Miles (b.1943), a key figure in the underground music and publishing scenes in London in the 1960s. The badges reflect his engagement with music, and with political activism – from CND to the campaign to free Nelson Mandela. They are a vivid record of their times and complement our holdings of music graphics and political posters and ephemera.

We have also collected graphic design in other formats. For example, we acquired a fine selection of the work of Clifford Richards (b.1934), who designed and produced hugely popular printed-paper products adorned with bold, brightly coloured illustrations. These included gift boxes, the 'Slottizoo' range of slot-together cardboard animals and the 'Polypops' products (pl.23) (made for Paperchase) – flat-packed card products that people could transform into three-dimensional objects at home. Richards' work featured, alongside posters, Pop Art prints and many of the badges, in a V&A display entitled *Sixties Graphics* (2006), a celebration of the explosion of innovative graphic design in the 1960s.

Commercial printed ephemera from earlier periods is represented by a rich diversity of material, ranging from a French placard, issued in 1793, advertising Revolutionary playing cards, to a fine metalwork pattern book with engraved designs for fire grates, stoves, balconies and fencing (pl.24 and see p.117), published in 1811 by the London firm Skidmore & Co. Equally rich as a source of design history is a volume of hand-coloured fashion plates from the Italian fashion periodicals *La Novita* and *Margherita* (pl.25 and see p.121), published in the 1880s. Such acquisitions demonstrate the importance

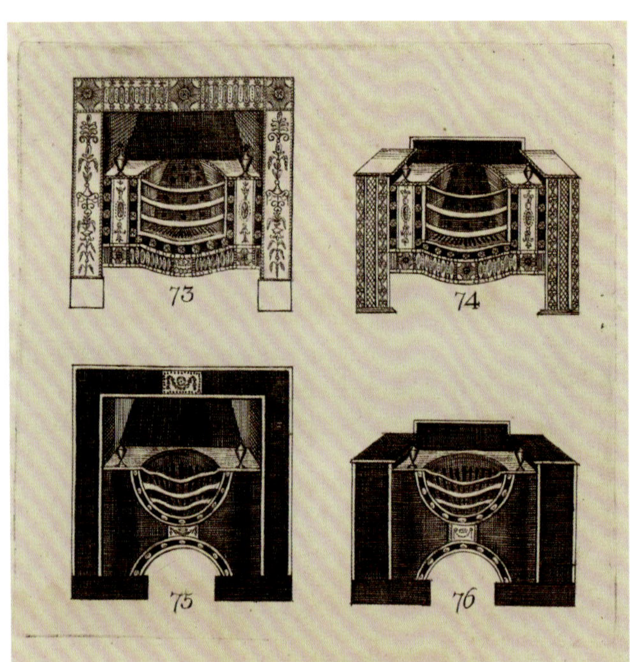

24. Page from a metalwork pattern book with fire grate, stove, balcony and fencing designs, c.1794, issued by Skidmore & Co., London
Engraving
V&A: E.444:43–2003
Purchased through the Julie and Robert Breckman Print Fund

of the print collections to the V&A as a whole, illuminating as they do other aspects of the Museum's holdings in such subjects as fashion and interior design, and offering evidence of their social and political context.

*

The V&A was founded on the idea of the educational potential of its collections and has provided facilities for public access to them, for individuals and for groups from schools, universities and art colleges. This access provision is very necessary for works on paper, which are held in store when not on display, to minimize their exposure to the damaging effects of light. Today, of course, a large proportion of the collection can be seen and studied online (and the dedicated programme of digitization is continuing), but there is no substitute for seeing the real thing, so the Prints & Drawings Study Room continues to be the key point of access for visitors wishing to see works that are not on show. The Study Room, originally located in the main South Kensington building, moved to the adjoining Henry Cole Wing in 1983. As part of the V&A + RIBA Partnership project, the Study Room was remodelled and improved in 2004 (by architects Wright & Wright) to accommodate a new adjacent study space for visitors to the Royal Institute of British Architects (RIBA) drawings collections, recently transferred to the V&A site.

Thanks to Robert Breckman, we were able to take this opportunity to commission the first of two important artworks for permanent display in the Prints & Drawings Study Room. This was a clock by the artist duo Langlands & Bell, designed specifically for the space (pl.26). It is set into the wall dividing the V&A and RIBA study rooms and has two faces, one with white lettering on black, the other black on white. In place of numbers,

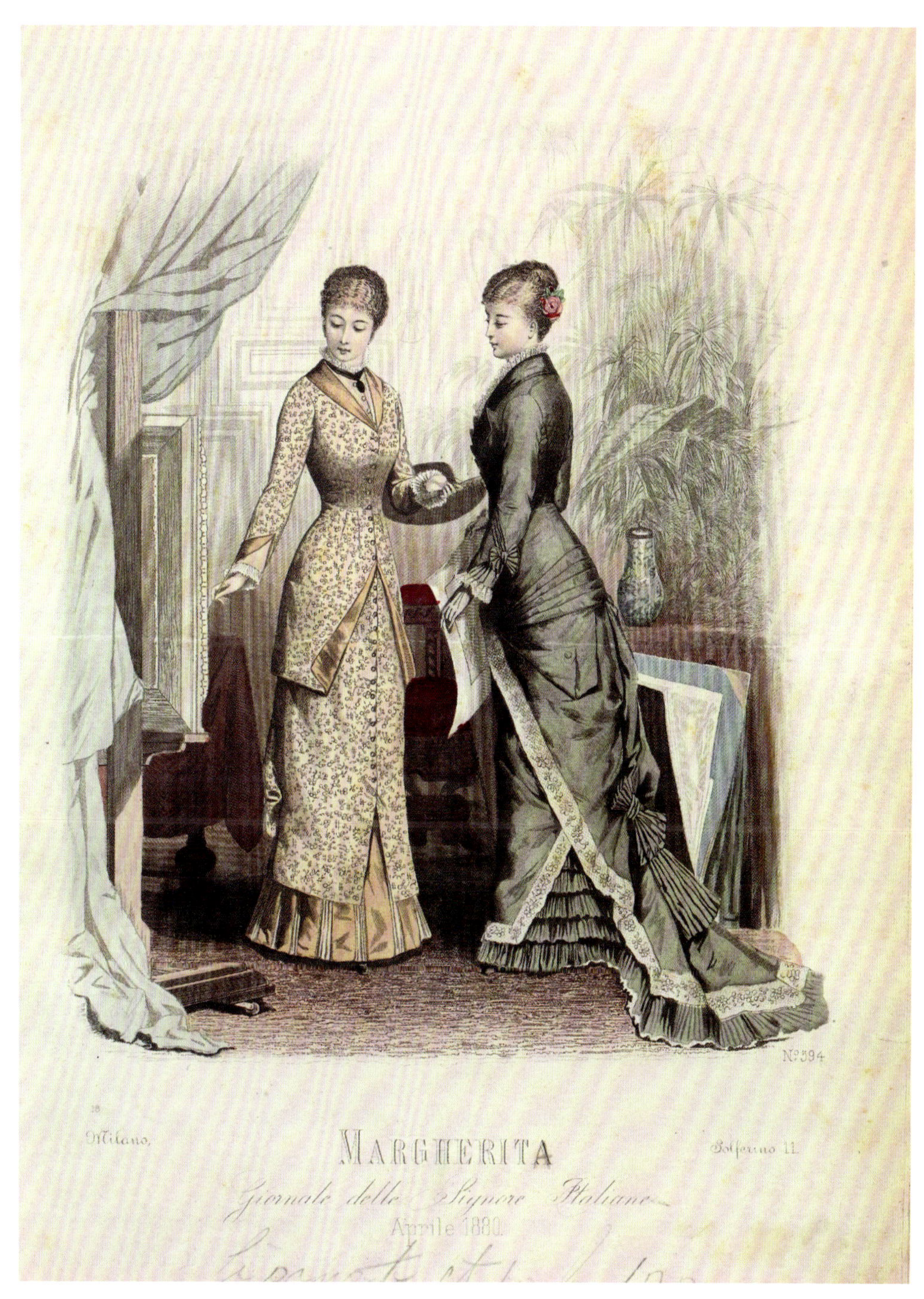

25. Fashion plate from *Margherita*, April 1880, Milan
Engraving, coloured by hand
V&A: E.151:19–2003
Purchased through the Julie and Robert Breckman Print Fund

the clock faces are printed with the three-letter codes that identify international airports around the world. The whole thing is animated, for not only do the hands of the clock move, but each face of the clock spins slowly clockwise, in a hypnotic display of perpetual motion.

Following this successful project, in 2011 we also commissioned a new print from the artist Liz Collini (b.1955) (pl.27 and see p.89), for the blank wall facing the Langlands & Bell clock. Robert and I had been talking for some years about finding a work to go on long-term display in the Study Room, but the challenge was to find something that would complement the other exhibits – the clock and the self-portrait by Marilène Oliver (b.1977), both of which were also donated by Robert. I was also keen that the work should be appropriate for the space, and ideally site-specific. So when I first saw Liz Collini's work I was excited by the idea of commissioning her to make a print for this room – not least because her work embodies the idea of 'word as image' (and the print collections are, of course, part of the Word & Image Department, which encompasses the V&A's National Art Library as well as the Museum's collection of prints, drawings and paintings).

In preparation, Liz came and spent some time in the Study Room, watching and listening to people working and studying there. In response, she devised the phrase 'among the indescribable sounds of paper, moving'; the words evoke the idea of people quietly turning the pages of books, and browsing through archival storage boxes full of prints and drawings. There is also a pleasing ambiguity to the phrase, because not only does it refer to the physical movement of pages and paper, but it also suggests that looking at works of art in a

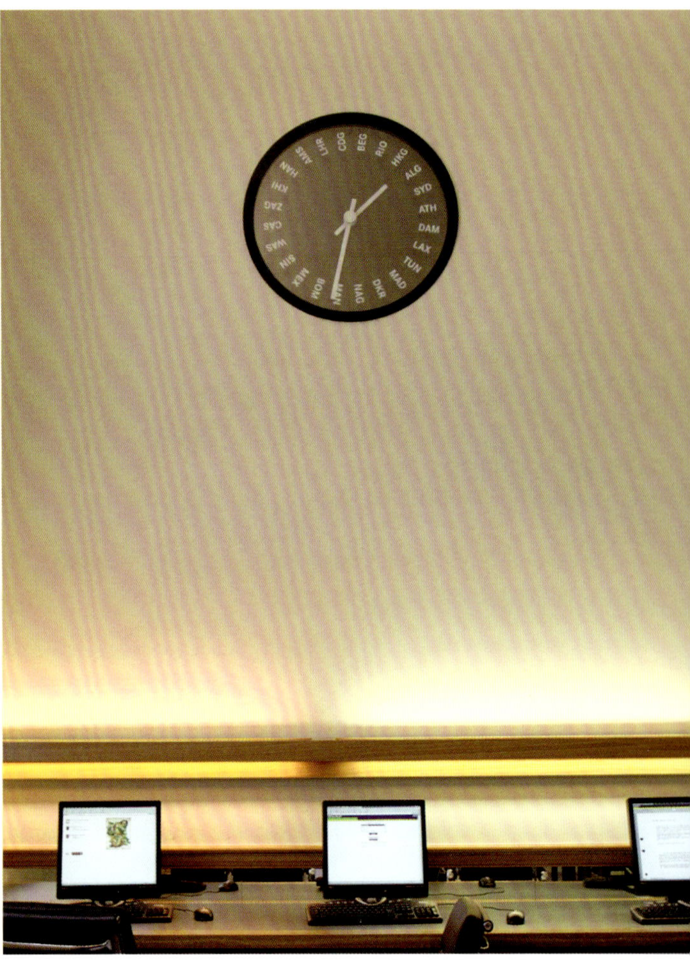

26. View of the Prints & Drawings Study Room showing the Langlands & Bell clock

spirit of quiet contemplation is in itself a moving experience. Visitors to the Study Room often tell us how privileged they feel to hold a work of art in their hands, and to have an opportunity to see it at close quarters, and not in a frame or behind glass; Liz's clever, subtle phrase conveys something of that sense of wonder and pleasure. In recognition of the significance of the work and its location, Robert chose to donate it in memory of Julie.

Over the past decade the V&A has been engaged in a major programme to refresh and revise its galleries, endeavouring to tell engaging and illuminating stories about the history of art and design, and to make the collections both physically and intellectually more accessible. Prints – as visual evidence of material cultures, and as works of art in their own right – have a vital place in these galleries, and thanks to the Print Fund we have been able to acquire key pieces. In the Medieval & Renaissance Galleries, which opened in 2009, there is a rare hand-coloured woodcut print of Ali Bassa (Ali Pasha) (see p.105), commander of the Turkish Ottoman fleet in the Battle of Lepanto (1571). An early example of political spin, it reports the victory of a European Christian alliance (the Holy League) over the Turks, adding layers of myth to the record of the event. In the Jewellery Gallery there is an intriguing copper printing plate from the Netherlands (pl.29), dated 1747, engraved with designs for jewellery. Works acquired through the Print Fund also feature in the Architecture Gallery, and in the spectacular new galleries devoted to Europe in the period 1600–1815. In the latter a prominent exhibit is an advertisement for playing cards (see p.113), part of a display on art and design during the French Revolution. It dramatizes very vividly the calls for racial, gender and political equality, exemplifying the early ideals of the revolutionaries.

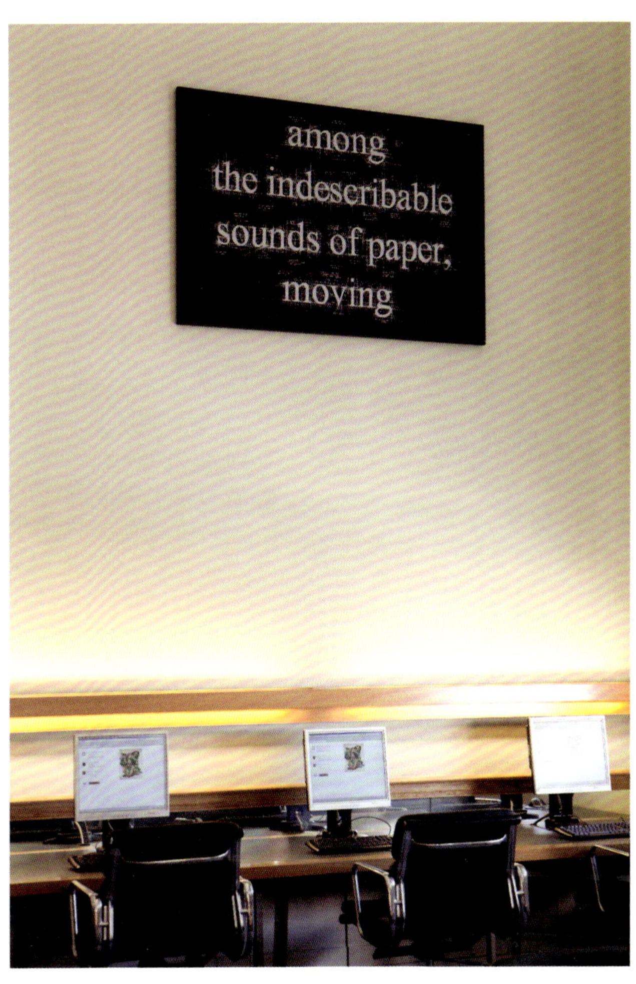

27. View of *Untitled (large text)*, 2011, by Liz Collini in the Prints & Drawings Study Room

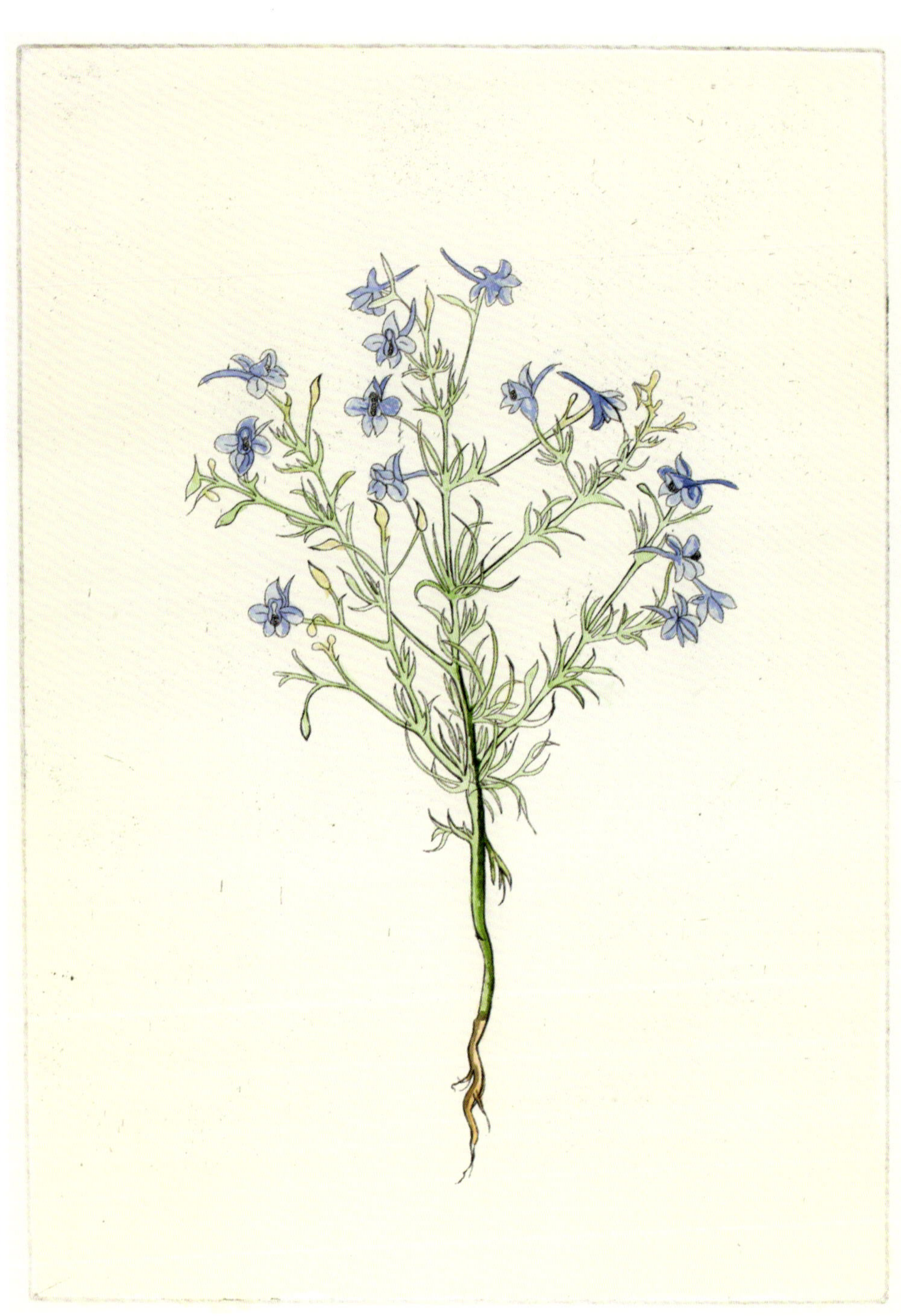

28. Plate from *The History of Plants, according to women, children and students*, 2002, by Christine Borland
Etching coloured by hand
V&A: E.2080:10–2004
Purchased through the Julie and Robert Breckman Print Fund

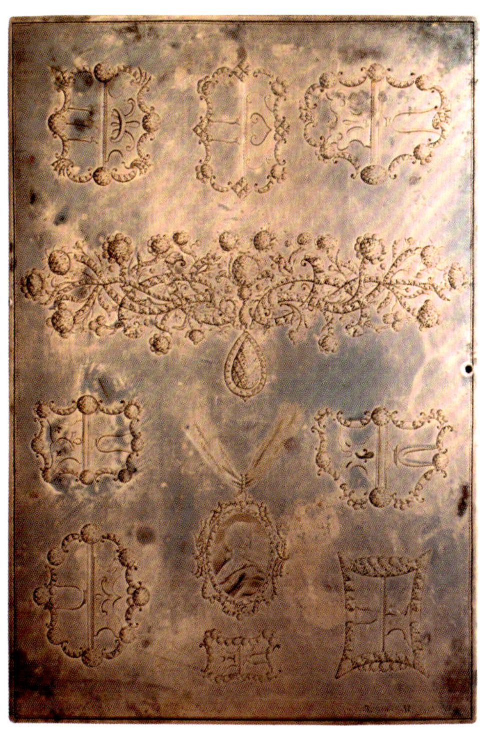

29. Copper printing plate engraved with jewellery designs,
1747, by Nicholas Mensma
V&A: E.3552–2004
Purchased through the Julie and Robert Breckman Print Fund

Prints purchased by the Fund have regularly featured in the changing displays curated by Tim Travis for the V&A Members' Room – where one of the first exhibits was a unique photograph by Susan Derges (b.1955) (pl.30 and see p.65), *Shoreline, October 5 1998*, donated by Robert Breckman in memory of Julie – and in our popular Print of the Month programme, which has won a devoted audience via its online presence. The V&A Directors Mark Jones and, now, Martin Roth have chosen several Print Fund acquisitions for their offices, focusing on prints and posters that reflect the Museum's priorities and act as talking points for the Museum's visitors. The Breckman-funded prints and ceramics are regularly shown in the Museum's own galleries and display spaces, but they have also been included in V&A touring exhibitions, notably *Street Art: Contemporary Prints from the V&A* and the poster show *A World to Win*, which were seen in museums and galleries around the UK. Both have proved very popular with audiences. Some of the best of the ceramic pieces have been exhibited internationally and have been seen as far afield as Damascus, Seoul, Istanbul and Sydney.

The value of the arts in healthcare has long been recognized, and since 2001 the Word & Image Department has worked in partnership with the Paintings in Hospitals charity, to design small loan exhibitions of prints for display in hospital buildings. The first of these was a selection of works purchased through the Print Fund during its initial 18 months; these were exhibited at St George's Hospital, Tooting, in the summer of 2001. This was followed by several further loans, all designed around Breckman Fund acquisitions, including *The Stations of the Cross* (the suite of colour linocuts by Adrian Wiszniewski, see p.69) at the Royal Brompton Hospital in 2002/3 and

Story and Tradition in Contemporary Printmaking, organized by Catherine Flood for Homerton Hospital in 2006. This featured narrative images by artists from Australasia, Russia and the UK. In 2009–10 Assistant Curator Sarah Grant devised *Contemporary Women Printmakers: Exploring the female tradition*, for the maternity unit, again at St George's, Tooting. The selected works, all by women artists, ranged from delicate botanical imagery by Christine Borland (b.1965) (pl.28), to intimate interiors by Giulia Zaniol (b.1979) and a lipstick kiss by Kate Moss (b.1974) (from the SHOWstudio portfolio). As for all these exhibitions, the feedback from staff and patients was positive and enthusiastic; most felt that the prints made the place feel more homely, and patients said that the art distracted them from their pain and anxiety. Above all, the prints stimulated conversations between staff, patients and visitors, helping to improve communication. Everyone agreed that it was a privilege to be able to enjoy artworks from the V&A in their local environment.

*

While collecting is the lifeblood of the Museum, and vital as a means of ensuring that we recognize and represent contemporary developments in art and design, it is also essential that new acquisitions are accessioned and documented in a timely manner by curators with the appropriate skills and expertise. The V&A has for many years offered training places through the Assistant Curator Development Programme. Curators on this five-year programme are obliged to undertake placements in two or three departments as part of their training in museum work. Given the pace of acquisitions through the Print Fund, and the great diversity of the material in terms of date, medium and place of origin, it was agreed early on that it would be valuable to employ a dedicated curator. This

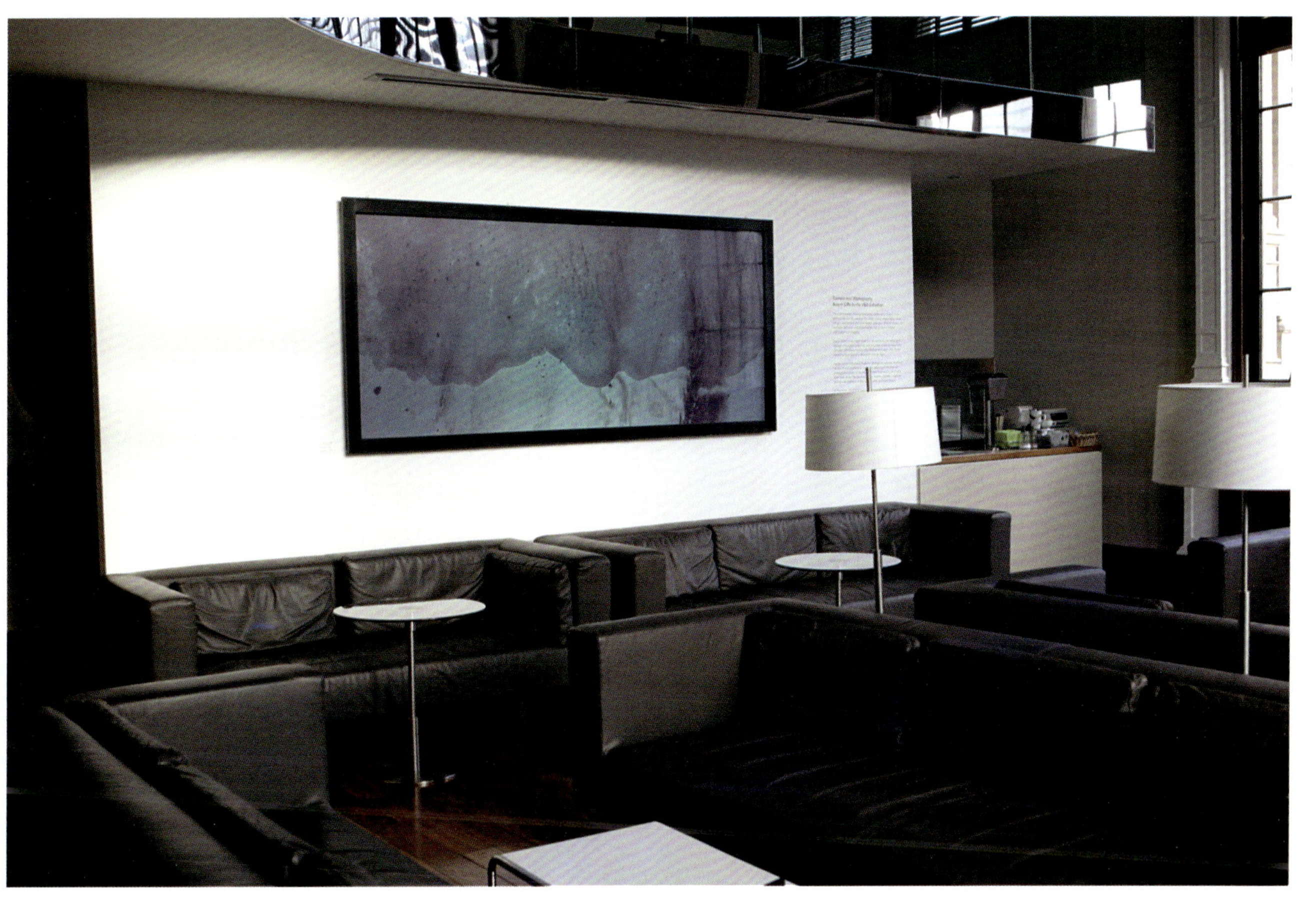

30. *Shoreline, October 5 1998*, by Susan Derges, on display in the
V&A Members' Room, January 2007

was envisaged as an opportunity for an early-career curator to specialize in prints, and to learn all the necessary skills: how to identify the many different media and techniques; how to catalogue prints to the appropriate standards; and how to handle, store and display such material. When the idea was broached by the then Senior Curator of Prints, Margaret Timmers, Robert was quick to agree to fund a Julie and Robert Breckman Bursary Curator, and in 2002 Catherine Flood was appointed to this role.

The value of the Bursary Curator opportunity was quickly evident. Catherine made the most of this opportunity to learn from the wide-ranging expertise of colleagues such as Stephen Calloway, Liz Miller and Margaret Timmers, and developed a particular interest in posters and graphic design. In due course she was appointed to a permanent post in the Word & Image Department, with special responsibility for the V&A's outstanding collection of posters and commercial graphics, assuring the long-term development and care of the collections, as well as maintaining the V&A's position as an international centre of excellence and expertise in this area.

The second Bursary Curator, appointed in 2003, was Riikka (Rikki) Kuittinen (pl.31). Rikki's contribution to the work of the department extended beyond her diligent cataloguing of Breckman Fund acquisitions, to include the creation of online records for more than 300 prints from the Ornament Gallery, as well as many other print acquisitions. She also demonstrated that young curators can bring valuable expertise of their own to an institution. Her in-depth knowledge of contemporary art and popular culture proved very useful, not least because she was quick to spot the importance of the rise

of street art, and initiated the acquisition of a
number of prints by graffiti artists from around the
world. As a result, the V&A was the first national
museum to collect such work. The Breckman Print
Fund enabled several purchases, including works
by Graeme Nimmo, Miss Tic (b.1958) and Sickboy
(see p.83), and Rikki curated an influential display,
Street Art, at the V&A in 2005. This was followed
by a hugely popular UK touring show, featuring
works by all the key figures of the street-art scene,
and a best-selling book. At the conclusion of
her Bursary role, Rikki went on to work in other
heritage organizations, but later returned to a
post in the V&A's Exhibitions Department, where
her previous experience of working with the print
collections has proved invaluable.

Looking back on more than a decade of
support from Julie and Robert Breckman, in the
preparation for this book, has been a heartening
experience. More than 1,200 prints, posters
and items of printed ephemera, and around
60 ceramic pieces, have been added to the
collection over a period of just 11 years. The
diversity of this material reflects the very particular
character and strengths of the V&A collections.
In the case of the print collections, we can
also see how curators seized the opportunities
provided by the ready support of the Print Fund
to strike out in new directions, too, collecting in
response to developments and innovations in
contemporary culture in the UK and beyond.
The V&A collections have been immeasurably
enriched by the enlightened generosity of Julie
and Robert Breckman, and together these
eclectic acquisitions stand today as an eloquent
memorial to Julie, just as Robert envisaged when
he approached the V&A in May 2000.

1 Anne Desmet in *Printmaking Today* (Winter 2006), p.30.

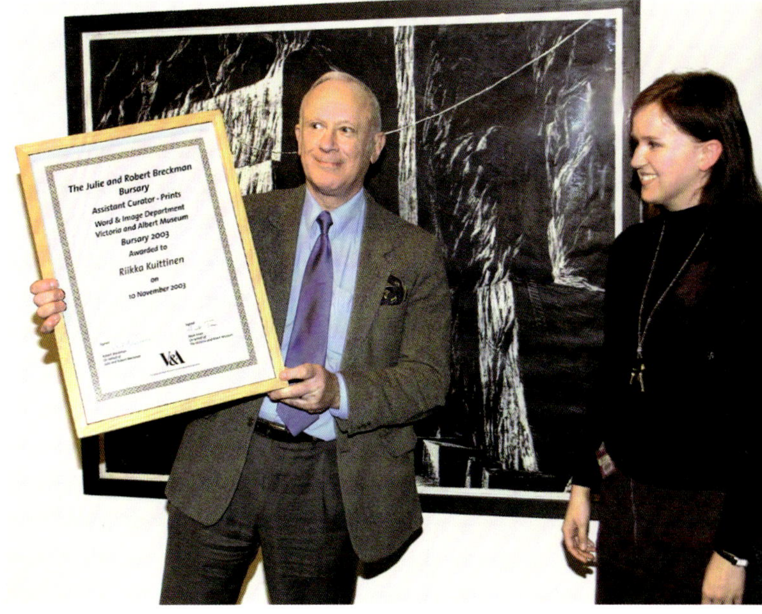

31. Robert Breckman presenting Riikka Kuittinen with a certificate to
mark her appointment as the Julie and Robert Breckman Bursary
Curator for Prints, on 10 November 2003

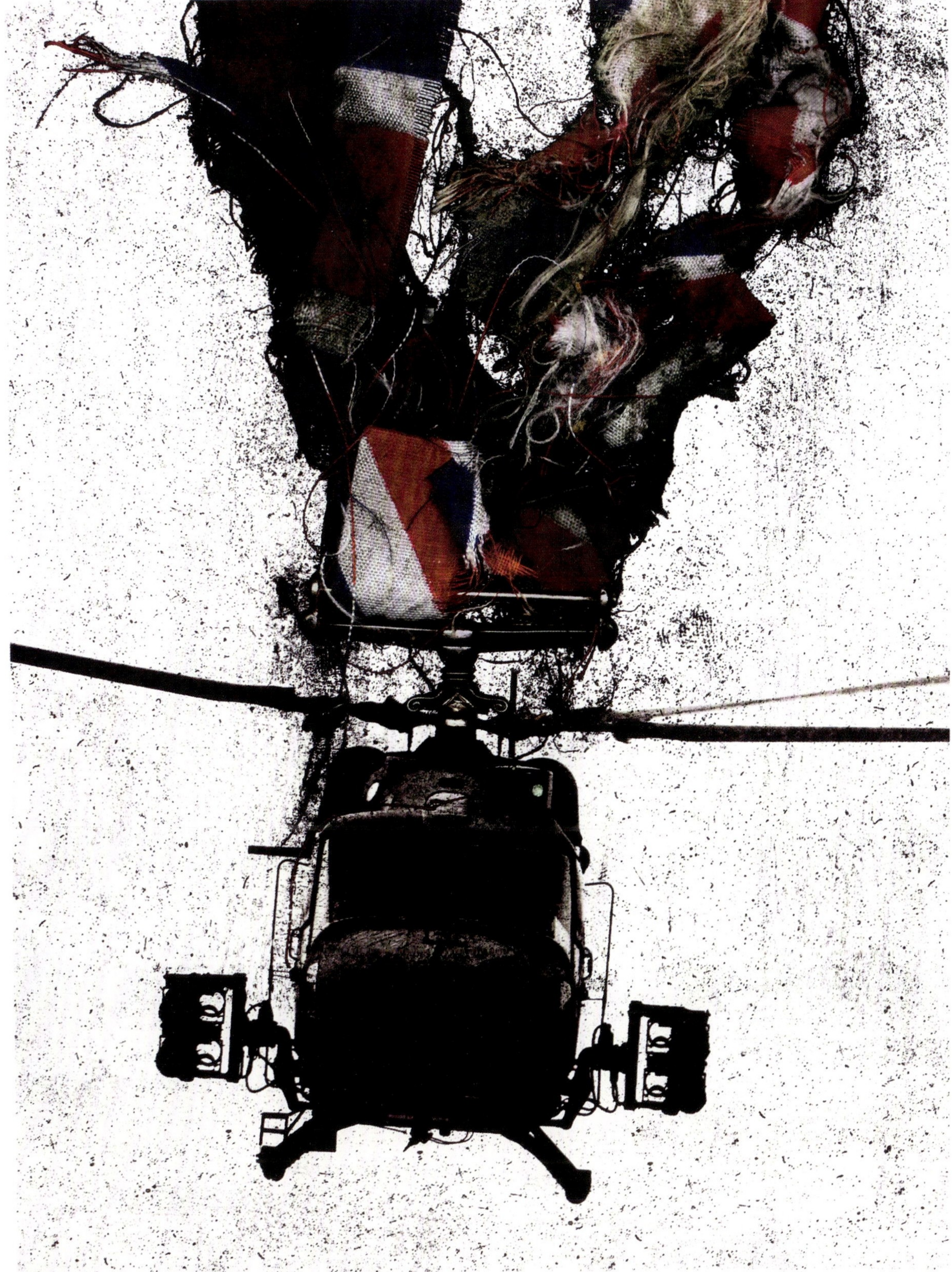

Fine-Art Prints

Gill Saunders

Though it is often considered to be a museum dedicated to the decorative arts, the V&A has extensive and internationally renowned holdings of fine art – paintings, prints, drawings and photographs. It is the only national institution that, from its foundation, collected contemporary fine-art prints in their year of publication or shortly after, without waiting for the verdicts of posterity; and this continues today, with curators presciently acquiring work by emerging talents, as well as from those with established reputations. However, we cannot be comprehensive in collecting from such a wide and diverse field of practice, so there is a particular V&A bias to our collecting, based on historical strengths, the Museum's founding purpose and the role of printmaking in a museum of design and the decorative arts.

It is in the contemporary field that 'the Julie Fund' (as Robert sometimes calls it) has been especially influential and effective, enabling us to collect important prints by art-world stars such as Damien Hirst (b.1965) (see p.71), Julian Opie (pl.32), Chris Ofili, Grayson Perry (see p.87) and Rachel Whiteread (b.1963) (see p.73), which would otherwise have been beyond our means. Many of these artists work primarily in media that fall outside the V&A's collecting remit – such as oil painting, sculpture and installation – but

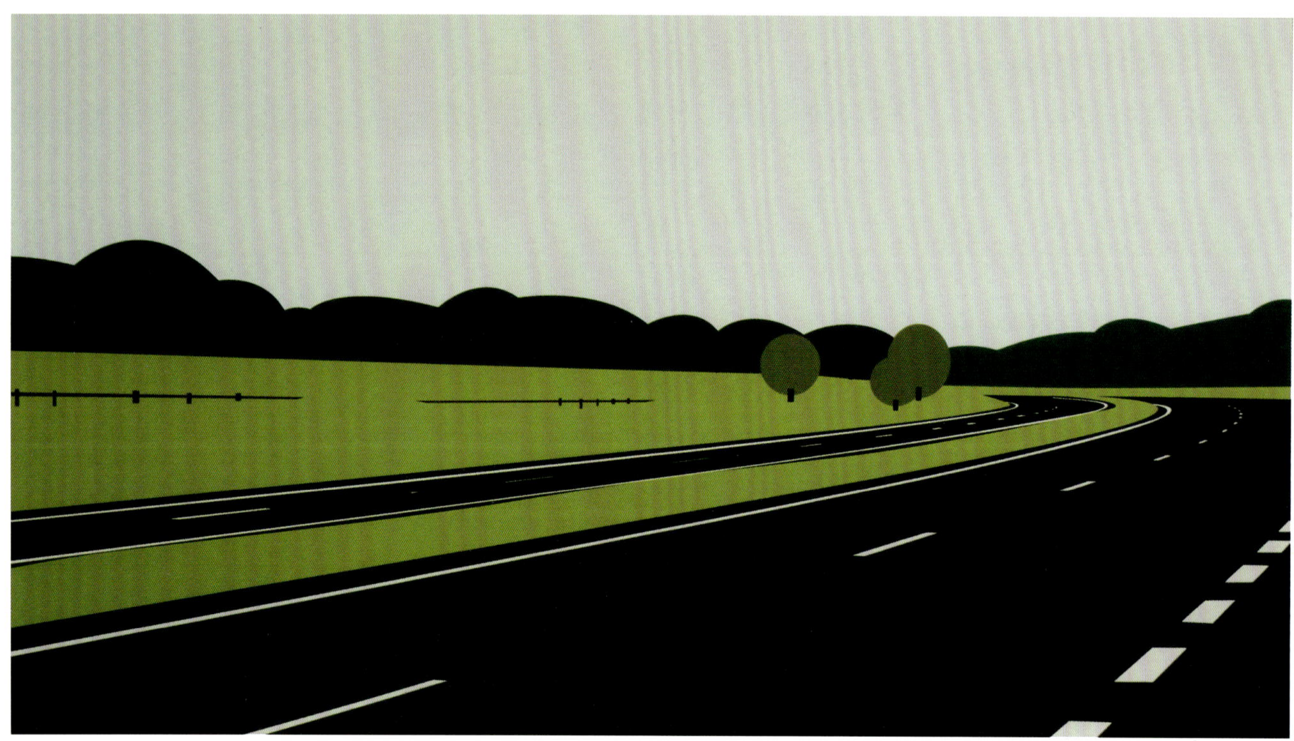

32. *I dreamt I was driving (motorway corner)*, 2002, by Julian Opie
Unique C-type print mounted on aluminium
V&A: E.3841–2004
Purchased through the Julie and Robert Breckman Print Fund

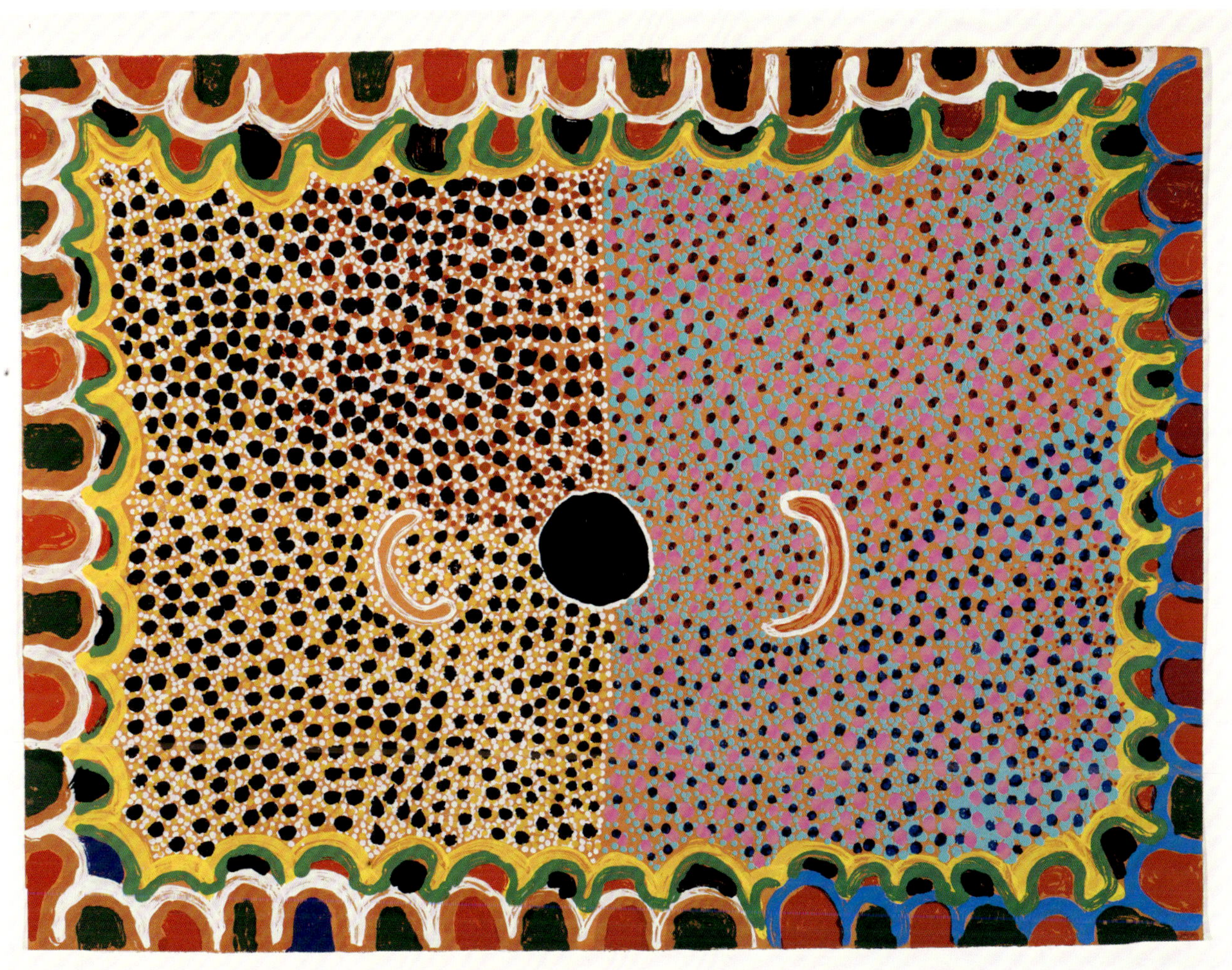

33. *Kaningarra*, 2002, by Susie Bootja Bootja Napangarti
Screen print
V&A: E.257–2005
Purchased through the Julie and Robert Breckman Print Fund

their work in print offers a fresh perspective on their practice and has been instrumental in revitalizing printmaking in the twenty-first century. By collecting such work, the V&A is able to demonstrate the extent to which printmaking has moved beyond stubborn misperceptions about its status and its historical associations with reproduction, and is now embedded in contemporary fine-art practice.

Inevitably our collecting has been focused on British artists and, to a lesser extent, those from Europe and the US. However, the V&A itself also has major collections of material from

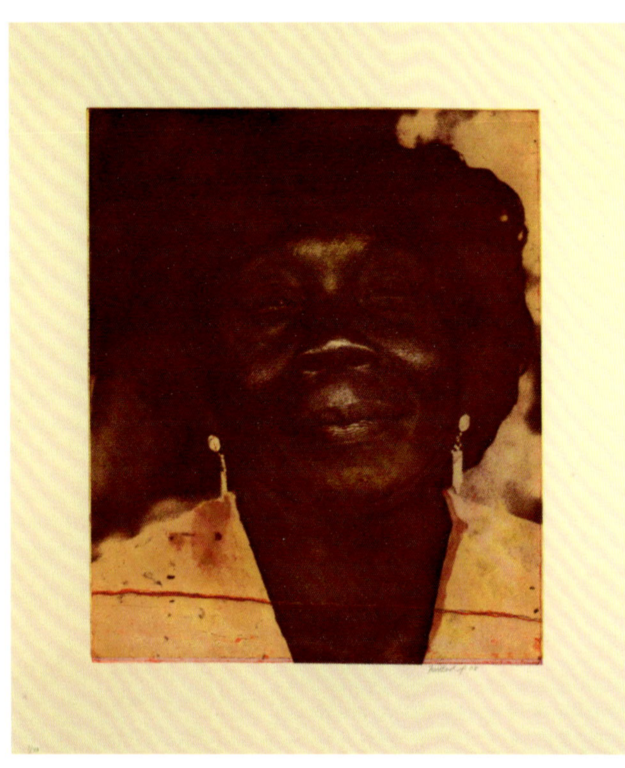

34. *Mother Approaching Sixty*, 2003, by Frank Bowling
Etching and aquatint
V&A: E.3581-2004
Purchased through the Julie and Robert Breckman Print Fund

non-western cultures and has been active in moving beyond Europe, Asia and the US, to explore art and design from other regions. The Word & Image Department has led this drive, and our print collecting in particular has become increasingly international in scope. In the past decade we have been proactive in collecting work by artists from the African and Asian diasporas, Australasia, Latin America and Russia, areas where new printmaking communities are emerging.

At the same time we have continued to address the history of fine-art printmaking, identifying gaps in the collections and seeking out key works from earlier periods, as well as reflecting the diverse approaches to print production here and now. The Print Fund has supported all of these initiatives and more, with acquisitions ranging from Rodolphe Bresdin's eccentric masterpiece of lithography, *Le Bon Samaritain* of 1861 (see p.55), and exquisite prints by Paul Drury (1903–87) (see p.57), a leading figure in the British 'Etching Revival' in the 1920s, to contemporary street-art prints from around the world. Many of the prints acquired through the Fund have a specific relevance to the V&A – for example, Lucian Freud's exquisite etching *After Constable's Elm* (2003) (see p.81), a homage in print to the oil painting by John Constable (1776–1837) of the trunk of an elm tree, in the V&A's collection.

The development and direction of the collections depend crucially on the expertise, enthusiasm and contacts of individual curators – and this has certainly been reflected in the acquisitions supported by the Print Fund. Print Curator Rosie Miles, alert to the fact that the V&A had unaccountably overlooked the work of black British and African American artists, led concerted efforts to acquire important prints

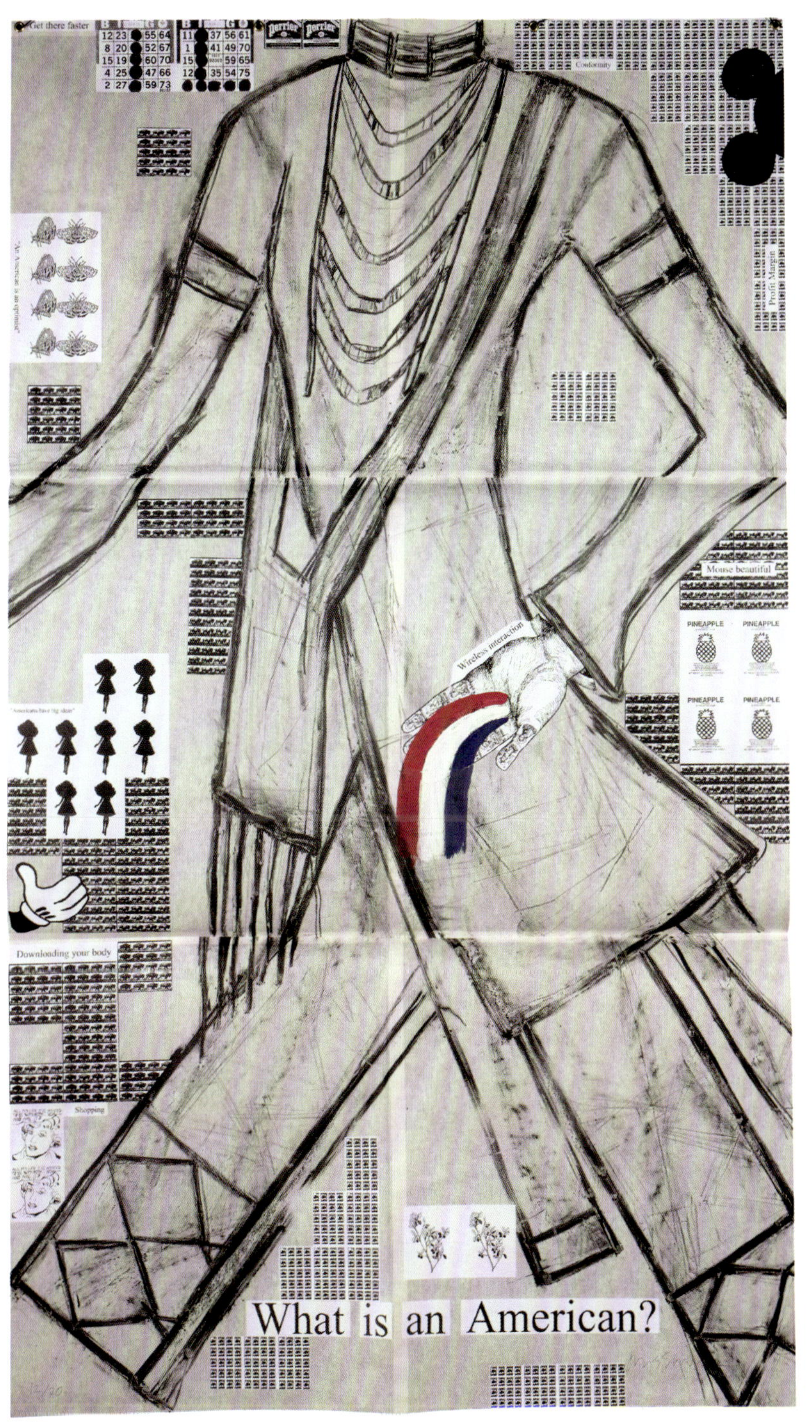

35. *What is an American?*, 2003, by Jaune Quick-to-See Smith
Lithograph, with *chine collé*, collage, hand-painting and grommets
V&A: E.3582–2004
Purchased through the Julie and Robert Breckman Print Fund

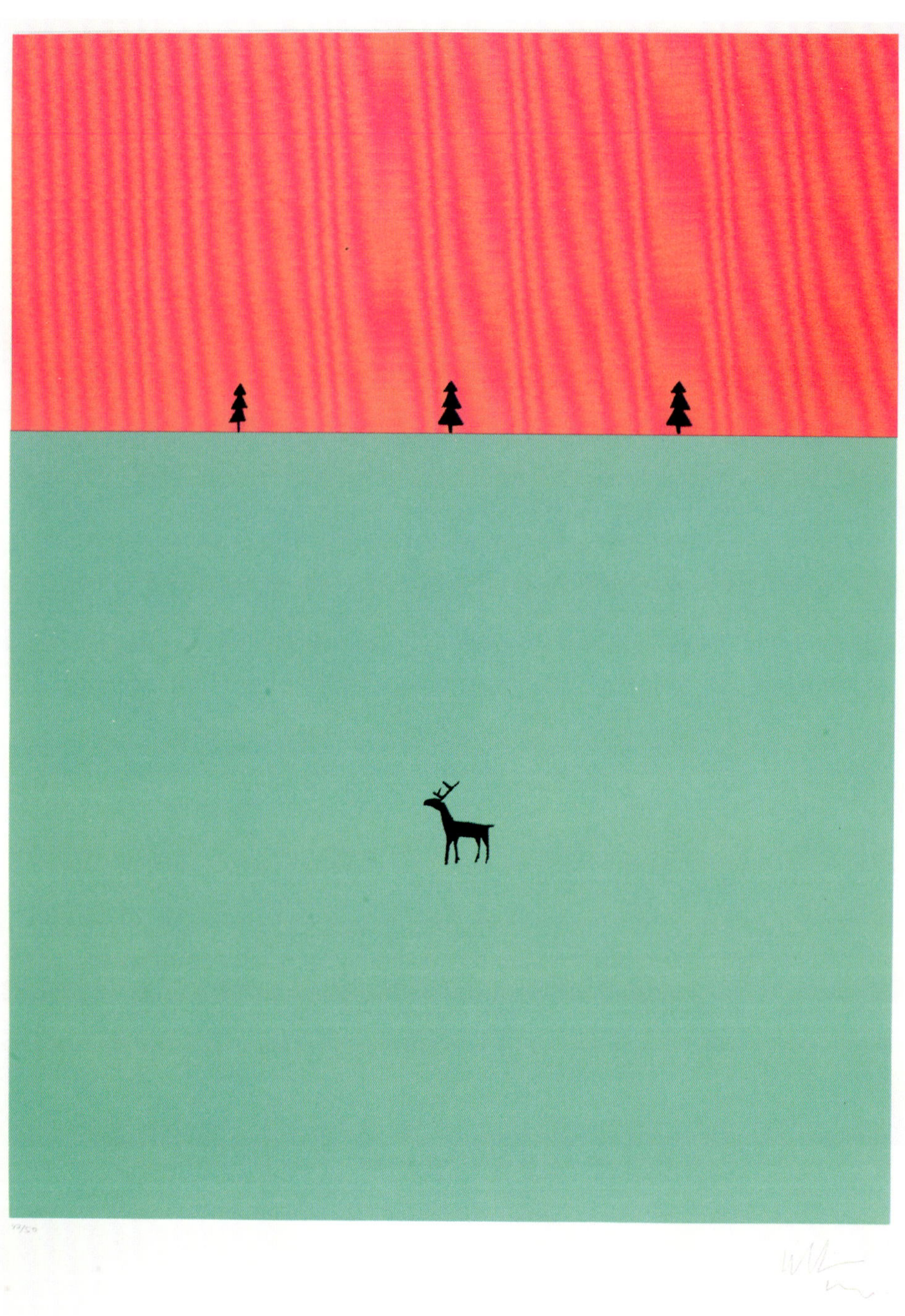

36. *The Deer*, 2000, from the series *Horizons*, by Timur Novikov
Screen print
V&A: E.2082–2004
Purchased through the Julie and Robert Breckman Print Fund

by major names such as Willie Cole and Faith
Ringgold in the US, and Frank Bowling (pl.34)
and Chris Ofili in the UK. She also established a
very fruitful relationship with the Rutgers Center
for Innovative Print and Paper (now the Brodsky
Center) in New Jersey. The Center's mission is to
enable artists – both established and emerging
– to create new work in paper and print. It also
promotes diversity and works with men and
women from a variety of cultural backgrounds.
The V&A has acquired innovative prints produced
at the Center by Cuban, African American and
Native American artists. Notable among these
are mixed-media pieces by artists of Native
American ancestry, in the form of moccasins
(Lynne Allen, b.1949) and a parfleche (a bag
or pouch made from rawhide) (Jaune Quick-to-
See Smith, b.1940; pl.35). Looking beyond the
US, Rosie also initiated the purchase of editions
by renowned Australian Aboriginal artists such
as Susie Bootja Bootja Napangarti (1935–2003;
pl.33), and magnificent colour linocuts by
artists David Bosun (b.1973) (see p.75) and Billy
Missi (b.1970) from the Torres Strait Islands. The
latter offer an eloquent demonstration of how
printmaking can be effective in preserving and
promoting a vulnerable cultural heritage.

Another member of the Prints team, Tim Travis,
has deployed his expertise and language skills
to explore the rise of printmaking in Russia and
Eastern Europe. Russian artists were hitherto barely
represented in the collection, but by working
with specialist dealers and other contacts,
Tim identified a number of gifted printmakers,
including Timur Novikov (1958–2002) (pl.36),
Alexander Florensky (b.1960), Alexander Kholopov
(1948–2016) and Natalia Lamanova (b.1964), and
the Print Fund enabled us to buy important works
by these and others. And, as described earlier
(see p.38), Breckman Bursary Curator Rikki Kulttinen

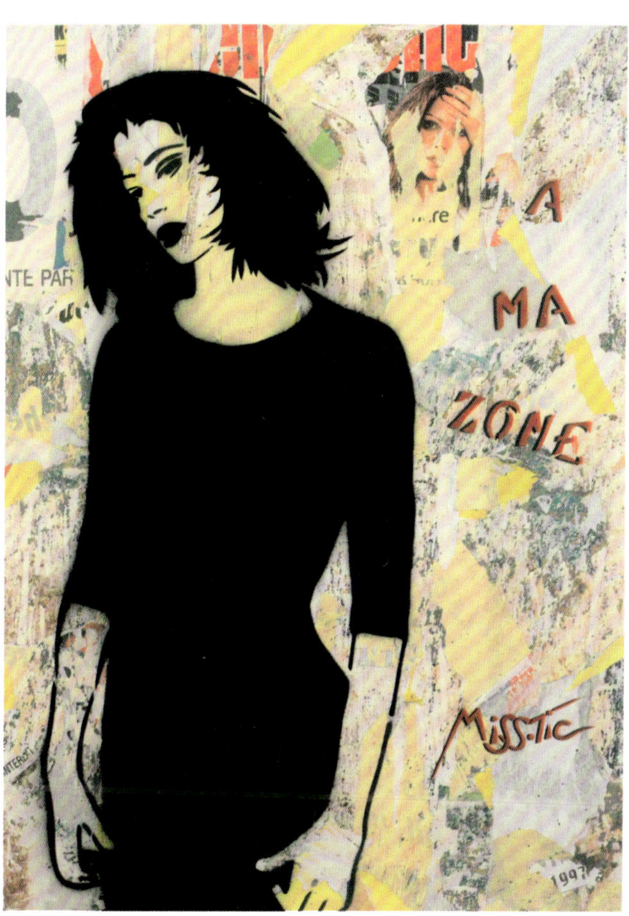

37. *A Ma Zone*, 2004, by Miss Tic
Screen print
V&A: E.274–2005
Purchased through the Julie and Robert Breckman Print Fund

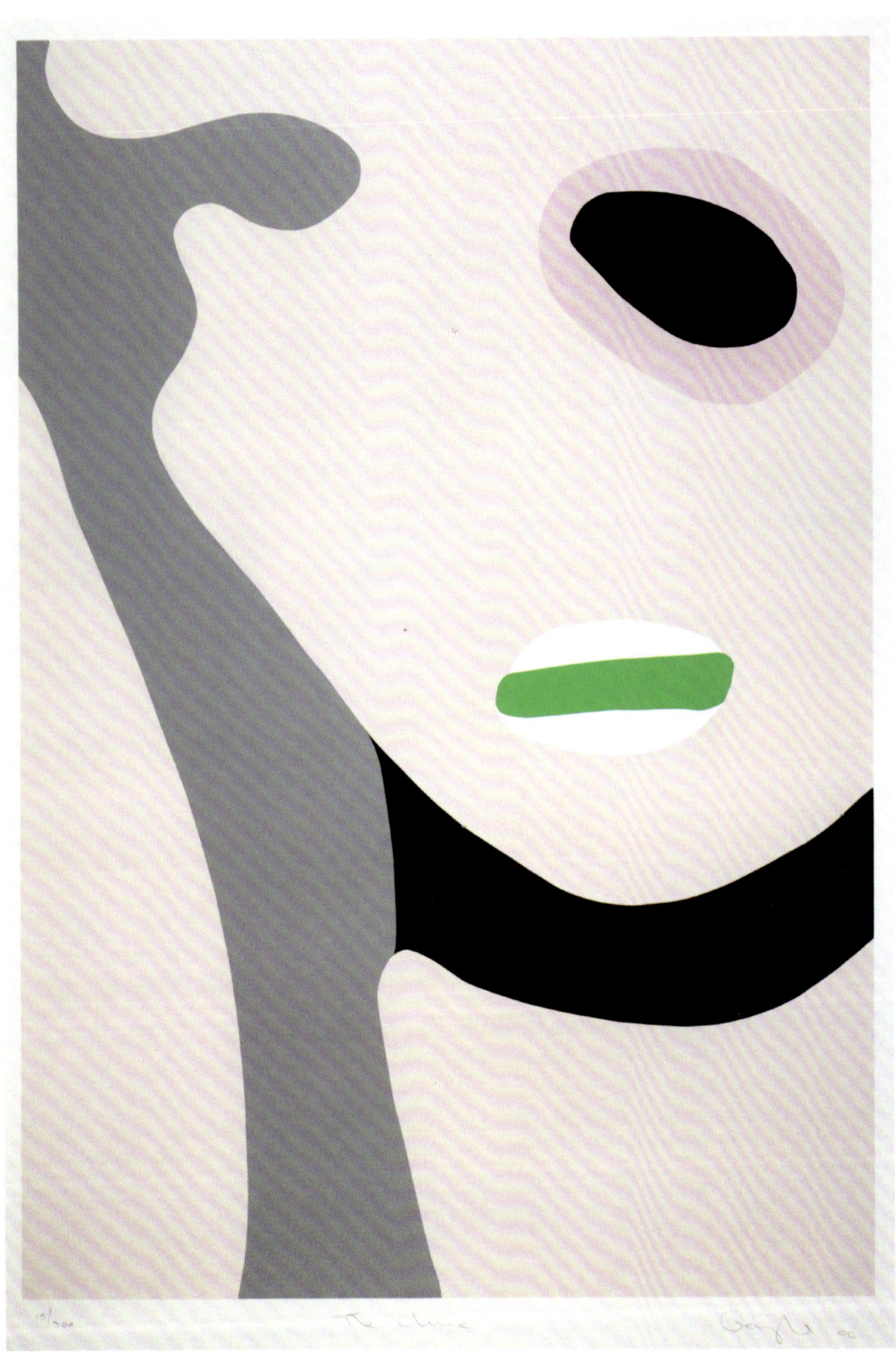

38. *The Cleric*, 2000, by Gary Hume
Screen print
V&A: E.1571–2001
Purchased through the Julie and Robert Breckman Print Fund

kick-started the V&A's unrivalled collection of prints by street artists, whose work reflects a confluence of graphic traditions from graffiti and poster art to caricature and comics (pl.37).

The establishment of the Print Fund was timely for the V&A because it coincided with a period of rapid expansion in fine-art printmaking as new players emerged in the field of print publishing, often working with artists who were new to the challenges of making prints or those keen to work with unconventional media. One effective way of reflecting the diversity of current print practice is to acquire mixed portfolios, and thanks to the Fund we have been able to buy exciting work published by novel enterprises such as Counter Editions and the Paul Stolper Gallery. The Counter Editions portfolio, published in 2000, contains prints by 14 artists, including the rising stars of the Young British Artists (YBA) generation – Peter Doig (b.1959), Tracey Emin (b.1963), Gary Hume (b.1962) (pl.38), Chris Ofili and Gavin Turk (b.1967). Later we added the Diamond Dust portfolio (published by Paul Stolper) to the collection. Inspired by the 'diamond dust' screen prints of the 1980s by Andy Warhol (1928–87), the works play with the visual legacy of Pop and punk, with icons of celebrity and objects of nostalgia further glamorized by their sparkling surfaces.

More established but hugely influential, the Paragon Press has published editions with some of the best-known names in British art and, thanks to the Print Fund, the V&A has been able to acquire selected prints from the *Nourishment* series by Michael Landy (b.1963) (pl.39), which reflect the traditions of botanical illustration, another strength of the V&A collections; a bold suite of colour screen prints, *Capital*, by Sarah Morris (b.1967), inspired by high-rise architecture; and three pieces from Damien Hirst's magnificent

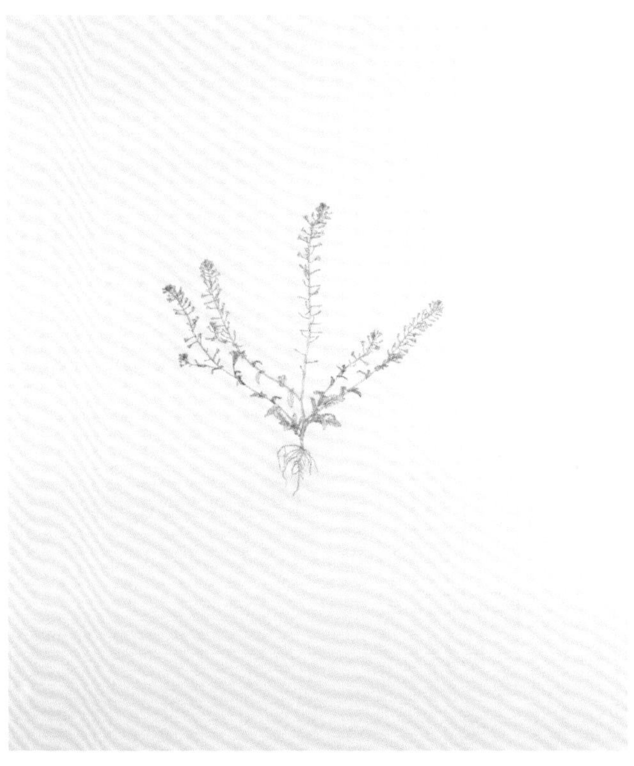

39. *Shepherd's Purse*, from the series *Nourishment*, 2002
by Michael Landy
Etching
V&A: E.1064–2003
Purchased through the Julie and Robert Breckman Print Fund

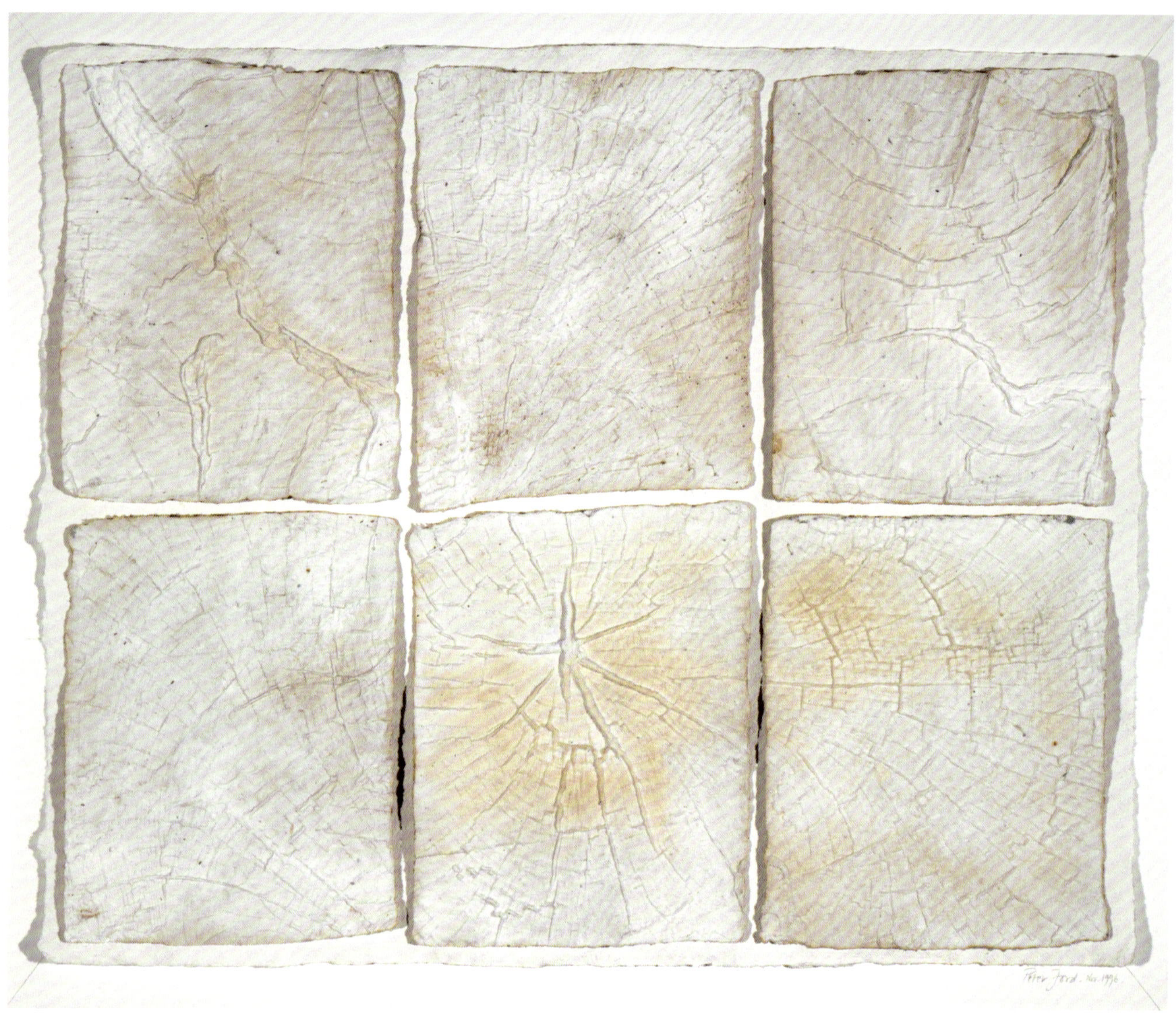

40. *Evidence 1*, 1996, by Peter Ford
Relief prints made from undyed paper pulp
V&A: E.1098-2002
Purchased through the Julie and Robert Breckman Print Fund

Last Supper suite (see p.71). Hirst's prints are clever amalgamations of fine art, graphic design and advertising; they pastiche posters and packaging, with a sly dig at the artist's own brand-name commercial success. The Fund also enabled the purchase of editions from the internationally renowned Glasgow Print Studio – including Adrian Wiszniewksi's *Stations of the Cross* (see p.69) and Christine Borland's suite *The History of Plants, according to women, children and students* (see pl.28) – both of which we have exhibited on several occasions.

Works of art and design that address social and political issues, either obliquely or directly, represent a significant theme in the V&A's collections, and this is reflected in the Breckman

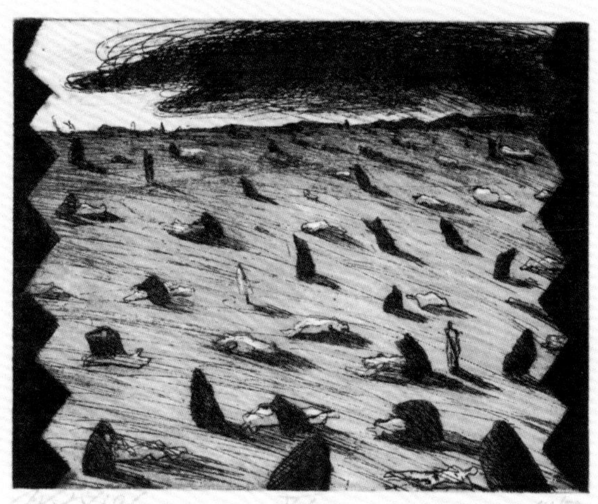

41. Plate VI from the portfolio *Dark Interludes*, 2001, by Walid Siti
Etching
V&A: E.108–2002
Purchased through the Julie and Robert Breckman Print Fund

Fund acquisitions. These range from mixed-media pieces by Sonia Boyce (b.1962) and Bill Woodrow (b.1948) exploring the experiences of migrants and refugees; and prints by Judy Brodsky (b.1933) on subjects as various as feminism (see p.63) and the Holocaust; to the subtleties of work by Conrad Atkinson (b.1940) about the use of landmines; and the caustic commentary by Peter Kennard (b.1949) on the US and UK engagement in the Iraq war (see p.85). Kennard's work is complemented by the series *Dark Interludes* by the UK-based Iraqi Kurdish artist Walid Siti (b.1954) (pl.41).

Many of the contemporary prints we acquire extend the concerns and practices of printmaking in the past, but one of the key

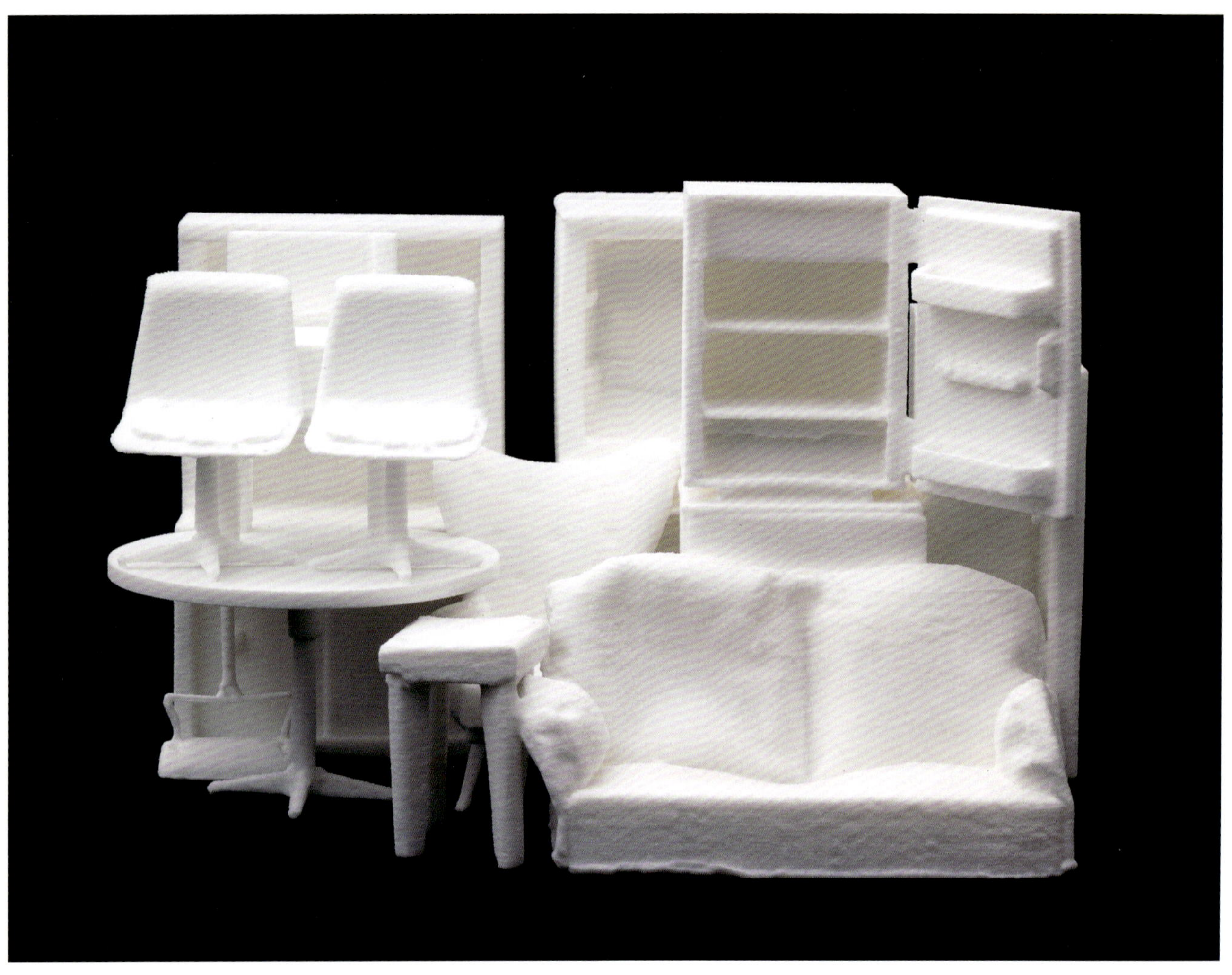

42. *Secondhand*, 2004, by Rachel Whiteread
Stereolithography or rapid prototyping in laser-sintered white nylon
V&A: E.502–2005
Purchased through the Julie and Robert Breckman Print Fund

drivers of our acquisition policy is technical and
conceptual innovation. The history of printmaking
is marked by successive inventions and by the
adoption of new technologies, driven both
by commercial imperatives and the ideas of
artists themselves. Artists have found inspiration
in accident and experiment, and in the need
to extend the capacity of the print media to
achieve their aims. It is a truism to observe that
printmaking has 'pushed the boundaries' to the
extent that it now defies easy definition. Enlisting
strategies from other fine-art disciplines, print
is continually shape-shifting. Print can now be
applied to almost any surface, and on any scale,
and can be realized in two dimensions or three.
The V&A, with its founding focus on materials,
processes and techniques, has continued to
acquire works in all media that demonstrate
such invention.

As the works acquired through the Print Fund
amply demonstrate, printmaking continues to
thrive, as artists continue to find in it the expressive
potential and the formal and material qualities
they seek. This might involve the innovative
application of a simple traditional process
such as blind embossing – seen in the lyrically
evocative *Evidence 1* by Peter Ford (b.1937),
paper-pulp impressions from the surface of a
cut tree trunk (pl.40); the adaptation of new
commercial processes for Rachel Whiteread's
stereolithograph *Secondhand* (pl.42), designed
to resemble her cast sculptures; or the use of
digital print to translate photographic imagery
from multiple sources, as employed by Catherine
Yass (b.1963) for *Northwest D6*. Lenticular plastic,
once used for advertisements and souvenir
postcards, has been co-opted by artists such as
Dan Hays (b.1966) (see p.77) and Julian Opie to
'animate' still images.

Rodolphe Bresdin (1822–85)
Le Bon Samaritain (The Good
Samaritan), 1861
Transfer lithograph on *chine collé*
Size of image 56 x 44 cm
V&A: E.473–2008
Purchased through the Julie and
Robert Breckman Print Fund

This magnificent and intriguing
print is considered to be one of the
masterpieces of pen-lithography;
drawn directly onto the printing stone
by the artist, it is Bresdin's largest
and most accomplished print and
attracted the admiration of a wide
circle of artists and writers, including
Victor Hugo (1802–85), Charles
Baudelaire (1821–67) and Théophile
Gautier (1811–72).

Little is known for sure of the
reclusive Bresdin, though his name
has consistently been linked with
the luminaries of Romantic and
bohemian circles in Paris. Born in
the Loire Valley, he headed for Paris
hoping to find artistic success, but
at the outbreak of the Revolution of
1848 began a walking tour of France
that extended to long sojourns in
Toulouse and Bordeaux. He returned
to Paris in 1861 with the massive,
near-completed printing stone of *Le
Bon Samaritain*, and exhibited one of
the first finished impressions to great
acclaim at the Salon that year.

Print connoisseurs of the day
admired the virtuosity of Bresdin's
handling of a technique then
usually associated with commercial
reproduction rather than original
graphic art, while contemporary
artists and critics were awed by the
prodigious fertility of invention –
coupled with minute observation
of detail – displayed in this print.
Flattering comparisons were made
between Bresdin's work and that
of great printmakers of the past,
including Albrecht Dürer (1471–1528)
and Rembrandt van Rijn (1606–69).
He had clearly profited, too, from
his study of prints by Jacques Callot
(1592–1635) and the grotesqueries of
early Flemish masters such as Pieter
Brueghel the Elder (*c.*1525–69).

The subject matter of the print also
alluded to contemporary political
events. Though it was subsequently
linked to the story in St Luke's Gospel
of the Good Samaritan, Bresdin
originally gave it the title 'Abd-el-
Kader giving aid to a Christian'.
This referred to the much-publicized
figure of Abdelkader el Djezairi, Emir
of Algeria, who had led his people's
fifteen-year insurgence against
French rule. Having surrendered in
1847, he was pardoned and allowed
to retire to Damascus. However,
caught up in violent disturbances
there in 1860, he gallantly intervened
to save the lives of Europeans and
Maronite Christians threatened by
religious conflict in the region.

Bresdin failed to capitalize on his
early success, and it was only the
sale of various reprintings of the
Samaritan that saved him from
abject poverty. In his last years he
was rediscovered by leading
Symbolist artists and writers.
Encouraged by this new wave of
attention, his daughter issued
further editions of the Samaritan.
This impression probably comes from
the second of these later printings,
taken from a transfer stone prepared
in about 1900.

SC

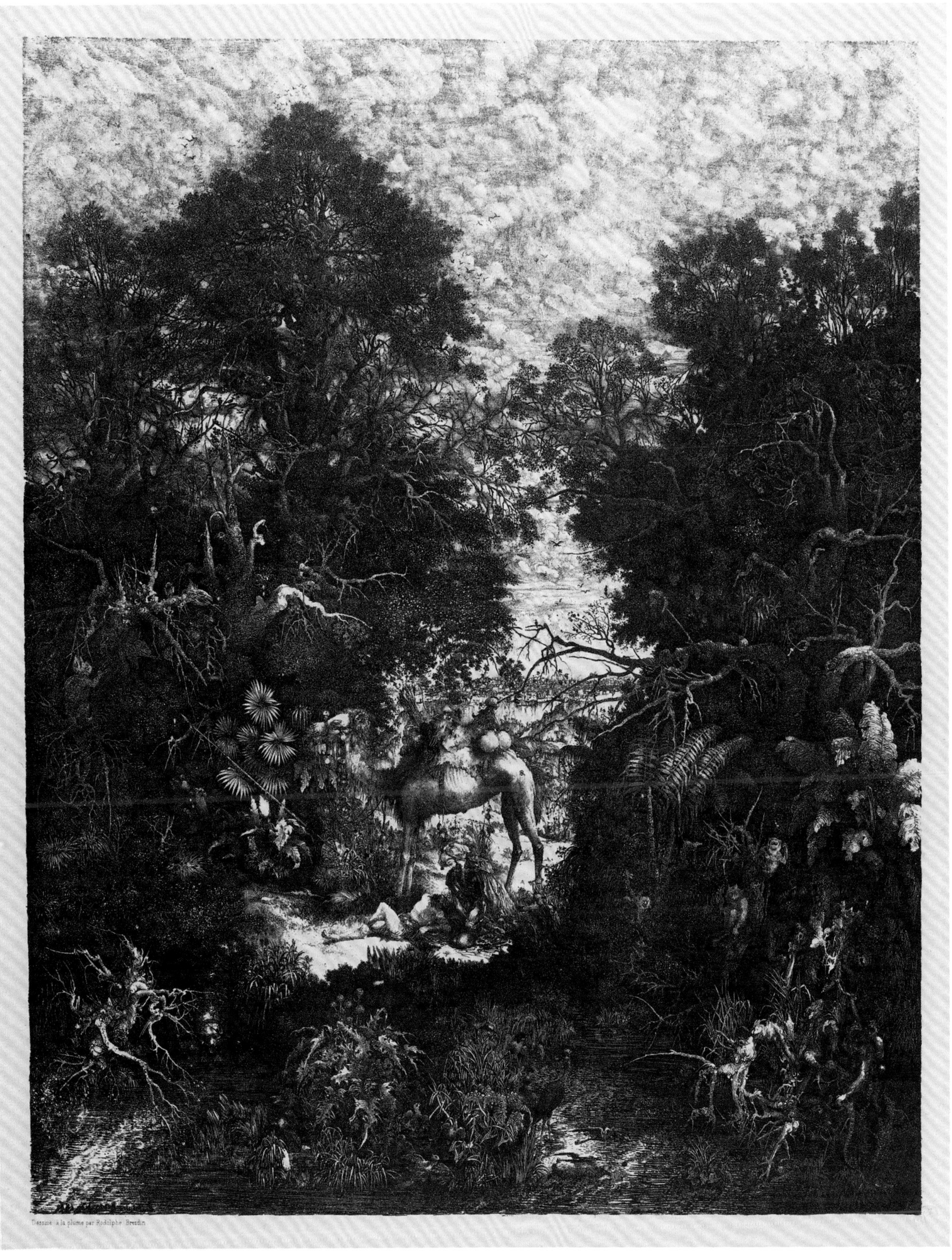Dessiné à la plume par Rodolphe Bresdin

Paul Drury (1903–87)
September, 1928
Etching; trial proof, 10th state
10.2 x 13 cm
V&A: E.3169–2004
Purchased through the Julie and
Robert Breckman Print Fund

Paul Drury was a key figure in the
last phase of the so-called 'Etching
Revival' in the 1920s, and belongs to
a group of British artists sometimes
called the 'Goldsmith's School', after
the London college where they all
studied or taught. In their prints of
rural subjects, made in the 1920s
and '30s, Drury, Graham Sutherland
(1903–80) and Robin Tanner
(1904–88) were all inspired by the
visionary landscapes of Samuel
Palmer (1805–81), most of which he
made during his time in the village
of Shoreham in Kent. Though Drury
had first seen Palmer's work in the
Tate in 1921, it was little known until
the seminal exhibition organized by
Martin Hardie at the V&A in 1926,
which revived Palmer's reputation.

Throughout his career Drury was
predominantly a portrait artist, but
he made a handful of etchings of
landscape subjects imbued with
the intense mystical spirit of Palmer's
Shoreham period. One of these
is *September*, which is generally
considered to be his masterpiece in
the genre.

The composition is a direct homage
to Palmer's Shoreham subjects, with
its thatched cottage, the conical
roofs of an oast house and the flock
of sheep, and at the centre figures
gathering windfalls from an apple
tree heavy with fruit. The image
started life as a drawing showing a
village church, some cottages, an
oast house and a small tree, but was
gradually modified until the apple
tree became the central motif, and
the sheep and figures (loosely based
on a drawing of gleaners by Jean-
François Millet (1642–79), owned by
Drury's father) were introduced. Drury
revised and reworked the image
repeatedly, through many states; this
impression comes from the 10th
state (of 12).

This is one of five prints, all of
landscape subjects, purchased from
the artist's son, Jolyon Drury, in 2004
through the Print Fund.

GS

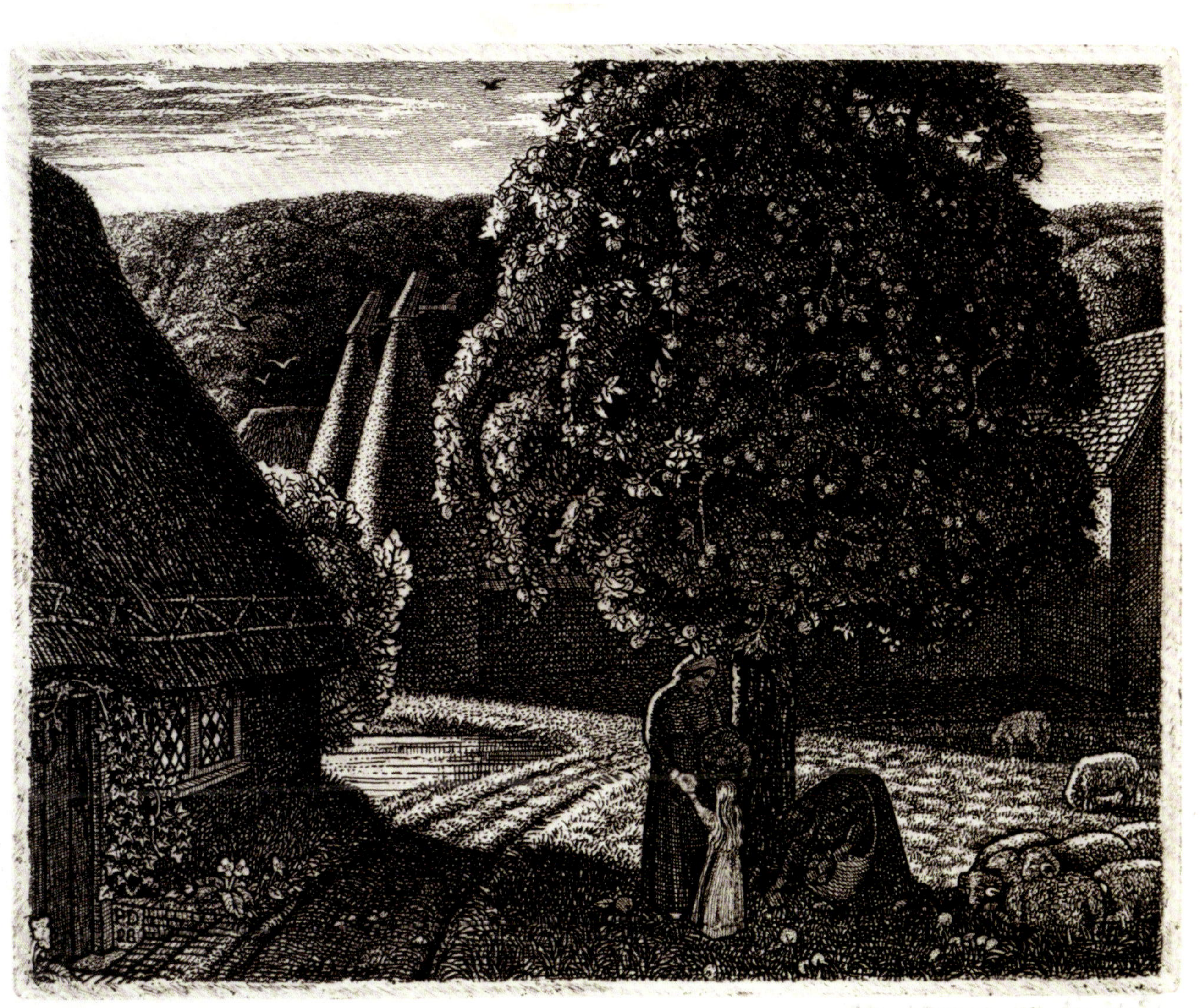

Peter Blake (b.1932)
Babe Rainbow, 1968
Published by Dodo Designs
Screen print on tinplate
66.4 x 43.4 cm
V&A: E.35–2006
Purchased through the Julie and
Robert Breckman Print Fund

Peter Blake was one of the founding
figures of British Pop Art, and his
work of the 1950s and '60s reflects
his love of working-class popular
culture – everything from pin-ups
and pop stars to tattooed ladies,
circus performers and wrestlers. He
has been going to wrestling matches
since he was about 16 and finds a
perverse glamour in the performers'
exaggerated characters, their
costumes and the choreography
of the battle between hero and
villain, which is as much theatre or
pantomime as it is a sporting event.

Though several of his prints and
paintings of wrestlers show real
people, Babe Rainbow is, in Blake's
account, 'a fictitious lady wrestler (…)
the most recent in a line of wrestlers
I have painted. These include *Irish
Lord X, Doktor K Tortur, Kamikaze* and
Les Orchidées Noires.' He invented
a biography for her, saying, 'She
is twenty-three years old and has
broken her nose in the ring. She
was born in New Cross, London and
wrestles mainly in Europe and the
USA as there have only been a few
contests between lady wrestlers in

London. She is the daughter of the
notorious *Doktor K Tortur*.' Blake has
given her a distinctively British identity
– her necklace features the word
'England' and the Union Jack; and
the belt at her waist has the word
'London' picked out in gilt letters, with
the cross of St George at the centre,
and other more arcane references
and motifs.

Much of Blake's work involved the
use of collage and the appropriation
of found images. When inventing
characters such as Babe Rainbow, he
reworked photographs and images
culled from other sources. For *Babe*,
he is said to have adapted the
image on the cover of a 1967 issue of
the French magazine *Marie Claire*.

Babe Rainbow was commissioned
by Dodo Designs, and reproduces
a painting dated 1967. It is unusual
because it is screen-printed on
tinplate. It was issued in an edition
of 1,000 and originally sold for
15 shillings (75 pence).

GS

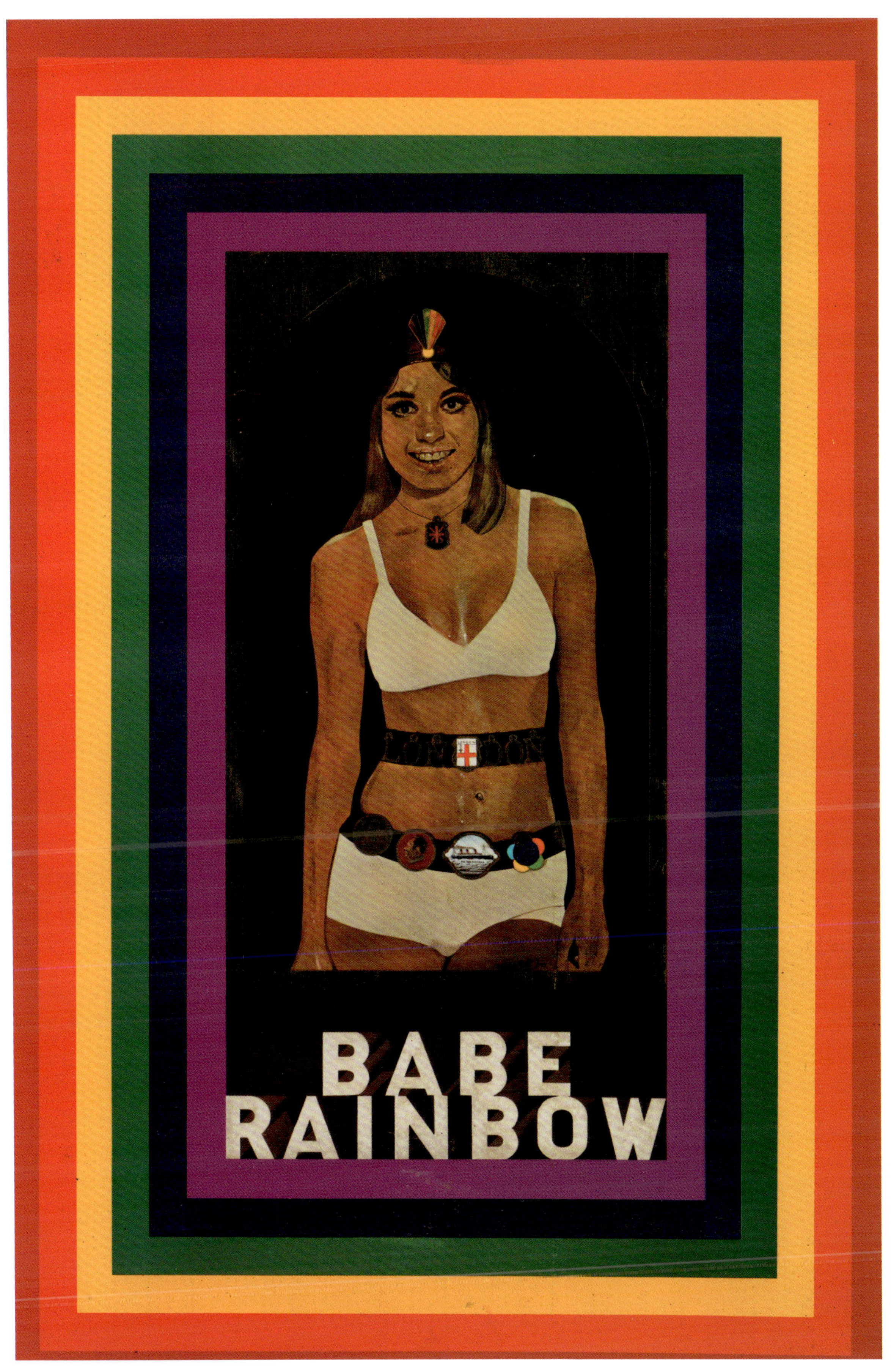

BABE
RAINBOW

Michael Druks (b.1940)

Druksland Physical and Social,
15 January 1974, 11.30 a.m., 1975
Printed and published by
Steendrukkerij de Jong & Co.,
Hilversum
Offset lithograph
47 x 37.8 cm
V&A: E.3010–2007
Purchased through the Julie and
Robert Breckman Print Fund

Israeli-born conceptual artist
Michael Druks has lived and worked
in Britain since the early 1970s. His
thematic preoccupations from
that time included the social and
political implications of boundaries
and borders, and the naming and
charting of territories. His self-portrait/
map evolved from a body of work
that explored personal and political
identity, adopting the idiom of
mapping as a universal system of
signs that was understood all over the
world. He called this 'an experiment
to use international and visual
language for individual purposes'.

In 1974 Druks was approached by
Steendrukkerij de Jong & Co., one of
the largest printing houses in Europe,
which was leading the progress
from photo-mechanical to digital
technologies in the printing industry.
Every year the company invited an
artist to collaborate with its printers
to create a print that was given
to clients as a promotional gift. To
create his piece, Druks 'mapped' the
landscape of his face by projecting
a grid of squares onto it using a
slide, and then photographed it
from different angles to build up a
contoured frontal view. The areas
of the face were coloured in using
the palette of mapmaking, and its
component parts were labelled like
geographical features – with a twist.
The naming of Druksland's facial
features alludes to the politics of the
state of Israel ('Occupied Territory',
'Left Druks'), the artist's psychological
make-up, his Jewish identity, places
he has been and people he has
known. The images portray the artist's
physical likeness, but at the same
time map his personality, situating
it as the product of political and
social influences and events, and
charting his biographical journey to a
particular moment in time.

TT

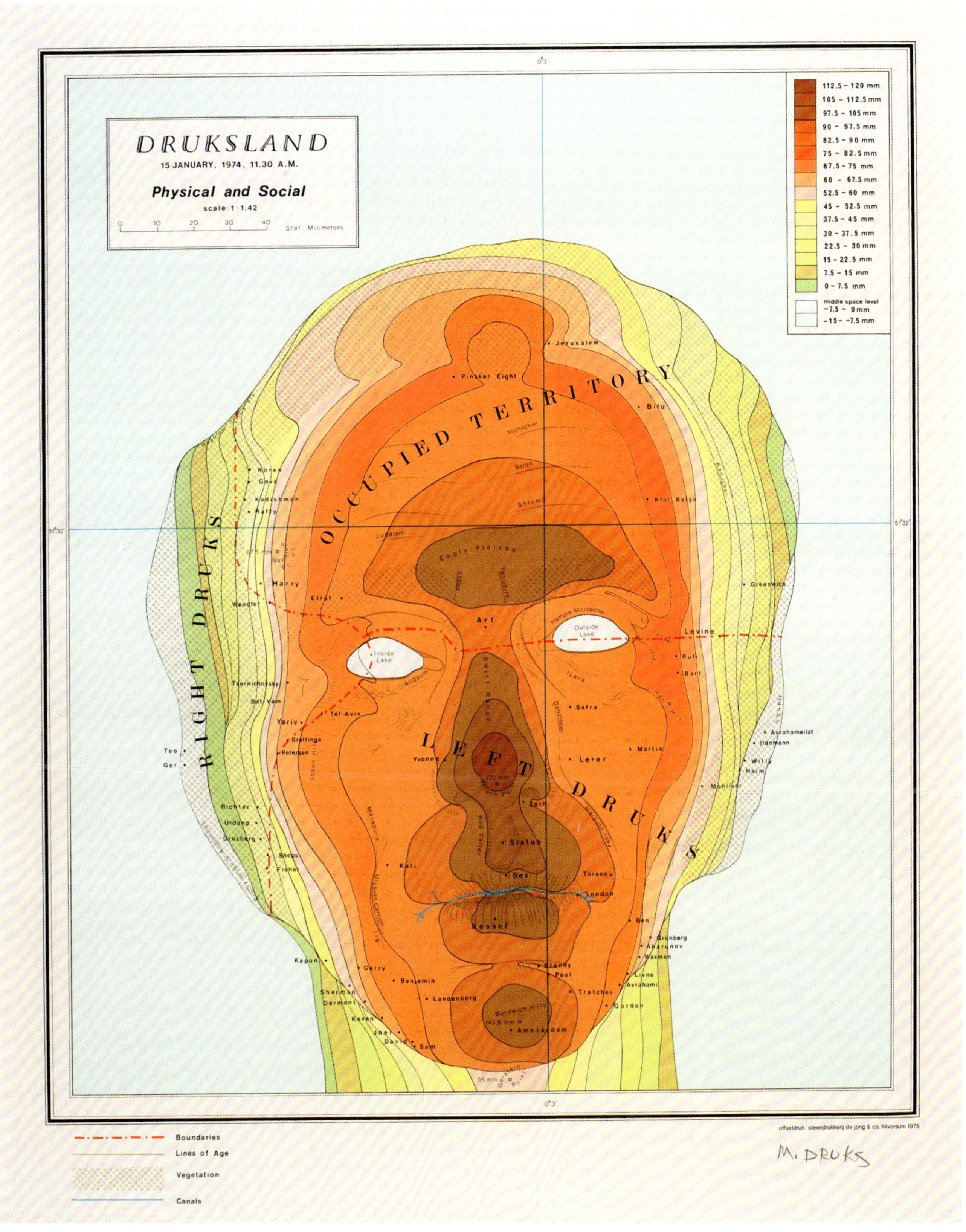

DRUKSLAND
15 JANUARY, 1974, 11.30 A.M.
Physical and Social
scale 1:1.42
0 10 20 30 40
Stat. Milimeters

112.5 – 120 mm
105 – 112.5 mm
97.5 – 105 mm
90 – 97.5 mm
82.5 – 90 mm
75 – 82.5 mm
67.5 – 75 mm
60 – 67.5 mm
52.5 – 60 mm
45 – 52.5 mm
37.5 – 45 mm
30 – 37.5 mm
22.5 – 30 mm
15 – 22.5 mm
7.5 – 15 mm
0 – 7.5 mm
middle space level
–7.5 – 0 mm
–15 – –7.5 mm

OCCUPIED TERRITORY
RIGHT DRUKS
LEFT DRUKS
Jerusalem
Pinsker Eight
Bilu
Yechezkiel
Sarah
Shlomo
Kfar Batya
Koren
Gevs
Kladshman
Rally
Judaism
Empty Plateau
Greenwich
Harry
Etrat
Wendle
Art
Hamore Mordechai
Outside Lake
Levine
Inside Lake
Ruti
Bart
Tsernichorsky
Ilana
Bat Yam
Safra
Yariv
Tel Aviv
Avrahameilat
Brattinga
Ilanmann
Teo
Petersen
Yvonne
Lerer
Martin
Willi
Ger
Haim
Mohilver
Richter
Zach
Urdang
Druzberg
Status
Sheps
Fisher
Kati
Sek
Torens
London
Ben
Kessef
Grünberg
Abarunov
Waxman
Kapon
Gerry
Blandy
Paul
Livne
Benjamin
Avrahami
Sherman
Landenberg
Tratches
Gordon
Dermont
Benowich Hills
Kevan
Joel
David
Sam
Amsterdam

Boundaries
Lines of Age
Vegetation
Canals

offsetdruk: steendrukkerij de jong & co, hilversum 1975
M. DRUKS

Judith K. Brodsky (b.1933)
Dishrag Diagrammatic, 1977
Etching; edition number I/XX
56 x 57 cm
V&A: E.135–2005
Purchased through the Julie and
Robert Breckman Print Fund

Judith Brodsky was an important
figure in the feminist movement in
the USA during the 1970s and has
been active as an artist, printmaker
and advocate for the arts. In 1986
she founded the influential Rutgers
Center for Innovative Print and Paper
(renamed the Brodsky Center in her
honour in 2006) at Rutgers, the State
University of New Jersey.

In her own prints and drawings
Brodsky works with imagery that
reflects on the intellectual, political
and social issues of our time, as
filtered through her own experience.
In particular, her work has engaged
with feminism, embodying such
slogans as 'The personal is political'
and co-opting domestic motifs
to comment on the struggles for
women's liberation. This colour
etching was made for a portfolio
published for the United Nations Year
of the Woman in 1977, alongside work
by 11 other New Jersey artists.

In this print a humble dishrag (or
a tea towel) is given an iconic
presence. It is presented like a flag,
and depicted in bold, vibrant colours
in a manner that is unmistakably

celebratory, held aloft like the stained
and tattered battle standard of a
victorious army that has fought long
and hard. The title suggests that it is
meant to be seen as instructive (like
a diagram) and therefore we should
read a message into it. Though it is
not explicit, it is easy to see this as
the physical evidence of 'women's
work', the constant struggle against
dirt and disorder in the home. But
perhaps it also signifies that women
are winning the fight against those
who would keep them corralled in
the domestic sphere, and that the
larger battles for women's rights are
also being won. The stripes of colour
at the bottom edge have no obvious
meaning, but there may be
some relevance in the choice of
purple and green, as these two
colours, with white, were the colours
of the Women's Social and Political
Union (led by Emmeline Pankhurst,
1858–1928), the most militant of the
women's suffrage movements in
the UK.

A second print by Brodsky, acquired
through the Print Fund, *Women, Love
and Philosophy III* (1998), represents
a piece of lace depicting the myth
of Danaë and the Shower of Gold,
a subtle meditation on violence and
war, and shows Brodsky still engaged
with issues of women and politics
20 years on.

GS

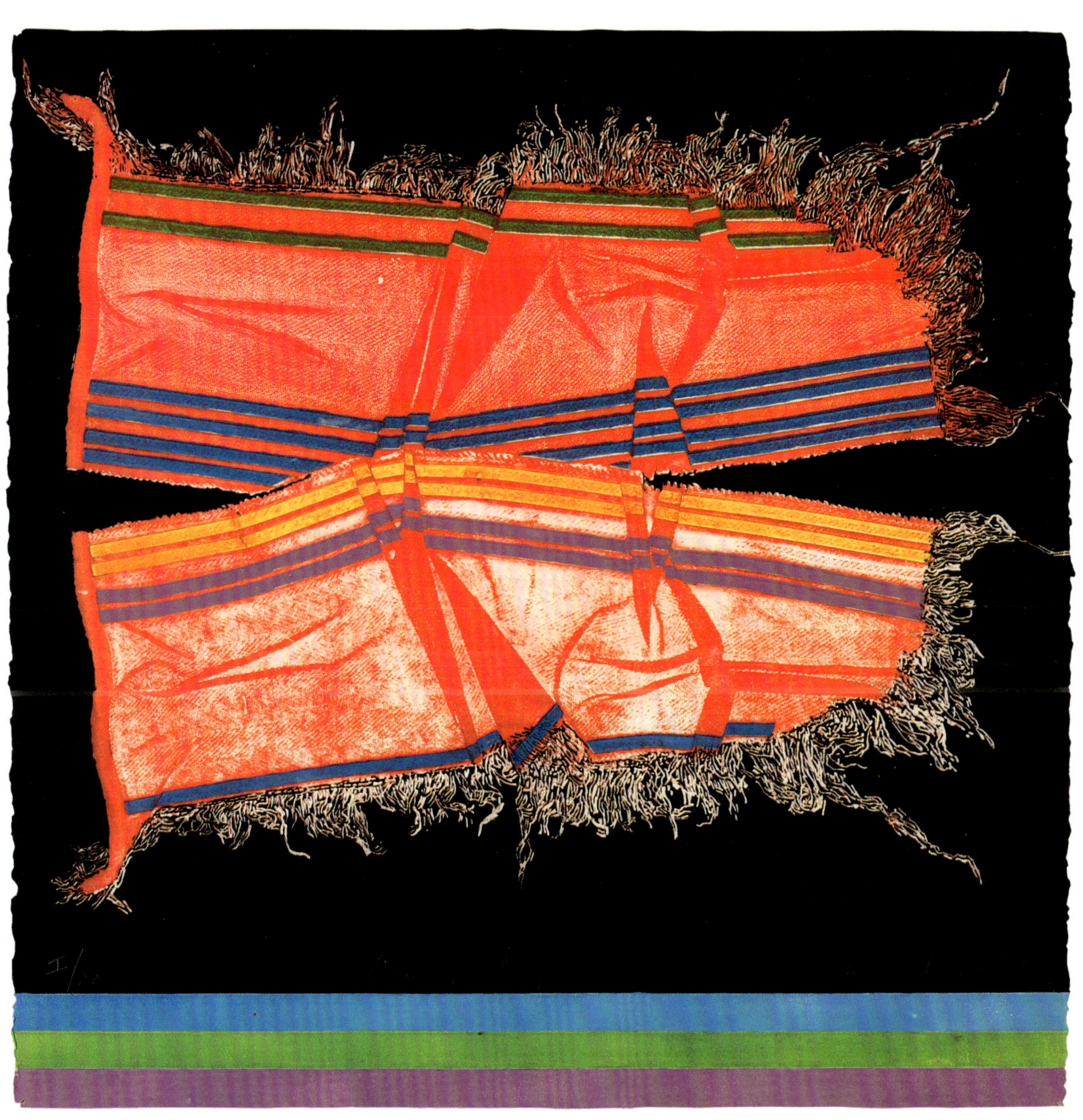

Susan Derges (b.1955)

Shoreline, October 5 1998, 1998
Dye destruction print
106.7 x 213.4 cm (framed)
V&A: E.528–2005
Donated by Robert Breckman in
memory of Julie

This photograph (or more correctly 'photogram') from the *Shoreline* series is a unique print made without the use of a camera. To make it, the artist went to the South Devon coast at night and laid a sheet of light-sensitive photographic paper on the beach. She then waited for the high tide and, as a wave broke over the paper, she set off a flash from above. Thus the photograph captures and fixes this moment, with the swirling rush of the water and the trails of stirred-up sand that the wave brought with it. With the *Shoreline* series, the pinkish tones are actually the result of light pollution from nearby street lights reflecting on the water.

From the beginning, Derges has eschewed conventional photography because she felt 'the camera always separates the subject from the viewer', and has instead worked with various experimental methods, seeking more direct connections with the natural world. She has regularly worked with water – and in particular water as an element of specific landscapes – usually in places that are local and familiar to her. Her huge photograms of waves on the seashore and of the waters of the River Taw are literal records of place, and eloquent metaphors for the natural rhythms and cycles of life. They also connect humans and nature, the body and the landscape.

This photogram has been exhibited in the V&A Members' Room, and was also a key exhibit in an important V&A touring exhibition entitled *Something I'll Never Really See: Contemporary Photography from the V&A*, which showcased photographs of places and people that viewers were unlikely to see in real life.

GS

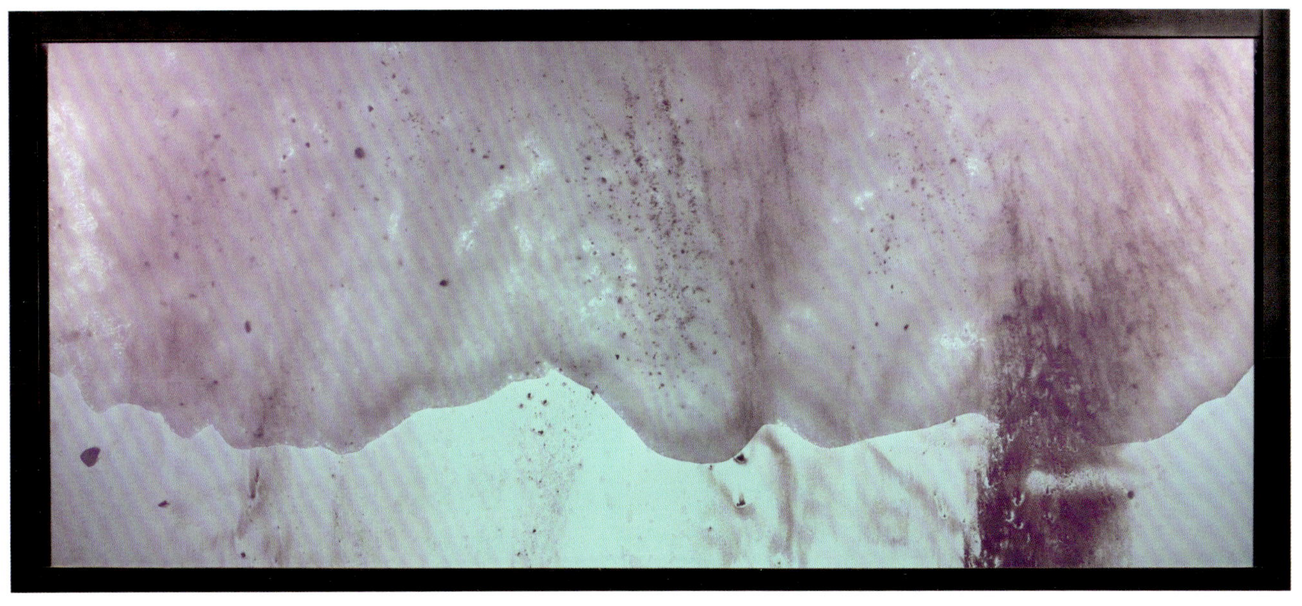

Maria Magdalena Campos-Pons
(b.1959)

Untitled, 1999
Colour photogravure on handmade
paper; edition number 9/14
51.4 x 44.5 cm
V&A: E.878–2003
Purchased through the Julie and
Robert Breckman Print Fund

Maria Magdalena Campos-Pons was
born in Cuba, of West African Yoruba
ancestry, and now lives in the US. Her
Nigerian ancestors were brought to
Cuba to work as slaves in the sugar
plantations. Much of her work is
autobiographical, and she explores
her complex Afro-Cuban identity
through works that engage with
history, memory and ideas of exile
and distance. She often includes
references to religious rituals and
storytelling, drawing on Cuban and
West African traditions. In this print she
has superimposed hand-drawn eyes
over an image of her own naked
back, emphasizing the centrality
of her colour and gender in her
experience of how others respond to,
and define, her.

These eyes, which echo the shape
of cowrie shells, may be a reference
to representations of Yoruba spirits –
Elegba, the male Yoruba *orisha*
(spirit or deity), is often depicted with
cowrie-shell eyes, and the female
orisha Oshun is frequently associated
with peacock feathers and their
decorative 'eyes'.

But the eyes may also allude to the
feminist theory that the female body
is subject to a controlling scrutiny or
gaze, in art and in life. The immigrant,
too, is subject to the surveillance of
authority in a new country, and may
be the object of suspicion in the host
society, an experience that would be
familiar to the artist herself.

GS

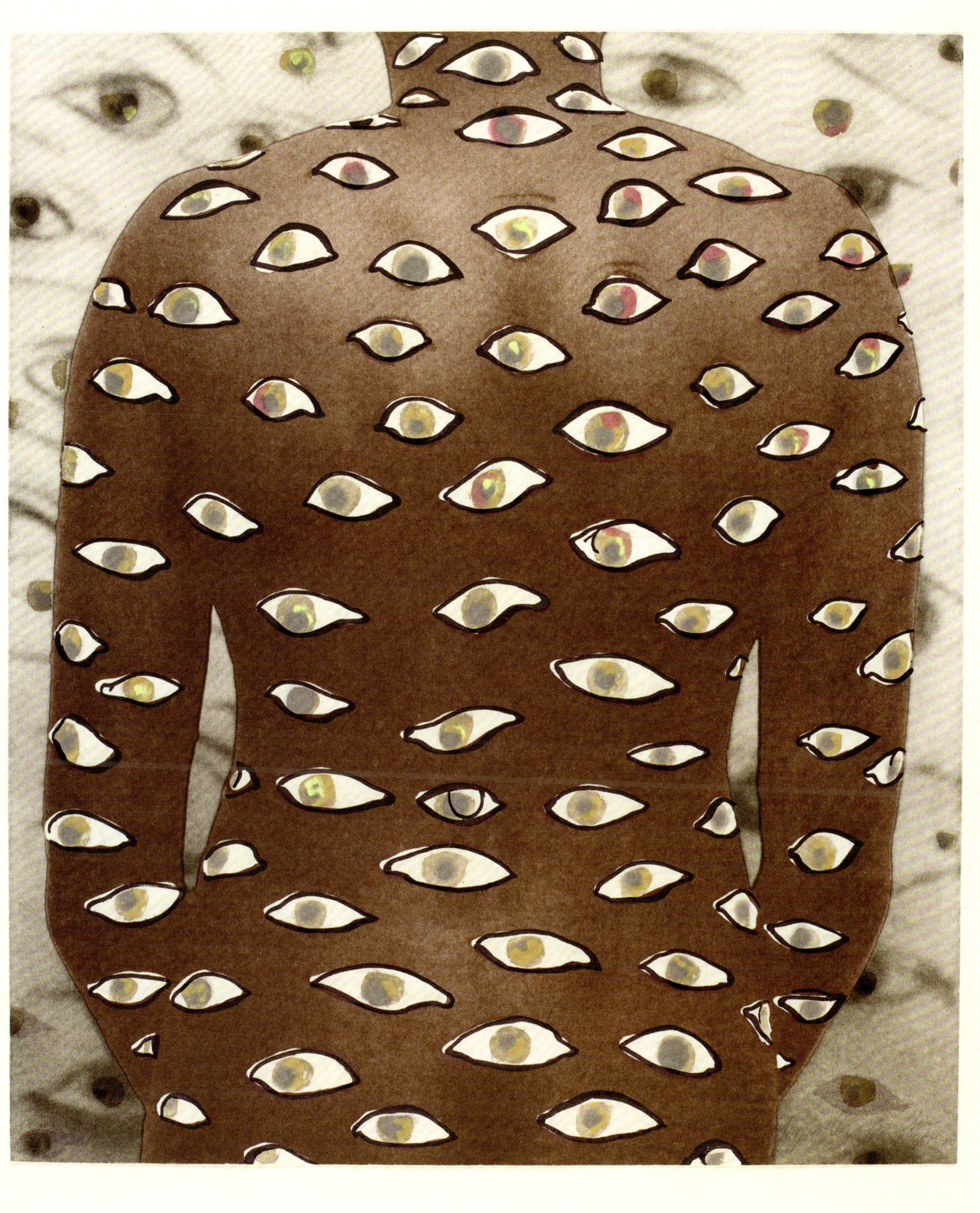

Adrian Wiszniewski (b.1958)
Stations of the Cross, 1999
Published by Glasgow Print Studio
Linocuts (14) on tenjin paper; edition
number 17/30
Each 62 x 50 cm
V&A: E.522:1 to 14–2001
Purchased through the Julie and
Robert Breckman Print Fund

This series of 14 prints was made to
celebrate the second millennium of
Christianity. In 1999, Bury St Edmunds
Art Gallery, in partnership with the
Diocese of St Edmundsbury and
Ipswich and the Council for the
Care of Churches, commissioned
13 contemporary artists to make
new sets of the Stations of the Cross,
a devotional sequence of 14 scenes
depicting the passion and death of
Christ. The finished sets of stations,
in various media, were exhibited
at the gallery, the cathedral and
several local churches during the
year 2000. Adrian Wiszniewski's
series of linocuts was shown at the
church of St Andrew, Wingfield. It
was also published in an edition of
30 by Glasgow Print Studio. This is
an organization founded in 1972 to
promote the art of printmaking by
running courses for artists who wish
to make prints, providing access to its
printing workshops and organizing a
programme of exhibitions in its gallery,
showcasing the work of local and
international artists. It is now one of
the largest publishers of original prints
in Britain, inviting leading artists from
around the world to collaborate with
its master printmakers.

Adrian Wiszniewski is one of a
generation of young Scottish artists
who came to prominence with
figurative paintings during the 'Neo-
Expressionist' mood that enlivened
the international art scene in the
early 1980s. Here he has illustrated
Christ's last hours in loosely drawn
compositions of white lines against
backgrounds of solid colour – just
one colour for each scene. The
colours are charged with symbolism:
faded purple for Christ's encounter
with imperial Rome, when he is
condemned to death by a world-
weary Pontius Pilate in the first
station; sky-blue, the colour sacred
to the Virgin Mary, for their poignant
meeting on the road to Calvary in
the fourth station. The characters
in the drama are shown in modern
dress, as though they were actors
in a contemporary mystery play.
This has the effect of associating
Christ's redemptive suffering with the
cruelties of our own age, abstracting
the scenes from their historical time
and place and projecting them
into the perennial here and now of
contemplation, a sacred realm where
Christ is always dying and Mary is
always weeping.

These prints were exhibited at the
V&A in 2005, alongside Albrecht
Dürer's famous woodcuts of the
same subjects, and have since been
exhibited at the Royal Brompton
Hospital as part of the V&A's
partnership with the Paintings in
Hospitals charity.

TT

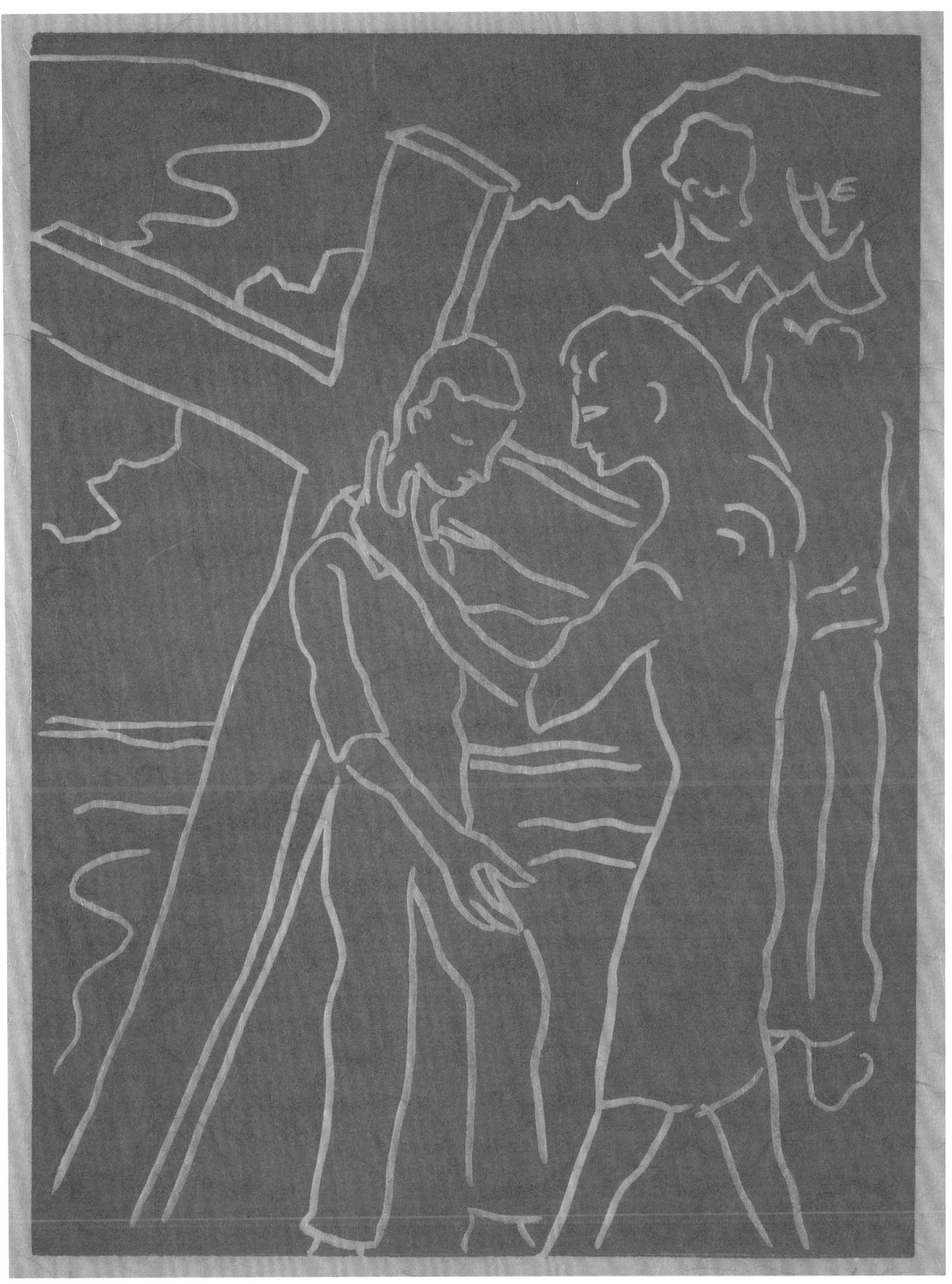

Damien Hirst (b.1965)

Steak and Kidney from *The Last Supper*, 1999
Printed by Coriander Studios and
published by Paragon Press
Screen print; from an edition of 150
152.5 x 101.5 cm
V&A: E.175–2002
Purchased through the Julie and
Robert Breckman Print Fund

This print comes from a set of 13
entitled *The Last Supper*. The image
– which is poster-sized – imitates
pharmaceutical packaging in its
colours, typography and layout,[1]
but the name of the drug has
been replaced with the name of a
food that is traditional to working-
class British café culture. Others
in the series include 'Sausages',
'Beans' and 'Cornish Pasty'.
Each print includes a variation
on the artist's name (here simply
'Damien') in place of the usual
drug manufacturer's logo, in a sly
allusion to his own art-world status
as a brand. There is a nostalgic or
'retro' feel to the design, and to the
foods themselves. The immediate
inspiration for the series can be
found in Hirst's own work, in particular
his installations of cabinets filled
with pharmaceutical packages, but
he has also acknowledged formal
parallels with minimalism. The
prints also reference Andy Warhol's
screen-printed images of
commodities such as Campbell's
soup cans and Coke bottles.

The series reflects Hirst's abiding
interest in death and religion,
explored here through ideas about
consumption. The prints address
our complex relationships with food
and medicines, substances that are
used and abused in contemporary
western societies. He suggests that
taking medicines has become as
routine and essential as eating,
but at the same time implies that
food itself has become an industrial
product stuffed with chemical
compounds – artificial colours and
flavourings, as well as antibiotics and
growth hormones. The series title
references the 'Last Supper' at which
Christ transformed bread and wine
into His body and blood, by which
they became agents of spiritual
sustenance and everlasting life. Here,
Hirst claims that art itself is a source
of sustenance, the equivalent of
religion, drugs and food.

The prints also refer to the London
restaurant called Pharmacy, which
Hirst and his collaborators had
opened a year earlier, in 1998;
the white minimalist interior was
decorated by Hirst, with displays of
pharmaceutical packaging in
the windows and artworks including
pill cabinets. The waiters wore
surgical gowns.

GS

1 The design of the prints was undertaken
by graphic designer Jonathan Barnbrook
working to Hirst's directions.

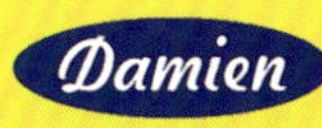

5036-23

Steak and Kidney*
Ethambutol Hydrochloride

Tablets
400mg

100 Tablets

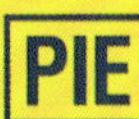

Rachel Whiteread (b.1963)

Herringbone Floor, 2001
Produced by Lasercraft and
published by Counter Editions
Laser-cut relief in birch plywood;
edition number 15/450
51 x 44 cm
V&A: E.20–2002
Purchased through the Julie and
Robert Breckman Print Fund

In 1992 sculptor Rachel Whiteread
was awarded a DAAD (German
Academic Exchange Service)
fellowship, and as a result she spent
a year living and working in Berlin.
She made several drawings of
the parquet floor of her Berlin flat;
some of these drawings are precise
and geometric, others are drawn
freehand so that the lines bunch
and waver, producing an irregular
pattern. It was one of these drawings
that inspired this delicate multiple.

Whiteread's work involves making
plaster or resin casts of spaces inside
or underneath everyday domestic
objects – baths and wardrobes,
mattresses and hot-water bottles. She
has cast whole rooms, and famously
a complete house, giving substance
to the intangible. This piece was
made by scanning her drawing onto
a sheet of very fine plywood. Using
laser-cutting technology, the space
between the drawn lines was cut
away, leaving a fine web of plywood
to represent the spaces between the
tiles of a parquet floor.

Floors have been a consistent motif
in Whiteread's work since she made
the Berlin drawings, and she has
made a number of casts of floors
that draw attention not only to
the surface texture, but also to the
pattern produced by laying each
block or board against the next. Her
casts are always made from objects
and spaces that carry traces of a
human presence, the wear and tear
of daily life. Though *Herringbone Floor*
is a work of precision and control,
by translating the uneven lines of
the original drawing, it alludes to
this 'lived-in' quality of a space and
has the character of something
uncertainly remembered.

Herringbone Floor is also intriguing
as a reference to prints and
printmaking, for it can be read as a
woodblock – the means of making
an impression of itself.

GS

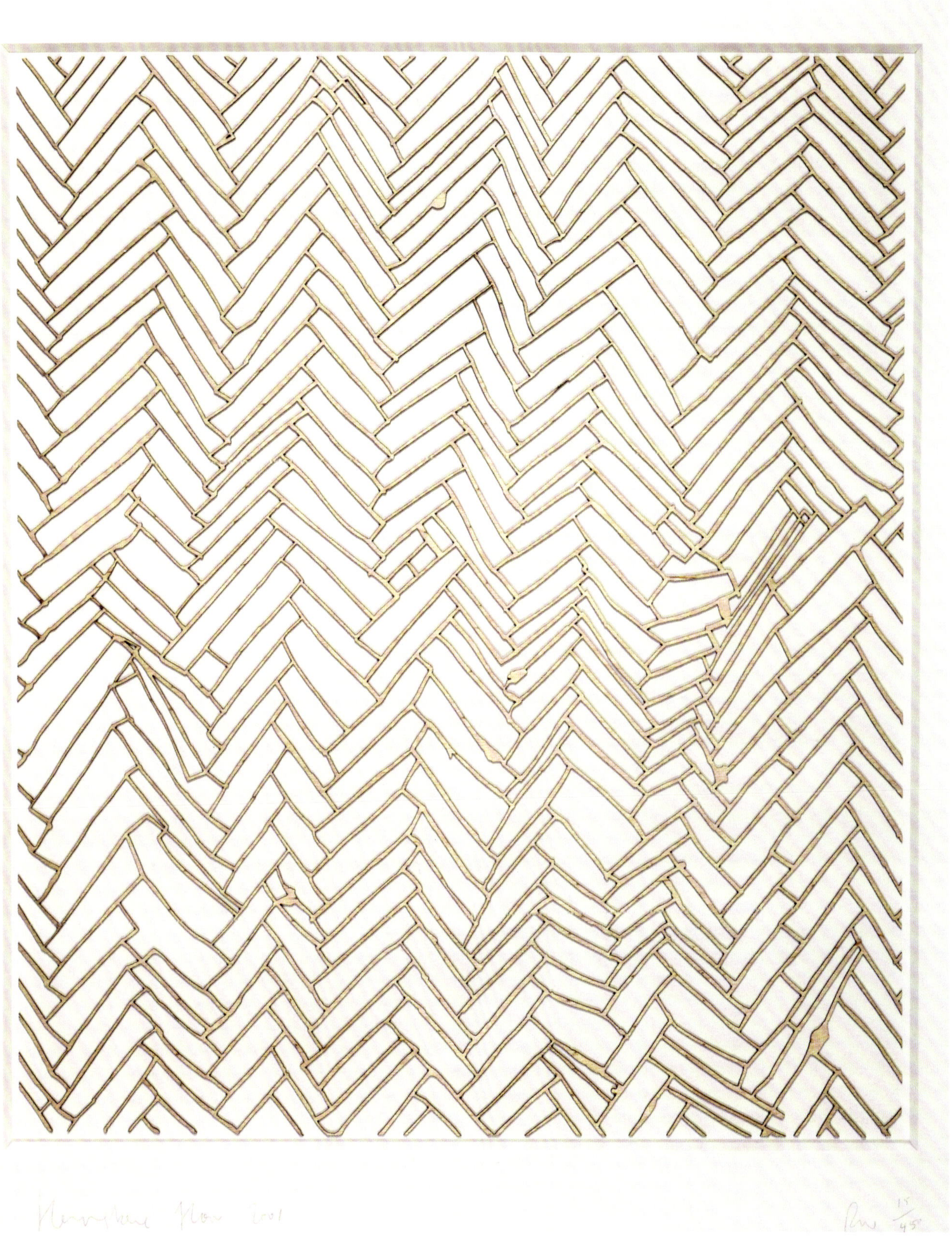

David Bosun (b.1973)
Gelam Nguzi Kazi (Dugong My Son),
2001
Linocut *(kaidaral)*; edition number
10/85
47 x 61.1 cm
V&A: E.1092–2002
Purchased through the Julie and
Robert Breckman Print Fund

The 1990s saw the emergence of a group of young printmakers in the Torres Strait Islands (situated to the north of Australia). All had studied at technical colleges in mainland Australia, where they were exposed to a wider range of artistic influences than was available at home. They combined this experience with their knowledge of traditional visual patterns and oral narratives, to develop a trademark style markedly more complex and ambitious than the images that then dominated a tourist-driven art market. Dennis Nona (b.1973), who is generally credited with initiating this new style, describes how the idea came to him in a dream to 'place around a single print all the elements of a large creation story…an entire narrative in one single work of art with all the characters and events linked by the clan patterning (or "minaral"), that bound the entire story to its place of origin'. The group became known as the Mualgau Minaral Artist Collective.

The 'minaral', specific to each clan, was traditionally engraved on objects such as ritual masks, but had been almost erased from the collective cultural memory through the proscriptions of nineteenth-century Christian missionaries and the removal from the islands of many such objects by anthropologists in the 1870s and '80s. Its revived use in printmaking, where the pattern is cut into lino, refers back to its original form. The principal image is black-and-white; colour is added by lifting the print on three margins and reapplying ink '*à la poupée*' (with a ball-shaped wad of cloth). In the Torres Strait Islands the process has been renamed *kaidaral* – literally, 'spirit that creates ripples on the surface of the water'.

This map-like print shows episodes from an island creation myth. A mother discovers that her son is keeping for himself the best of his catch (his fire burns brighter than hers, with fat from his roasting pigeon). She punishes him by disguising herself as a witch, to frighten him while he is hunting. However, he discovers her trick (cleaning lice from her hair, he sees traces of the mud she has used to mask herself). Disgusted, he makes a raft in the shape of a dugong, or sea cow (at the centre), and abandons her for ever. Weeping on the shore, she is transformed into a rock, which, it is said, can be seen on Moa Island (Bosun's birthplace) to this day.

GS

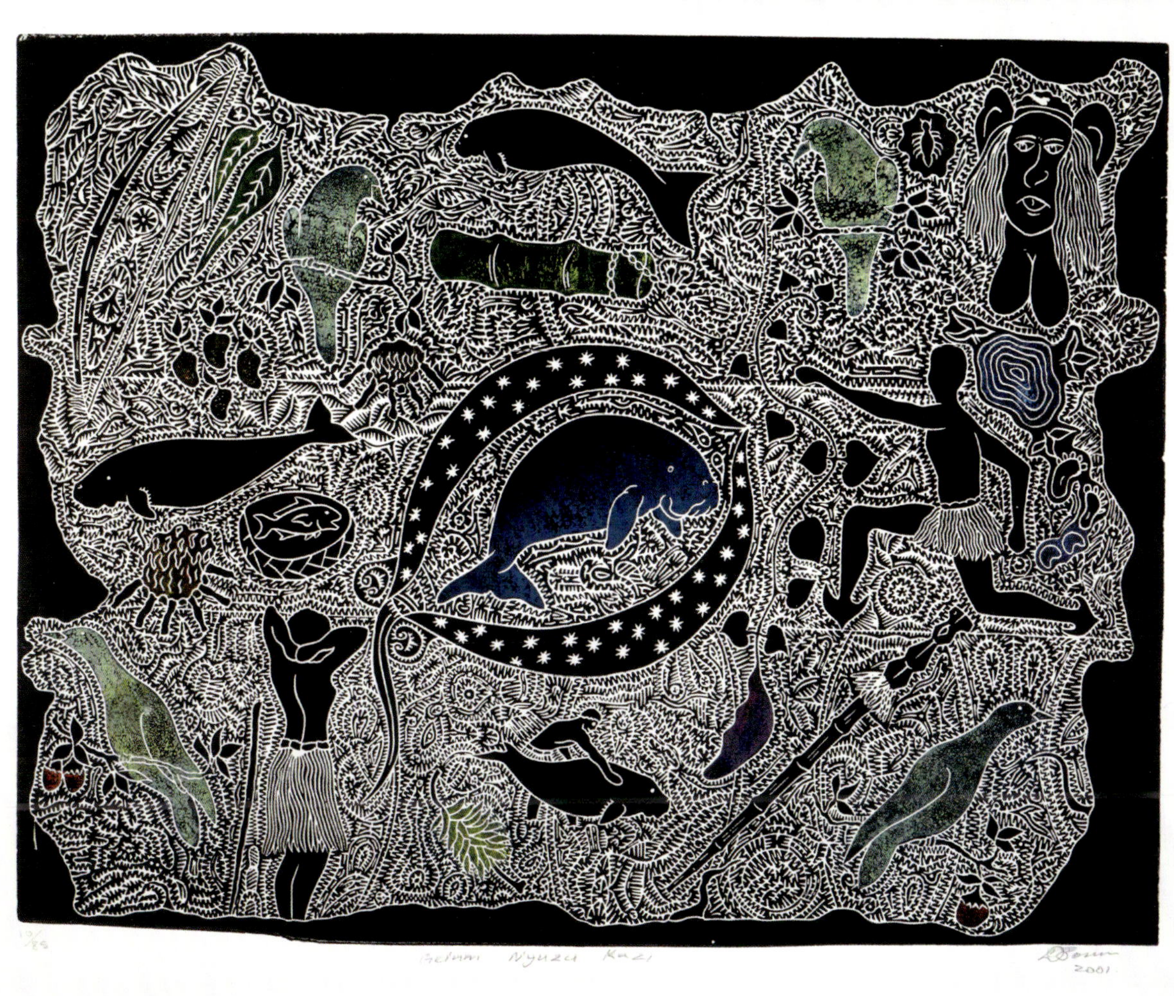

Dan Hays (b.1966)
Sanctuary, 2001
Published by the Multiple Store,
London
Digital cibachrome print with
lenticular plastic; edition number
32/50
46 x 68 cm
V&A: E.334–2003
Purchased through the Julie and
Robert Breckman Print Fund

Dan Hays made this print in
collaboration with the Multiple Store,
which was established in 1999 to
publish limited-edition objects by
artists in various media, bringing
them to new audiences and often
introducing them to unfamiliar
materials in the process. Since 1996
Hays had been making paintings of
empty cages, a sly reference to his
famous guinea-pig paintings, but
also a vehicle for his experiments with
subtly shifting colour relationships and
spatial ambiguities. The first painting
in the series had been derived from
a found photograph, and Hays'
concern with mediated imagery –
gradually evolving as it is translated
from one medium to another – was
given a further twist in this project.

Hays' invitation to create an edition
with the Multiple Store fortuitously
coincided with a digital technology-
driven revival in lenticular printing.
This was a process combining two
or more spliced-together views with
a plastic screen made up of tiny

lenses or prisms to create a three-
dimensional image, which appears
to move as it is viewed from different
angles. Hays used a 3D modelling
software program to create a version
of his 1997 cage painting *Harmony
in Green*, which he then turned into
a 24-frame lenticular animation,
rotating the view by just a few
degrees around a central axis. As well
as the whole view shifting slightly, the
areas of flat colour between the bars
of the cage constantly switch and
change, albeit within a harmoniously
related band of values. The viewer
experiences an illusionistically realized
three-dimensional space, rendered
in a calm palette, but one that is
unsettlingly destabilized and, in
ideological terms, problematized. The
title *Sanctuary* takes on an ironic or
wistful tenor, with political overtones.
It suggests an analogy with the
modern state, which offers its citizens
security at the price of their freedoms,
or holds out to refugees the prospect
of asylum, only to detain them in
processing camps.

TT

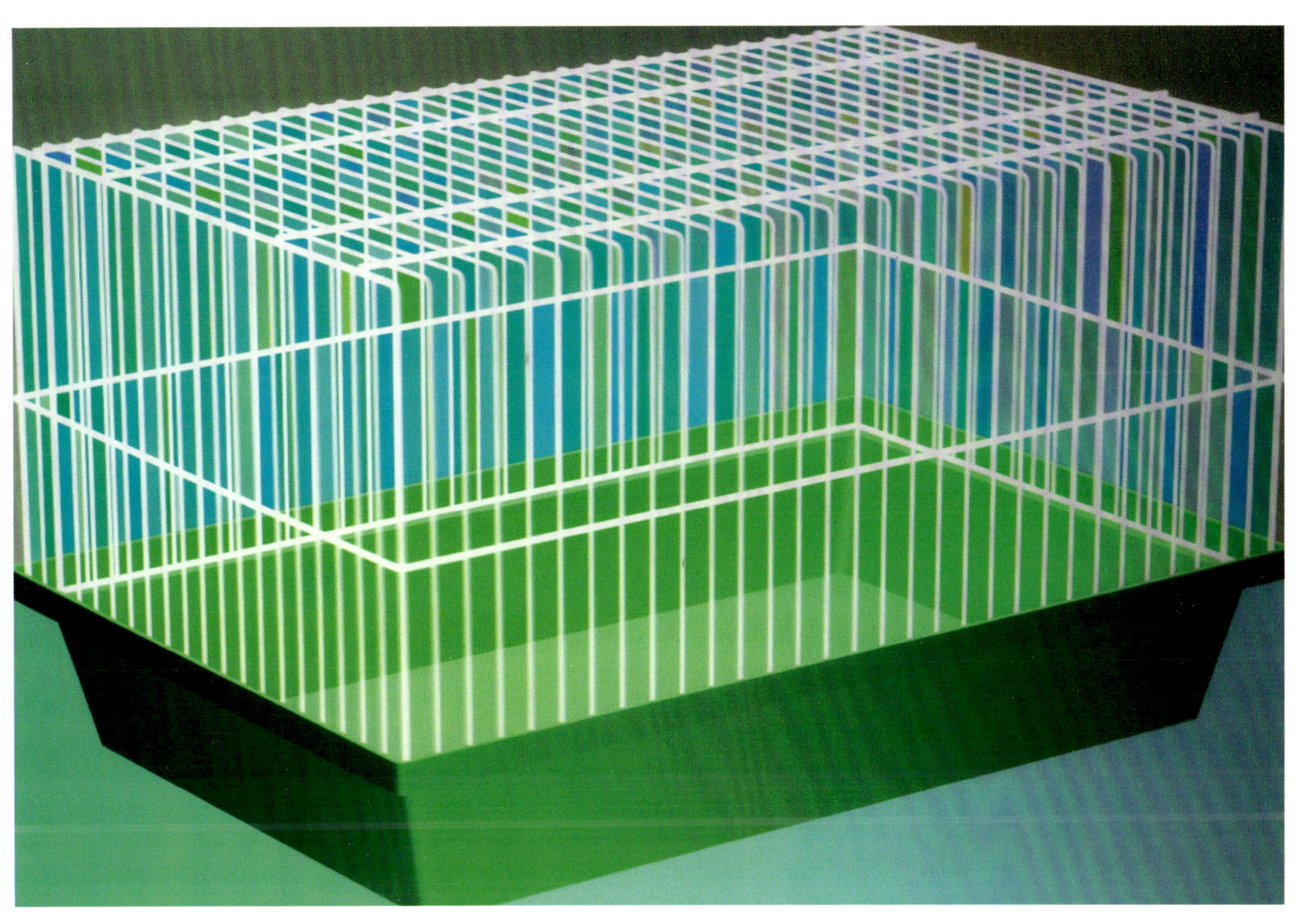

Langlands & Bell (Ben Langlands,
b.1955, and Nikki Bell, b.1959)
Air Routes of the World (Night) and
Air Routes of the World (Day), 2001
Screen prints in painted wood frames
Each 84 x 143.8 x 3.8 cm
V&A: E.9, 10–2002
Purchased through the Julie and
Robert Breckman Print Fund

Langlands & Bell have been
collaborating since 1978, working
in a variety of media to explore
the systems of communication
that codify our world. Their artistic
appropriation of diagrams and
plans recalls the movement
towards 'de-materialization' in the
conceptual art of the 1960s and
'70s, which scrutinized the qualities of
non-aesthetic systems of information.
Typically this was a strategy that
eschewed the traditional artistic
craft values of technique and 'touch'
or the visual rhetoric of pathos,
restricting itself to a cool, pared-
back idiom. In their approach,
however, Langlands & Bell manage
to suggest narrative possibilities,
evoking a range of emotional and
psychological responses.

This print diptych is from a series of
works based on the global network
of international airline routes,
including a digital animation related
to the present piece and a public
sculpture at Heathrow Terminal 5. In
black on white (day) and white on
black (night), two otherwise identical

diagrams appear as webs of lines
arcing between the variously sized
circular dots, representing flight paths
criss-crossing the curvature of the
Earth's surface between the airports
of the world. The busier the airport,
the larger the dot. No geographical
features are shown and none of the
routes or airports are labelled.
In its black-on-white incarnation, the
resulting abstract form resembles
a Constructivist mobile or the
schematic drawing for the wing of
some imaginary flying contraption,
while the white-on-black version
seems to chart constellations of stars
in the night sky. The viewer is offered
an alternative map of the world: one
shaped by the constant to-and-fro
of air travel, suffused with longing for
adventure and escape, for flight in
more than one sense of the word.

TT

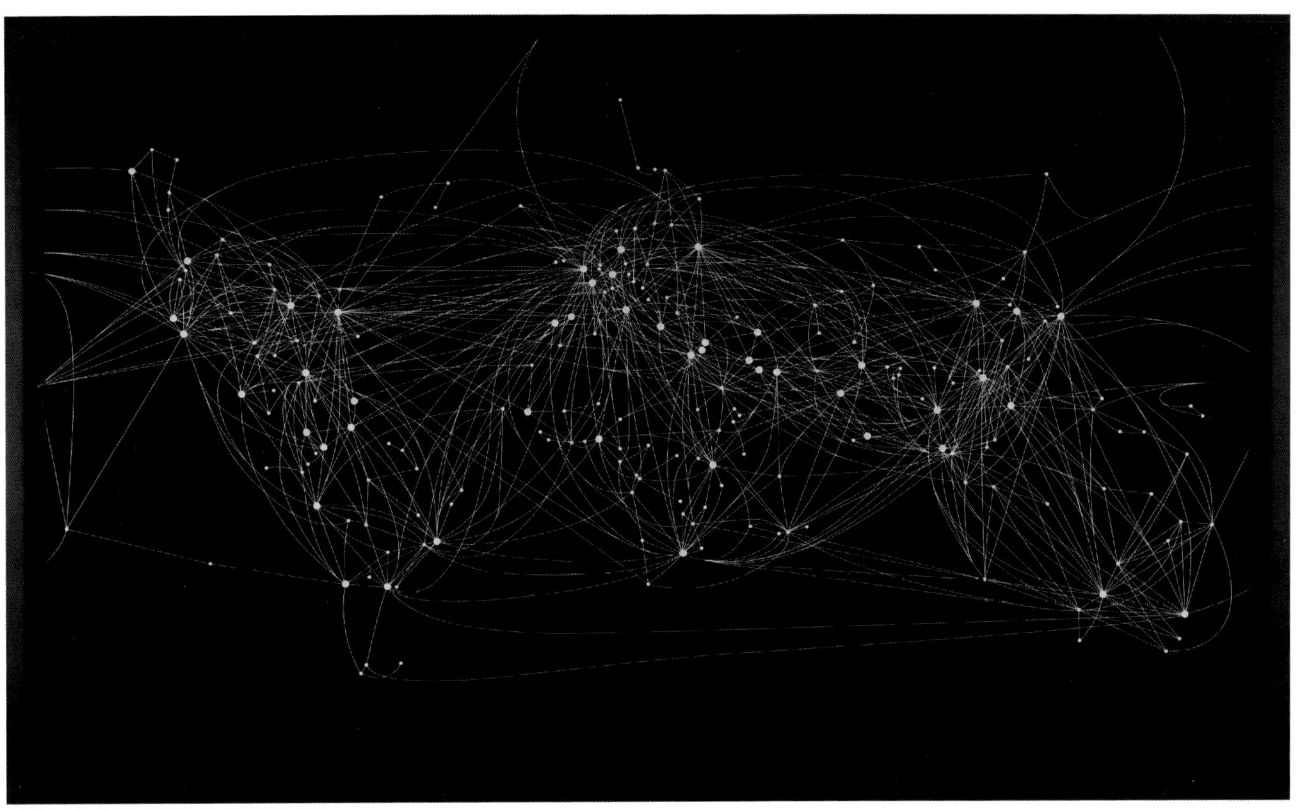

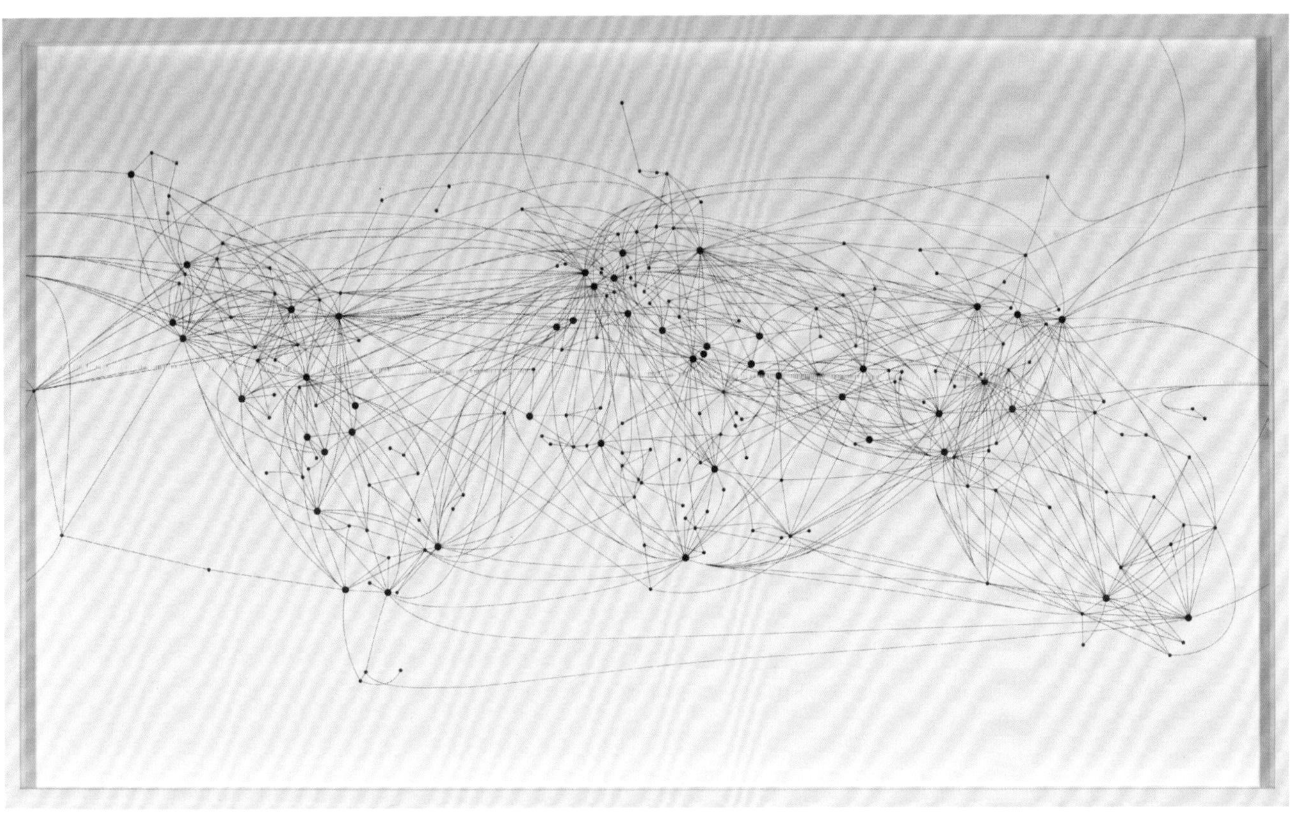

Lucian Freud (1922–2011)
After Constable's Elm, 2003
Printed by Studio Prints, London, and
published by Matthew Marks Gallery,
New York
Etching; edition number 40/46
48 x 38 cm (size of sheet)
V&A: E.1063–2003
Purchased through the Julie and
Robert Breckman Print Fund

Lucian Freud is renowned as a
painter, but he also worked
extensively with etching. He was
fascinated by the printmaking
process, and enjoyed what he called
the 'element of danger and mystery',
the unpredictability inherent in
etching, with the biting of the printing
plate in the acid bath and the
reversal of the image in the transfer
from plate to paper.

Freud's prints were produced in
parallel with his paintings, though
they are never reproductions of
them. They explore the same subjects
and often portray the same sitters,
but were always conceived as
independent works of art. In addition
to the nudes, and the 'portrait heads'
as he called them, he also produced
a handful of landscape subjects
in paint, and in print. Most of these
were drawn from the life, but *After
Constable's Elm* had a different origin.

John Constable's modest oil, *Study of
the trunk of an elm tree*, was painted
around 1821 and came to the V&A

in 1888, part of an extensive gift from
Constable's daughter, Isabel. Freud
had admired this study since he first
saw it at the age of 17, and it was
among the pictures he selected for
an exhibition of Constable's work
in Paris in 2002. The catalogue
included a conversation between
Freud and the art critic William Feaver
(b.1942), published in 2003 as 'Freud
on Constable'. There he recalled,
'I'd seen the little painting of the
tree-trunk, close-up in the V&A and
I thought what a good idea. That's
the thing, I thought. Trees. They are
everywhere. Do one of those. A close-
up. Real bark. So I took my easel out
and put it down in front of a tree and
found it completely impossible'. As an
art student in Dedham (in 'Constable
Country'), Freud also tried – and failed –
to copy the Constable painting.

Prompted by this memory of
challenge and frustration, he
engaged with the picture once more,
and made an etching to accompany
the book. Freud's image is an
eloquent translation of the Constable –
it is not an exact copy (not least
because it is reversed in the printing),
and it is in black-and-white, yet
through etched lines and subtle plate
tone it achieves a richly textured
rendering of its subject that is
respectful of its source, yet
unmistakably a Lucian Freud print.

GS

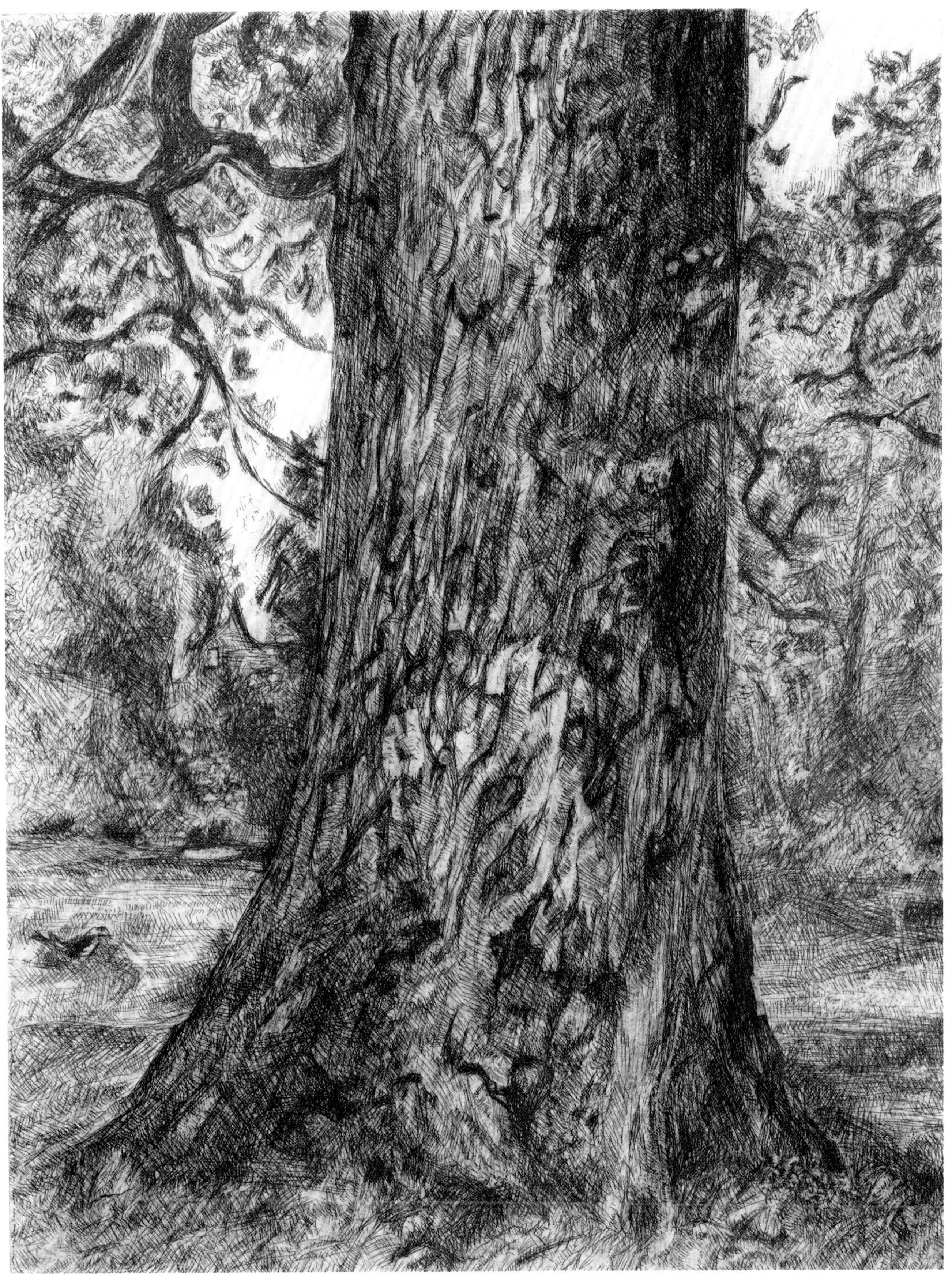

Sickboy

Love Supreme, c.2004
Screen print; edition number 37/250
70 x 50 cm
V&A: E.382–2005
Purchased through the Julie and
Robert Breckman Print Fund

In recent years graffiti has evolved
into a rich and accessible form of
visual expression that has come to
be known as 'street art'. While there
is no single aesthetic, street art has
a common means of transmission as
an unsanctioned and unfiltered form
of public art. Images range from
self-promotion to playful reworkings of
pop culture, to irreverent reflections
on society and the state of the world.
In an era when public spaces are
becoming increasingly privatized
and gentrified, the very presence of
street art can be a political comment.

Street art encompasses many
techniques, including forms of
printmaking such as stencils sprayed
on walls and digitally printed stickers
that invite people to embellish
the built environment. While street
art is essentially an urban genre,
many street artists in the 2000s
started translating their work into
limited-edition prints, offering the
opportunity to capture and collect
images that usually only have a
fleeting life on the street before they
are scrubbed off, painted over or
simply degraded by the weather.
The V&A began collecting

street-art prints in 2004, building an
international collection that includes
work from British, French, American
and Brazilian artists.

Sickboy is a Bristol-based artist who
works in a range of media, including
canvases and clothing. His work
can be found around Bristol, which
has become a creative centre for
British street art, often in the form of a
brightly coloured cartoonish minaret.
This print, *Love Supreme*, counters
negative views of street art as a
form of antisocial behaviour. It is a
joyful homage to graffiti, suggesting
that the spray-can art form has the
potential to spread love and make
us happy. In an era when space in
cities is increasingly privatized,
sanitized and commercialized,
street art has offered a means of
reclaiming public space for
alternative forms of expression.

CF

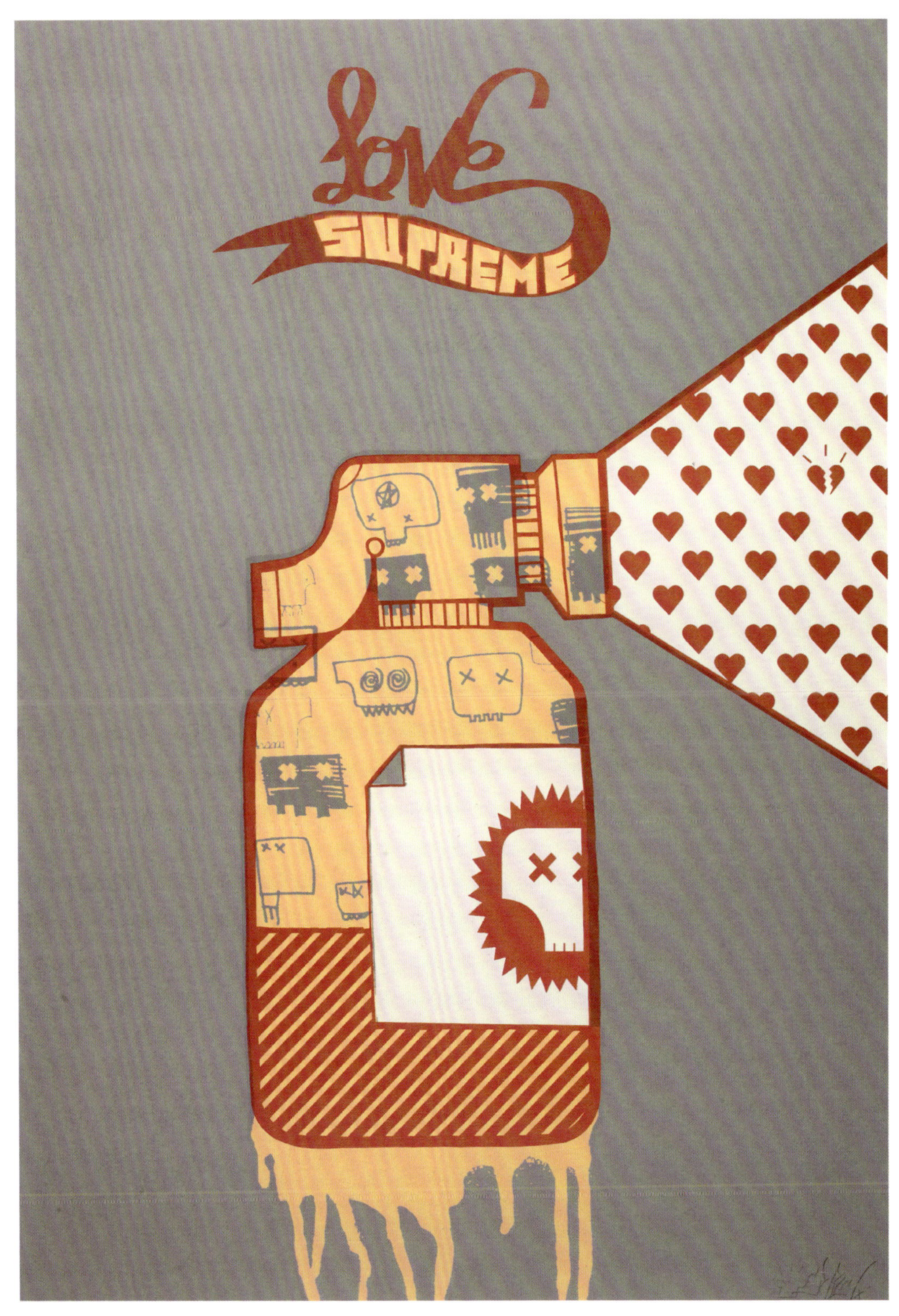

Love
SUPREME

Peter Kennard (b.1949) and
Cat Picton Phillipps (b.1972)
*Award Made During the Invasion and
Occupation of Iraq 2003 to Now*, 2004
Published by Martello Press in
association with Henry Peacock and
Gimpel Fils
Portfolio of 15 plates; digital inkjet
prints from an Epson 9600 on
Hahnemühle cotton rag paper;
edition number 2/100
V&A: E.231:1 to 22–2005
Purchased through the Julie and
Robert Breckman Print Fund

Kennard is an avowedly political artist,
and the political intent of this suite of
prints is made explicit in the title. His
art has become synonymous with left-
wing protest and support for causes
such as the Campaign for Nuclear
Disarmament, as well as anti-war and
anti-poverty movements. His earlier
work took the form of photomontage,
an effective but laborious method
of splicing together images from
disparate sources to craft provocative
visual messages, but since 2002 he
has used Computer-Aided Design.
Supported by the technical expertise
of Cat Picton Phillipps, he has worked
with computers, scanners and inkjet
printers to develop a process that has
enabled a more seamless marriage
of diverse pictorial elements, to
telling effect.

Kennard titled his autobiography
*Dispatches from an Unofficial War
Artist* (2002), and *Award* reflects his
anti-war views, embodying a caustic
critique of the Iraq war and its after-
math. Kennard has explained that

> The series (…) arose out of our
> need to find a way to express
> our disgust with the war against
> Iraq and attempt to revoke our
> impotence in the face of the raging
> terrorism committed in the name
> of democracy. We wanted to use
> digital technology to make visceral
> images that used everyday stuff
> as directly as we could in order to
> respond to the war's full horror with
> thousands of Iraqis being killed.[1]

The prints were made by scanning
some old medals that Kennard had
bought in Camden Market; for each
plate, the medals were progressively
'distressed', the ribbons torn and
frayed, the medals themselves
bashed and battered. Documentary
photographs – of military helicopters,
gun-sights, bomb craters – sourced
from the *Guardian*'s picture library
were incorporated. Blood, sand,
dirt and dust were thrown onto the
scanner, too, offering a kind of visual
equivalent for the deteriorating
situation in Iraq and the corrosion of
moral values in the conduct of the
Occupation. In the V&A collection,
Award has a particular resonance
with historical prints by Francisco
Goya (1746–1828) and Jacques
Callot addressing the horrors of war;
and a suite of etchings entitled *Dark
Interludes* (2001) – made by Walid Siti,
an Iraqi Kurd, as a personal response
to the experience of living through
the Iran–Iraq war of 1980–8
– which was also purchased for the
V&A through the Julie and Robert
Breckman Print Fund.

GS

1 Quoted at www.kennardphillipps.com/
blood-on-the-scanner/#more-112, accessed
14 December 2015.

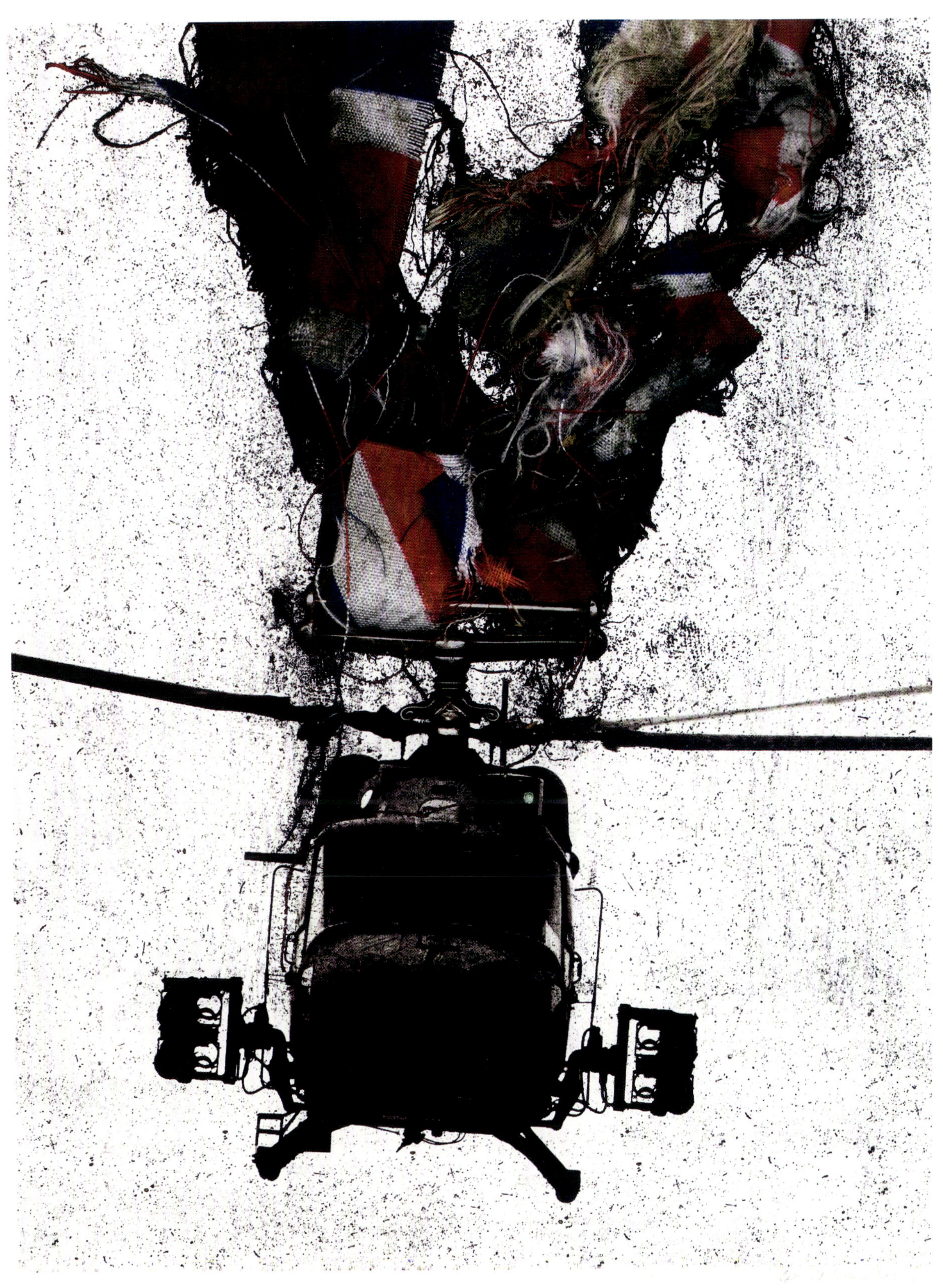

Grayson Perry (b.1960)

Mr & Mrs Perry, 2006
Published by the Paragon Press
Linocuts on patterned papers
Each 45.5 x 36 cm
V&A: E.475–2008, V&A: E.476–2008
Purchased through the Julie and
Robert Breckman Print Fund

Grayson Perry is one of Britain's
leading artists. His is best known for
his pots with drawn, incised and
transfer-printed decoration, but also
makes prints, designs tapestries and
has even designed a house (albeit
a rather eccentric holiday-let). His
imagery is a potent combination
of contemporary urban themes,
often autobiographical, with social
and political critiques, but often
represented in the idiom of historical
exemplars and incorporating
decorative styles and motifs from
earlier periods.

These prints were made for his
exhibition *The Charms of Lincolnshire*,
held at the Victoria Miro Gallery,
London, 2006 (and first shown at The
Collection, a new museum of art
and archaeology in Lincolnshire).
For this show Perry selected historical
artefacts – everything from toys,
costume and bibles to gamekeepers'
traps, coffin plates and a wooden
hearse – from museums of rural life
and social history in Lincolnshire.
These were shown alongside his own
new works – including dolls, vases,
plates and an embroidered sampler,

all of which were designed to blend
together in what was described as
'a three-dimensional narrative poem'
exploring death, childhood, religion,
folk art, hunting and the feminine (a
theme of particular interest to Perry, a
transvestite who often makes public
appearances as his female alter
ego, Claire).

The prints were inspired by American
folk-art portraits of the kind made
by amateur or jobbing artists in
the nineteenth century, before
photographic portraits had become
commonplace. Perry has imitated the
naïve style of these artists, using the
cheap and relatively crude medium
of linocut on commercially printed
patterned papers (from Paperchase),
so that the background appears to
be wallpaper. Each pair of prints has
a different combination of patterned
papers, so each pair in the edition is
unique. The Victorian style suggests
that these might be portraits of
Perry's ancestors, but in fact they
represent the artist and his wife,
Philippa. By his own admission, these
are poor likenesses, but their crude
style is intended as a 'celebration
of the naïve folk tradition', in which
Perry recognizes a sincerity that is
often lacking in more sophisticated
productions. The prints also draw on
the tradition of 'pendant portraits',
in which husbands and wives are
depicted separately, to be hung
together as a pair.

GS

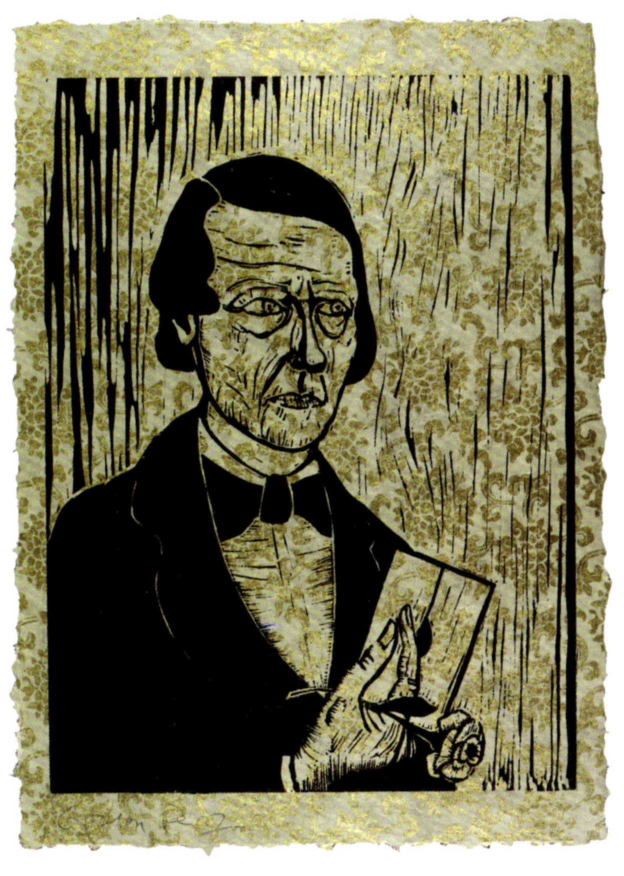
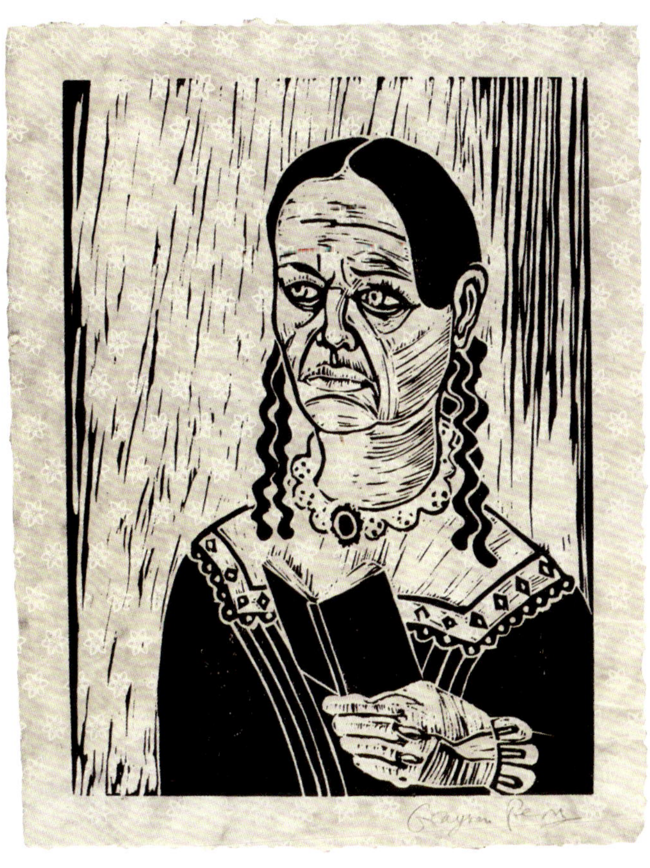

Liz Collini (b.1955)

Untitled (large text), 2011
Screen print on board; edition
number 1/2
100 x 150 cm
V&A: E.327–2011
Donated by Robert Breckman in
memory of Julie

Liz Collini produces prints and
drawings that are short texts
comprising ambiguous words and
phrases. She has described her work
as follows: 'The written word holds
many paradoxes, not least those of
absence and presence. There are
gaps and overlaps between reading
and viewing, text and image, the
hand and the machine. I try to create
breathing spaces in which we can
pause and look back at language.
Whole narratives can be compressed
into a single word or familiar phrase.
The drawings' resemblance to plans
and blueprints reflects the strange
provisionality of written language;
the things about which we write are
always elsewhere. I work only with
Times New Roman (the default font)
and my own handwriting to minimize
questions of typography.'

In 2010 the V&A commissioned
Collini to make a site-specific print
for long-term display in the Prints &
Drawings Study Room. The resulting
work is a literal embodiment of word
as image. The simple but ambiguous
phrase 'among the indescribable
sounds of paper, moving' was
devised by the artist after she had

spent some time in the Study Room
watching and listening. It not only
suggests the turning of pages and
the careful perusal of prints and
drawings, but also hints at the more
spiritual pleasures that can come
from looking at works of art. The artist
includes the measurements and
other annotations generated in the
process of drawing the lettering. With
its allusions to typography, the design
process and architectural plans, this
print has a particular resonance
when seen in the context of the Study
Room and the collections there.

Along with the print itself, we
acquired a proof and the artist's
working drawing.

GS

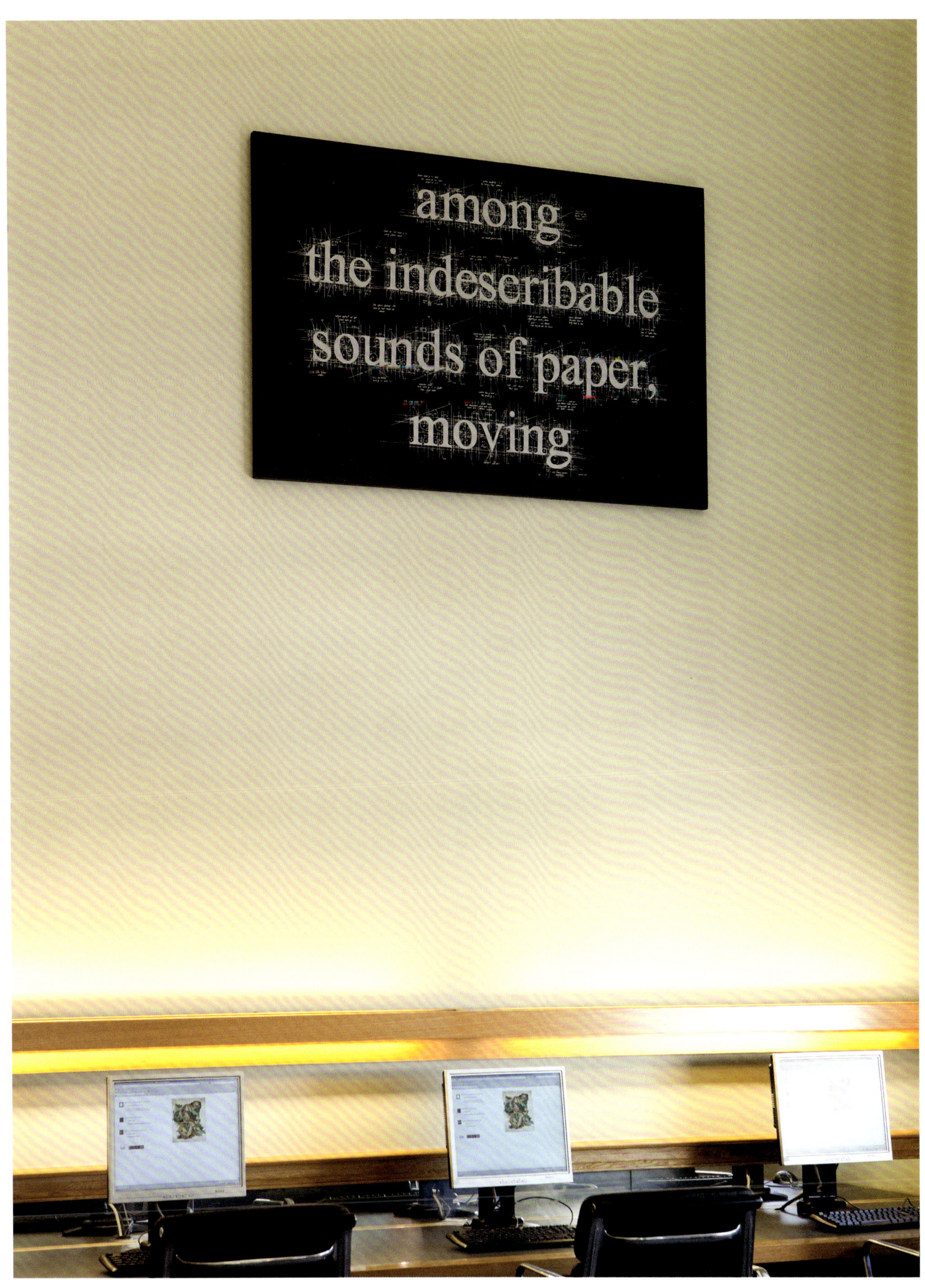

among
the indescribable
sounds of paper,
moving

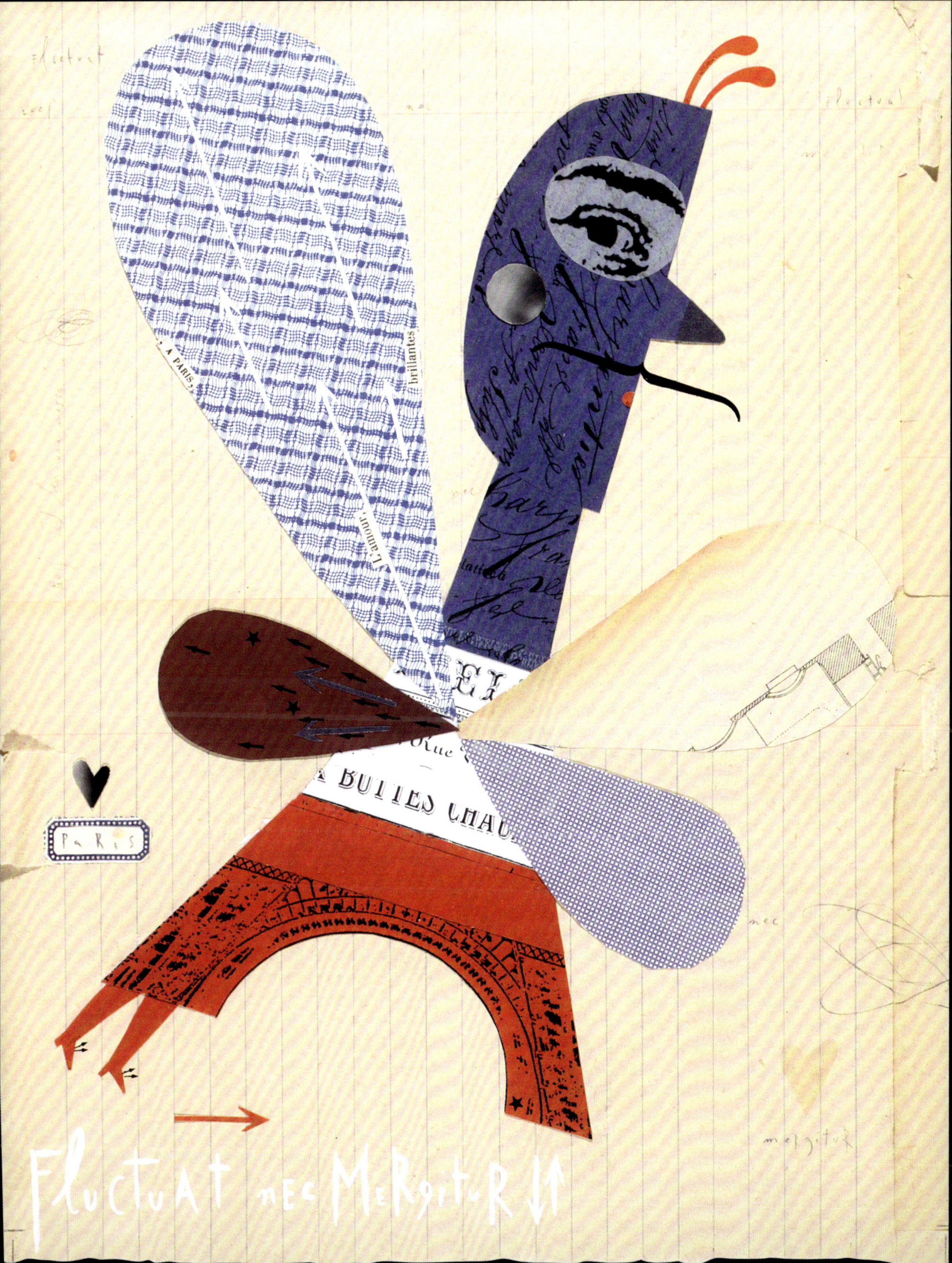

Posters and Popular Prints

Posters and Popular Prints

Catherine Flood

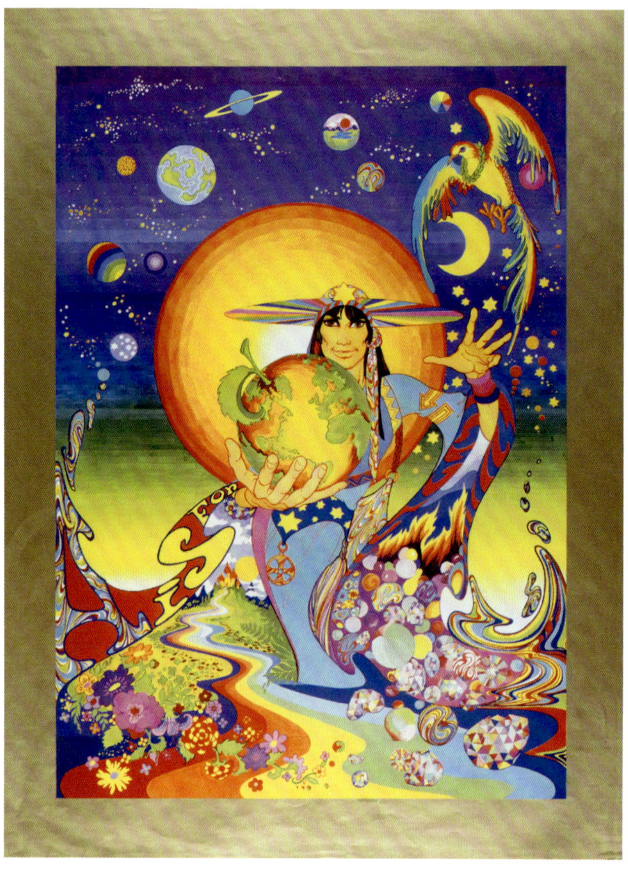

43. Poster designed by The Fool for the Beatles' Apple Boutique, Baker Street, London, 1960s
Colour photogravure
V&A: E.277–2002
Purchased through the Julie and Robert Breckman Print Fund

Throughout history the vast majority of printed images have been produced for specific practical purposes and not purely as art. Reasons for printing pictures include the desire to communicate and disseminate ideas, to persuade people, to sell things to them, to inform, educate or regulate them, to entertain or simply to embellish and decorate. It is these imperatives that have driven the development of printing technologies, while the expressive qualities of a process are generally realized later. The V&A print collections encompass an enormous variety of applied print and ephemera, from fifteenth-century playing cards (see p.113) to Greenpeace posters from 2014 protesting against Shell's extraction of oil in the Arctic. Our holdings span centuries during which print was as essential a feature of everyday life as photographs and digital media are today, and one that was relatively democratic. Indeed, while the V&A has historically tended to focus on objects of elite production and private consumption, the print collections have also drawn material to some extent from the public realm and the lives of ordinary people.

In supporting the development of the V&A print collections, the Julie and Robert Breckman Print Fund has therefore engaged with a very diverse field of print activity. This essay looks briefly at three key areas of the V&A's collection of ephemeral prints and popular graphics, and at how the Breckman Fund has contributed to them. Prints produced in the context of popular culture are often discarded, or at least not actively treasured and preserved, once they have served their initial purpose. A mass-produced print, such as a broadsheet, a poster or even a wallpaper, can therefore become a rare historical survival – sometimes with considerable monetary value. Robert Breckman's support has enabled us

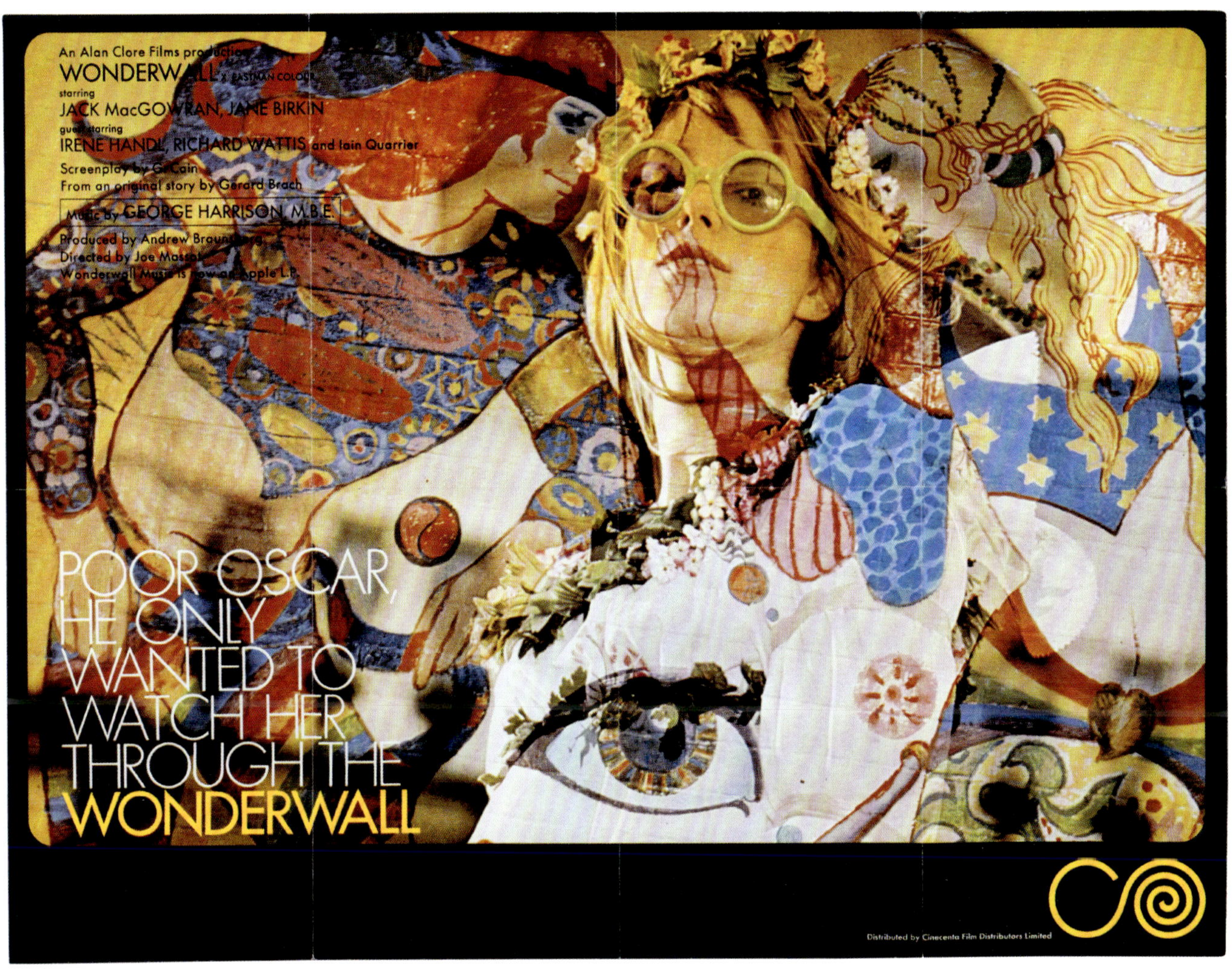

44. Poster advertising the film *Wonderwall*, produced by Apple Films
(part of the Beatles' Apple Group), 1960s
Colour offset lithograph
V&A: E 276–2002
Purchased through the Julie and Robert Breckman Print Fund

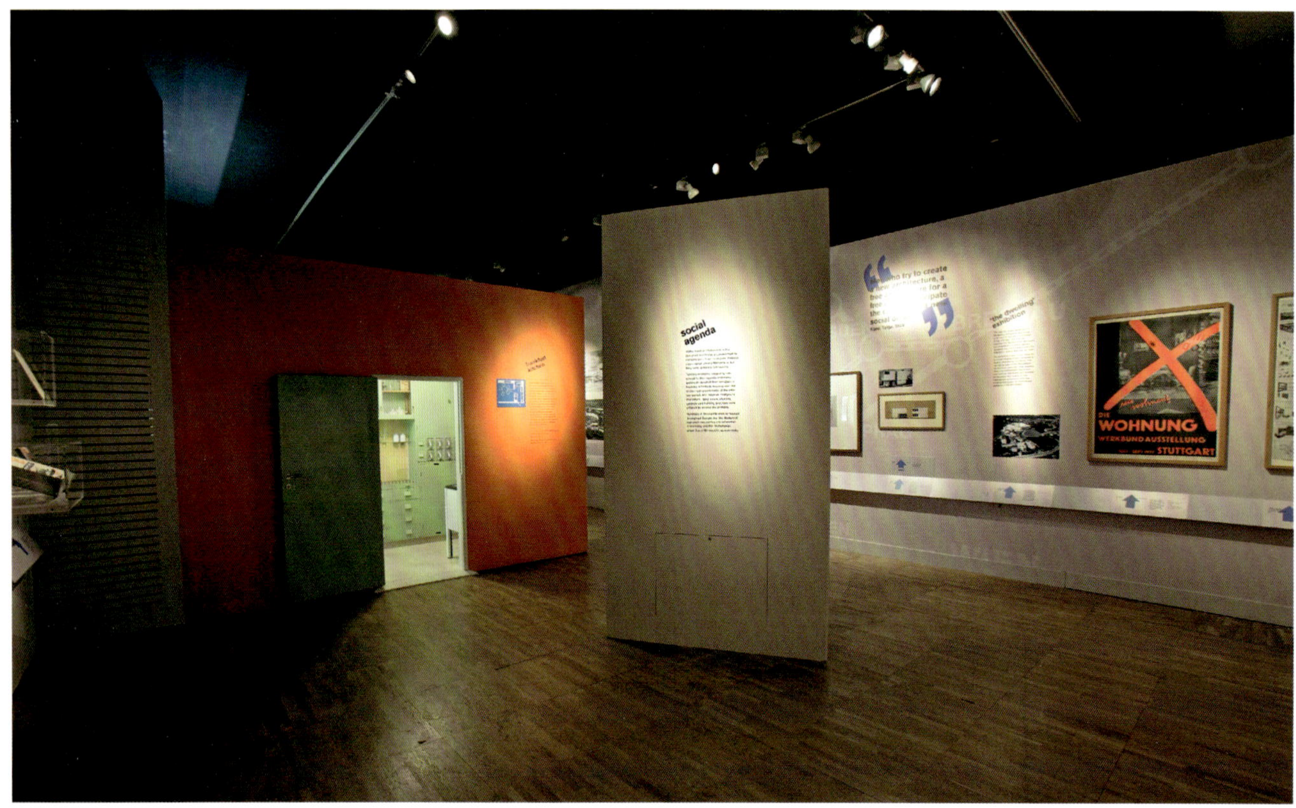

45. Installation view of the exhibition *Modernism: Designing a new world 1914–1939*, 2006, showing poster *Die Wohnung* by Willi Baumeister

to track down and purchase elusive prints for specific projects, and to take advantage of the exciting discoveries that come to light in auction sales rooms and people's attics.

Prints and everyday life

Since its foundation the V&A has collected ephemeral prints as examples of best design in commercial printing processes; these range from satirical prints to fashion plates, to packaging and advertising. The interest these prints inspire, however, is not confined to their formal qualities. In his seminal 1864 essay on art and modernity Charles Baudelaire singled out fashion plates and graphic satire as worthy of attention because they depicted everyday life, at a time when academic art dealt almost exclusively with grand themes from history, mythology and

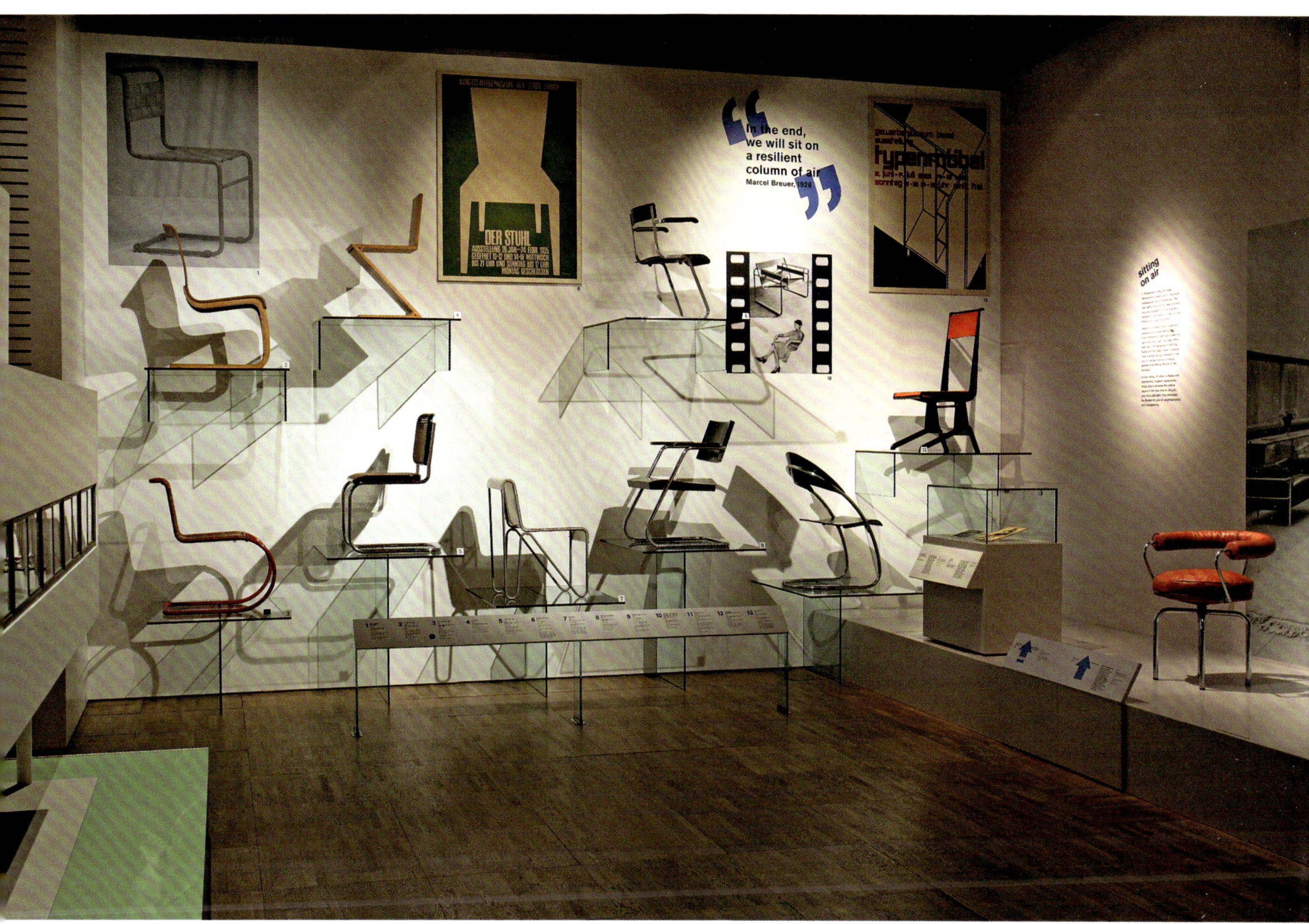

46. Installation view of the exhibition *Modernism: Designing a new world 1914–1939*, 2006, showing poster *Typenmöbel* by Ernst Mumenthaler

religion. To Baudelaire, such prints reflected the thrilling immediacy of the modern world.[1] For later generations, they can satisfy a curiosity to know what everyday life looked like in the past. *A Handbook to the Department of Prints and Drawings and Paintings* at the V&A, published in 1964, grouped popular and reproductive prints under a heading of 'Social History' and pointed to their value as 'illustrations of how people lived and dressed, how their towns looked, what their tools and technical processes were, and their customs in matters of food and drink'.[2]

The Breckman Fund has enabled several acquisitions of this kind (see p.107 and p.117) that offer multiple avenues for research. A set of fashion plates published in Italian periodicals in the 1880s (see p.121), for example, can support technical studies of the V&A's dress collections,

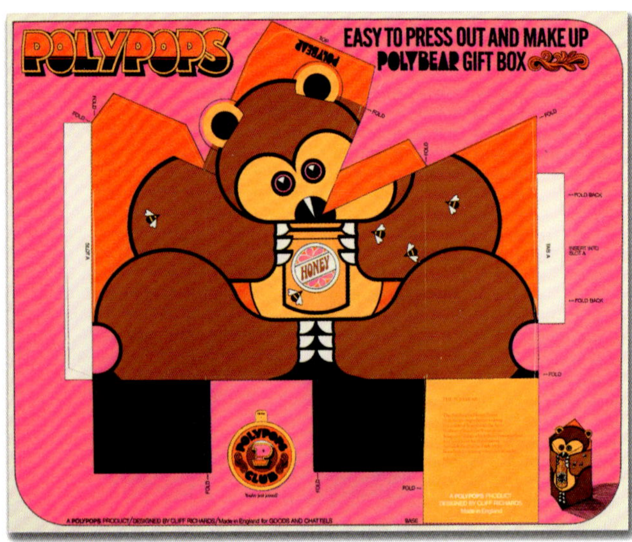

47. *The Polybear*, c.1968, gift box from the 'Polypops' series
designed by Clifford Richards
Litho-print on card, varnished and die-cut
V&A: E.3677:1 to 3–2004
Purchased through the Julie and Robert Breckman Print Fund

help us to date paintings and photographs precisely, provide source material for the history of magazine publishing and illuminate an aspect of nineteenth-century visual culture in terms of how people were prompted to look at fashion. Indeed, over the past 40 years the profile of the V&A's 'Social History' prints has grown, as art historians have begun to pay closer attention to popular prints, studying them not just as illustrations of social life, but as active agents in determining how people saw the world around them and their place in it.

Increasing academic interest in popular prints has mirrored changing perceptions of the importance of graphics within contemporary culture. In the late 1950s and early '60s Pop Artists such as Richard Hamilton (1922–2011) in Britain and Andy Warhol in America embraced the products and printed paraphernalia of mass consumerism as valid subjects of aesthetic interest. In Britain the profile of graphics was raised further in the late 1960s by the emergence of a vibrant, youth-led counterculture and underground press, which used graphic art as a primary means of expression. Prints acquired through the Breckman Fund have expanded the V&A's representation of this extraordinary explosion in graphic creativity, including seminal images of the Sixties such as solarized photographs of the Beatles (produced for poster prints) by Richard Avedon (1923–2004), posters designed for the Beatles' Apple Group (pls 43 and 44) and a poster by psychedelic designer Martin Sharp (1942–2013) promoting the underground magazine *Oz*. These were included in the V&A's 2006 exhibition *Sixties Graphics*, and some also feature in the 2016 exhibition *You Say You Want a Revolution: Records & Rebels 1966–70*.

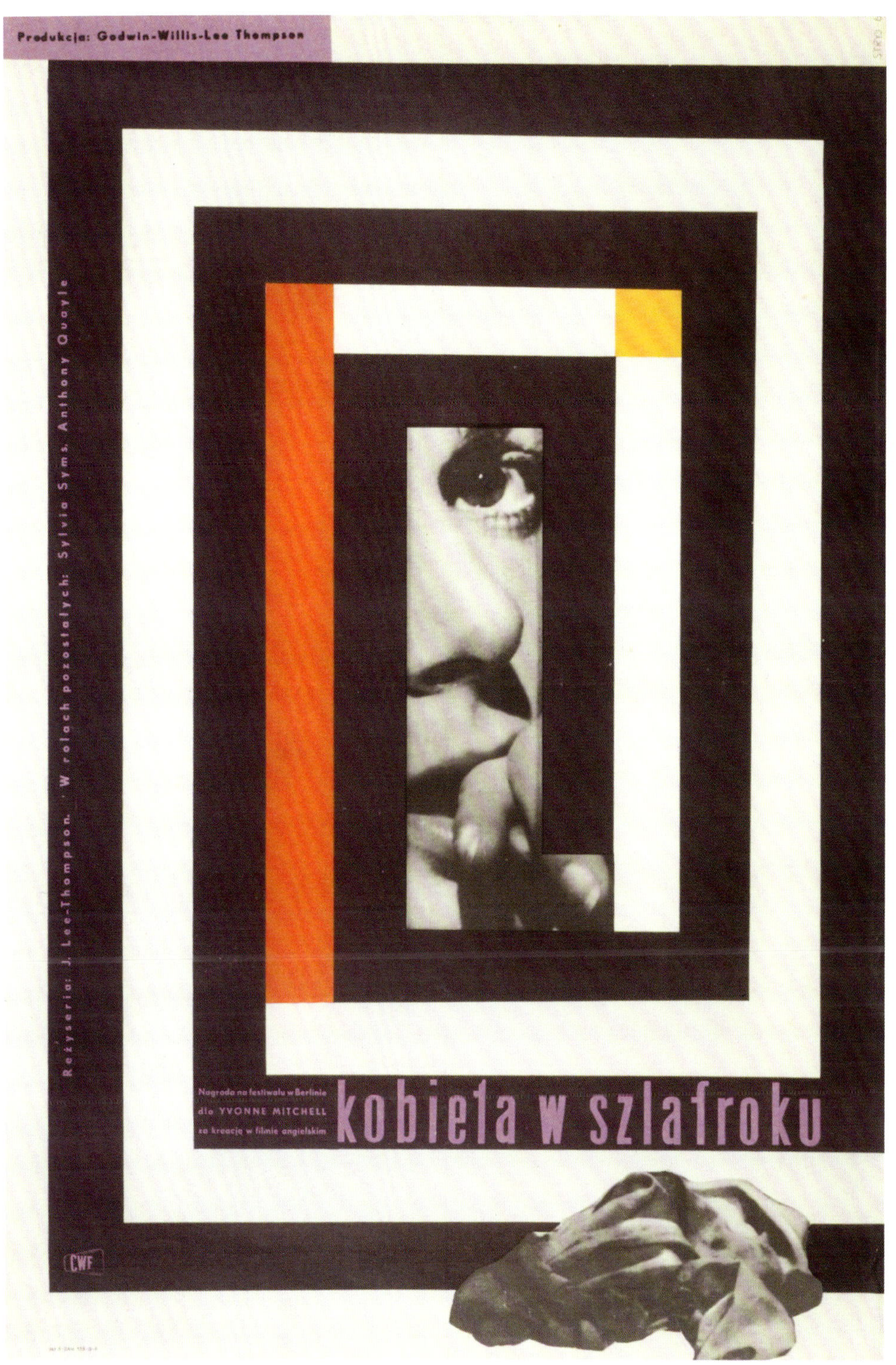

48. Film poster for *Woman in a Dressing Gown* (UK, 1957, director
John Lee Thompson), *c*.1961, by Maurycy T. Stryjecki, Poland
Lithograph
V&A. E.354–2003
Purchased through the Julie and Robert Breckman Print Fund

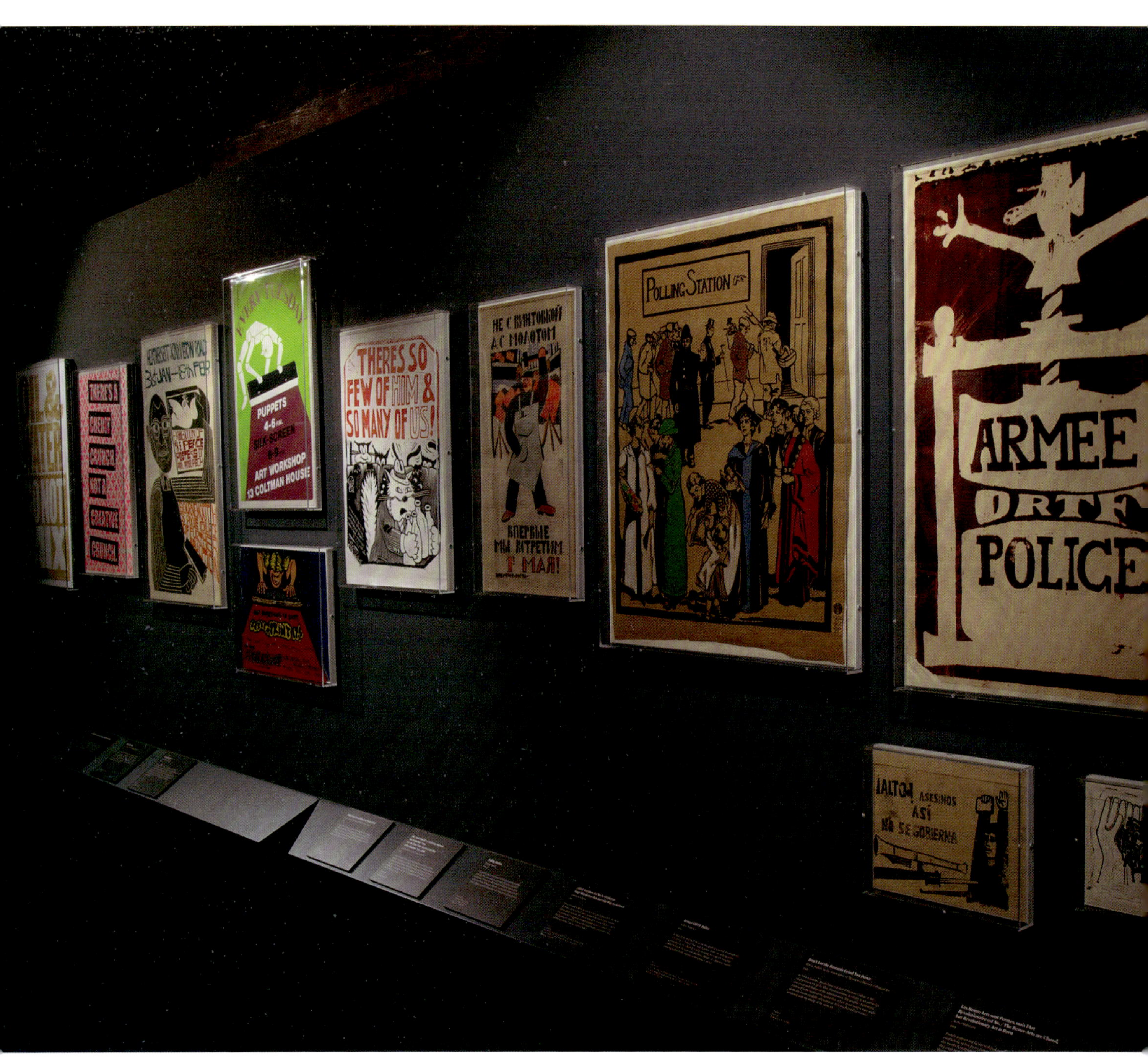

49. Installation view of the exhibition *A World to Win: Posters of protest and revolution*, National Print Museum, Dublin, 2015

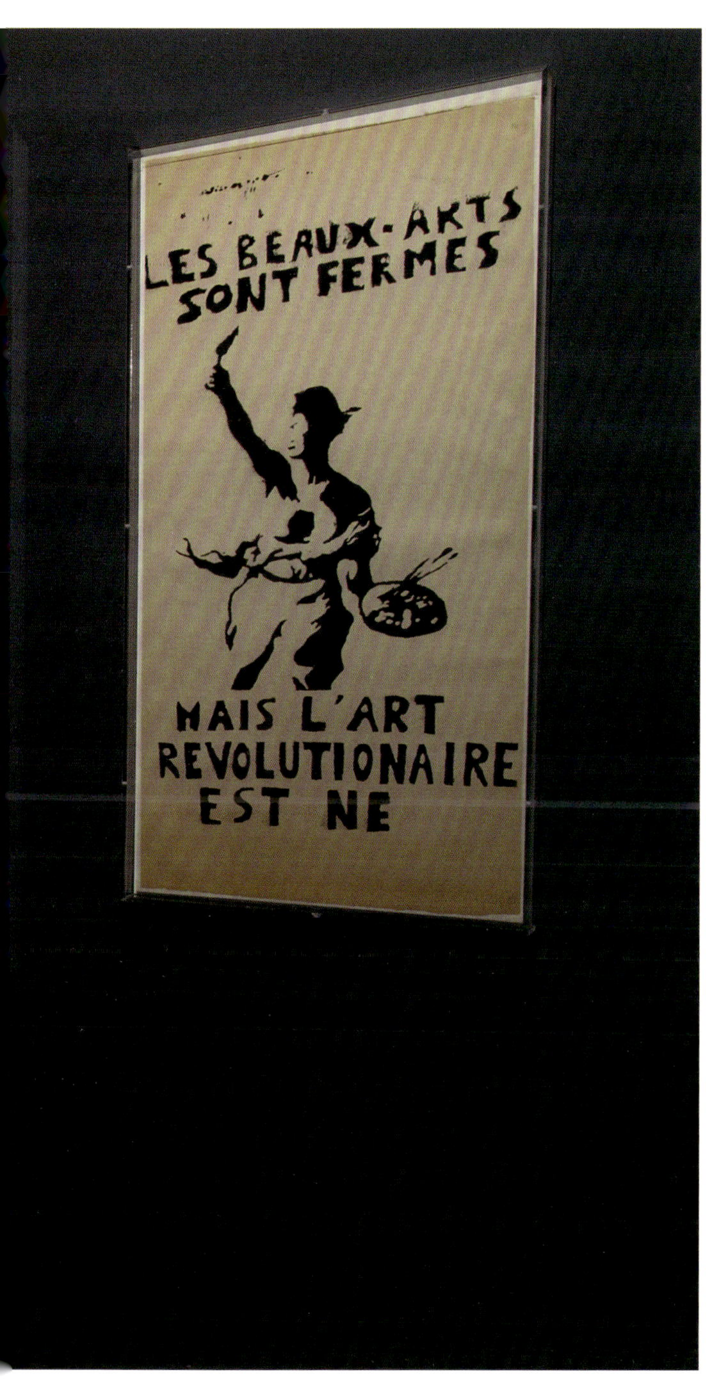

As the public became increasingly receptive
to graphics in the Sixties, new printed products
emerged, including posters designed as cheap
art prints, record covers and badges emblazoned
with band names, humour and political slogans
(see p.137). The very disposability of such objects
(although they sometimes proved irresistibly
collectible) allowed young people a constant
engagement with design, and the ability to try
out different identities through the statements
they pinned to their walls and clothes. One of
the talented artists and designers who began
exploring the potential of printed paper artefacts
in the Sixties was Clifford Richards, a personal
friend of Robert Breckman. Richards created
cult decorative paper objects such as pop-
ups, 'slotties' (free-standing 3D figures created
by slotting pieces of card together) and doll's
houses – all adorned with bold, colourful graphic
illustration that captured the exuberance and
optimism of the decade (pl.47). Introduced to
Richards by Robert, the V&A has since collected
pieces from his archive and commissioned him
to create new printed products for the V&A shop.
A growing appreciation for tactile graphic art that
departs from today's ubiquitous screen culture
means that Richards' work is being valued anew
by contemporary audiences.

Masterpieces of graphic design

During the twentieth century, graphic design
became an important discipline within
the European avant-garde and Modernist
movement, as influential artists and designers
experimented with new forms of visual
communication that prioritized functional
objectivity and social purpose. The Breckman
Fund has enabled us to acquire key posters by
important Modernist graphic designers, such
as Willi Baumeister (1889–1955; see p.123).

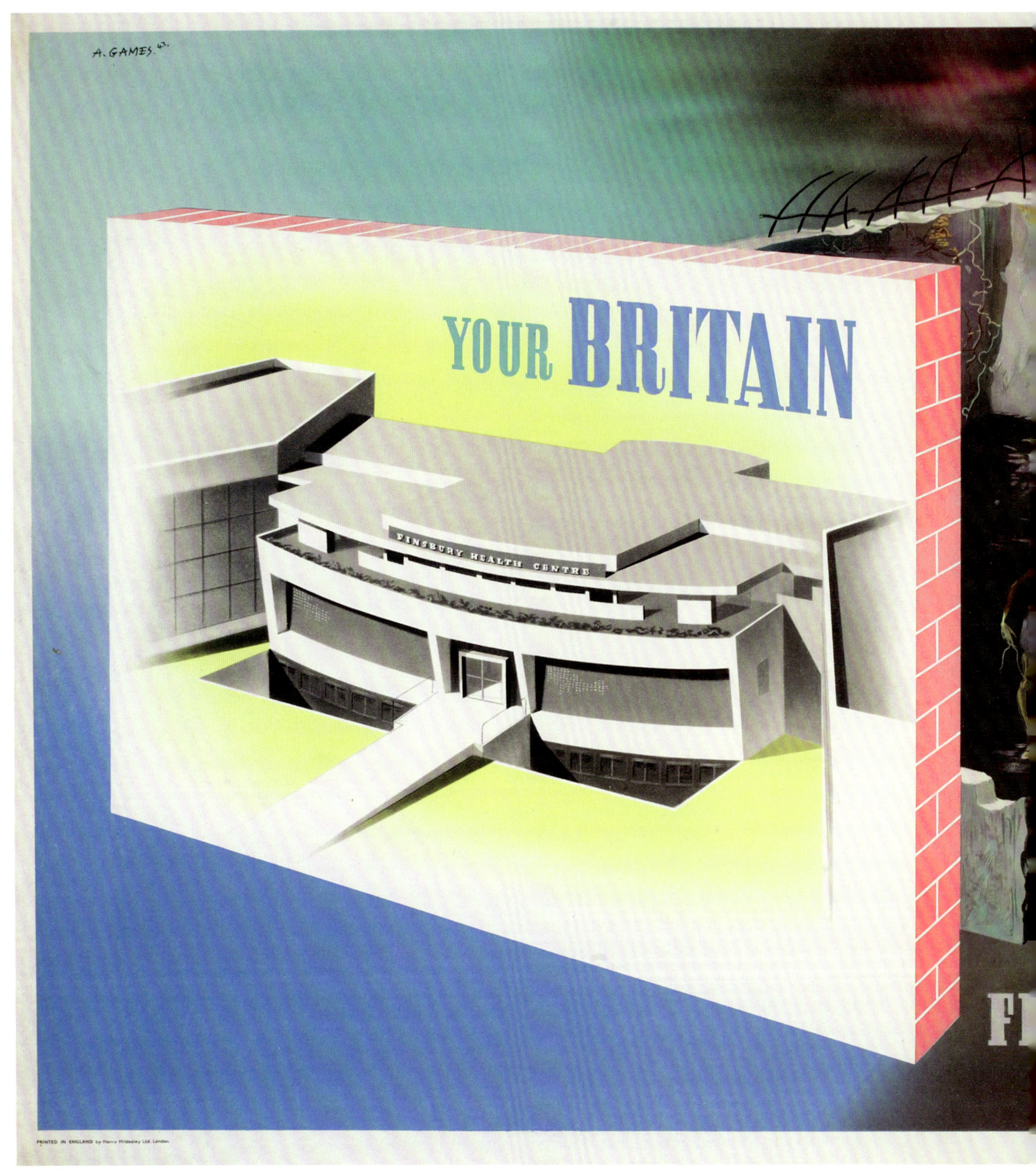

50. Poster, *Your Britain – Fight for it Now*, 1942, by Abram Games
Colour offset lithograph
V&A: E.295–2006
Purchased through the Julie and Robert Breckman Print Fund

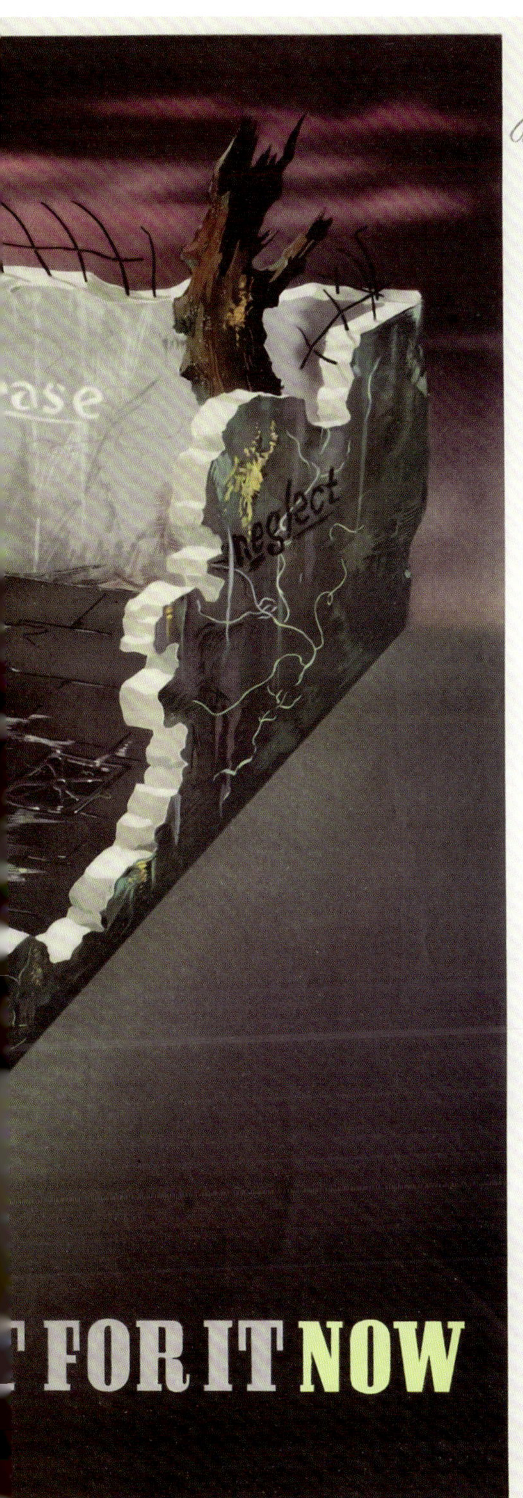

Ernst Mumenthaler (1901–78; see p.125), Lester Beall (1903–69; see p.127) and Armin Hofmann (b.1920), which have enhanced the V&A's capacity to represent the development of the Modern movement in design. Some were acquired specifically for the V&A exhibition *Modernism: Designing a new world 1914–1939* (2006) (pls 45 and 46).

Another high point of twentieth-century poster design is the Polish Poster School. Under communism in Poland, poster design was considered a more socially legitimate medium than painting for artists to engage in, but was not subject to the kind of stylistic controls that were imposed in the Soviet Union. As a result, Polish cultural posters became the focus of great creativity, characterized by a painterly expressive execution and a poetic use of metaphor and suggestion. Here, too, the Breckman Fund has enabled us to increase our holdings through the acquisition of works by masters of Polish poster design, such as Waldemar Świerzy (1931–2013; see p.133), Maurycy T. Stryjecki (b.1923) (pl.48), Maria Syska (b.1932) and Jan Szmatloch (b.1950).

Weapons of mass communication

War has provided, and continues to provide, a powerful impetus for the creation and distribution of images as propaganda, and such political prints and posters are one of the strengths of the V&A print collections. The Print Fund has supported some star acquisitions to this field, notably an early woodcut celebrating the victory of the Holy League over the Ottoman Empire in the Battle of Lepanto in 1571 (see p.105). The print is contemporary with the battle, one of the first major events to occur on the European stage after the use of printing technology became

widespread. Now in the Medieval & Renaissance
Galleries, it is a key object in a display about
Europe's interactions with the rest of the world.
While many objects in the V&A's collections
provide evidence of international trade links,
it is far harder to find objects that offer insights
into what Europeans thought about world
events, other peoples and religions. It is through
this ability to enter into the realm of ideas and
perceptions that seemingly modest prints can
contribute to major narratives within the Museum.

The First World War proved the power of the poster
as a medium of propaganda on a grand scale
and stimulated the V&A's collecting of posters
in general, and of political posters in particular.
Immediately after the war, V&A curator Martin
Hardie gathered together several hundred war
posters, which he published in a book entitled
*War Posters issued by Belligerent and Neutral
Nations* (1921). For Hardie, the experience of the
war (in which he had fought) had created a new
measure for what felt culturally important – and
therefore relevant for the Museum to acquire.
As he wrote in *War Posters*: 'Never in the history
of the world have the accessories of ordinary
civilised life met with so searching a test of their
essential quality as during the war.' While most
V&A departments at this date had a policy
of collecting only historical artefacts, Hardie's
engagement with war posters demonstrated
the potential of the Museum as a space for
reflecting on contemporary political events – an
approach that the print curators have continued
by collecting (and displaying) posters in the
moment, as events unfold.

Contemporary collecting, however, inevitably
leaves gaps, and the Breckman Fund has
supported some significant retrospective additions
to our holdings of political posters (see p.135).

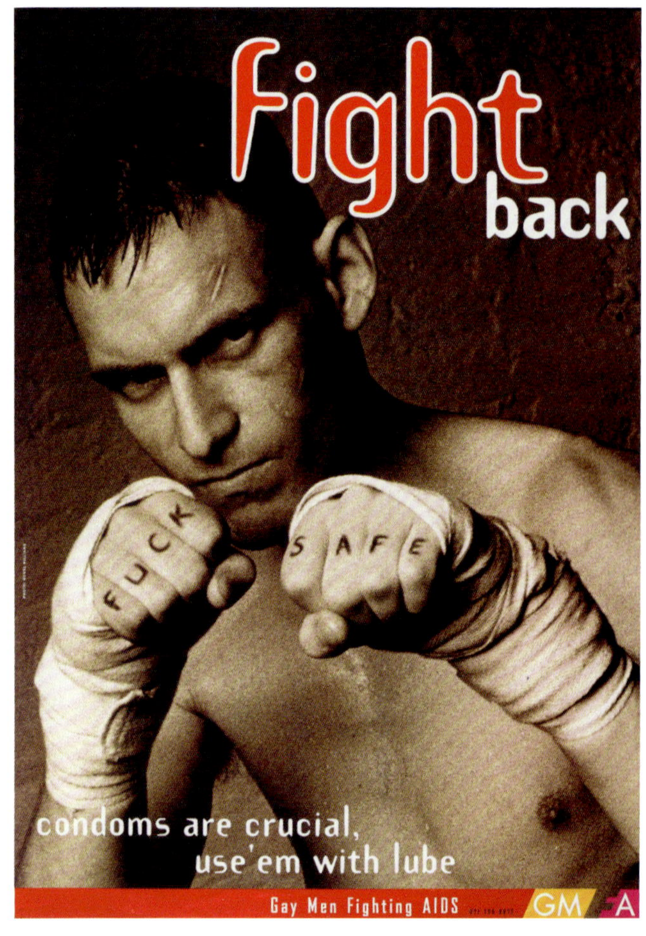

51. Poster, *Fight Back*, c.1990, for Gay Men Fighting AIDS (GMFA)
Colour offset lithograph
V&A: E.948–2002
Purchased through the Julie and Robert Breckman Print Fund

One fascinating example was designed by Abram Games (1914–96) for the Army Bureau of Current Affairs during the Second World War, entitled *Your Britain – Fight For It Now* (pl.50). It depicts a scene of dereliction and disease replaced by a health centre built in a modern architectural style, and was one of a series designed to inspire the war effort by encouraging people to imagine how Britain could change for the better in a post-war future. When first exhibited in 1943, the poster sparked controversy – the Minister for Labour, Ernest Bevin (1881–1951), actually tore it from the wall, outraged by the socialist tone and the exposure of poverty and deprivation. Today it is an important document in the story of design and social reform in Britain and has been selected for a gallery in the new Shekou Design Museum in China (opening in 2017), which will provide a history of design through highlights from the V&A collections.

Alongside state-sponsored propaganda, the V&A has extensive holdings of protest posters. A key acquisition supported by the Breckman Fund is a poster roughly screen-printed by the Atelier Populaire (the People's Workshop) – a group of French art students who set up a guerrilla press in support of the anti-government strikes and demonstrations that rocked Paris in May 1968. The poster (a hitherto-unknown example of their work) announces the group's intent to use art as a form of direct action: 'The Fine Arts Are Over, But Revolutionary Art Is Born' (see p.135). It is significant because it makes explicit the ideological spirit that inspired the Atelier Populaire, and the many artists and activists who followed their lead in using cheap hand-printing techniques to produce their own propaganda materials. It has featured in the V&A's touring exhibition *A World to Win: Posters of protest and revolution* (2014–16) (pl.49).

Further Breckman-funded acquisitions demonstrate different graphic strategies of protest, from posters produced in the early 1990s by Gay Men Fighting AIDS (GMFA), which use slick advertising-style production to forge an affirmative visual identity for gay men (pl.51), to a portfolio of prints sold to raise money for the Stop the War Coalition on the eve of the Iraq war in 2003 (see p.141).

1 Charles Baudelaire, *The Painter of Modern Life* (London, 2010; first published 1863 in *Figaro*).
2 *Handbook to the Department of Prints and Drawings and Paintings* (London, 1964), p.34.

Anonymous

True Likeness of the beheaded Turkish officer Ali Bassa
Broadsheet published in Germany (possibly Nuremberg), *c.*1571
Woodcut with stencil and hand-colouring on laid paper with letterpress
42.6 x 33 cm
V&A: E.912–2003
Purchased through the Julie and Robert Breckman Print Fund, and supported by the Friends of the V&A

This fascinating and rare print was published in Germany, probably shortly after the allied Christian naval victory over the Turks at the Battle of Lepanto in 1571. Ali Pasha, the defeated Turkish naval commander, is shown full-length, wearing a kaftan of costly woven, figured silks. His exotic clothes, turban and long feathery headdress denote his high rank. Although he is shown alive, in the background is a detail of his head on the end of a pole. Behind Ali Pasha is the Turkish flagship on which he was wounded and subsequently beheaded. It is being engulfed by the smoke and flames of battle.

The text at the top of the print on the left is taken from a Nuremberg newspaper of 1571 and explains events relating to the battle. It captures the time when news of the victory was fresh, but its significance not fully understood. The text on the right of the print thanks Almighty God for His intercession. The defeat of the Turks at the Battle of Lepanto was of great significance for Europe, and this broadsheet was published when European fear of the Ottoman Empire was at its height. It is a very rare survival of a propaganda print with a grim but reassuring message to Christendom.

Prints such as this would have been made and sold in large numbers and may have been pasted up on walls for display. They were designed for wide distribution at low cost and their imagery was simple and direct. The vast majority of such prints were bought casually and treated carelessly, and very few have survived. This print has been folded at some stage and was perhaps inserted in a book, which may have ensured its survival. The back of the sheet has been used for doing some hasty sums. The only other recorded example of this image is a cut-down and damaged print in the Zentralbibliothek in Zurich. The V&A's impression is a key exhibit in the Medieval & Renaissance Galleries that opened in 2010.

FR

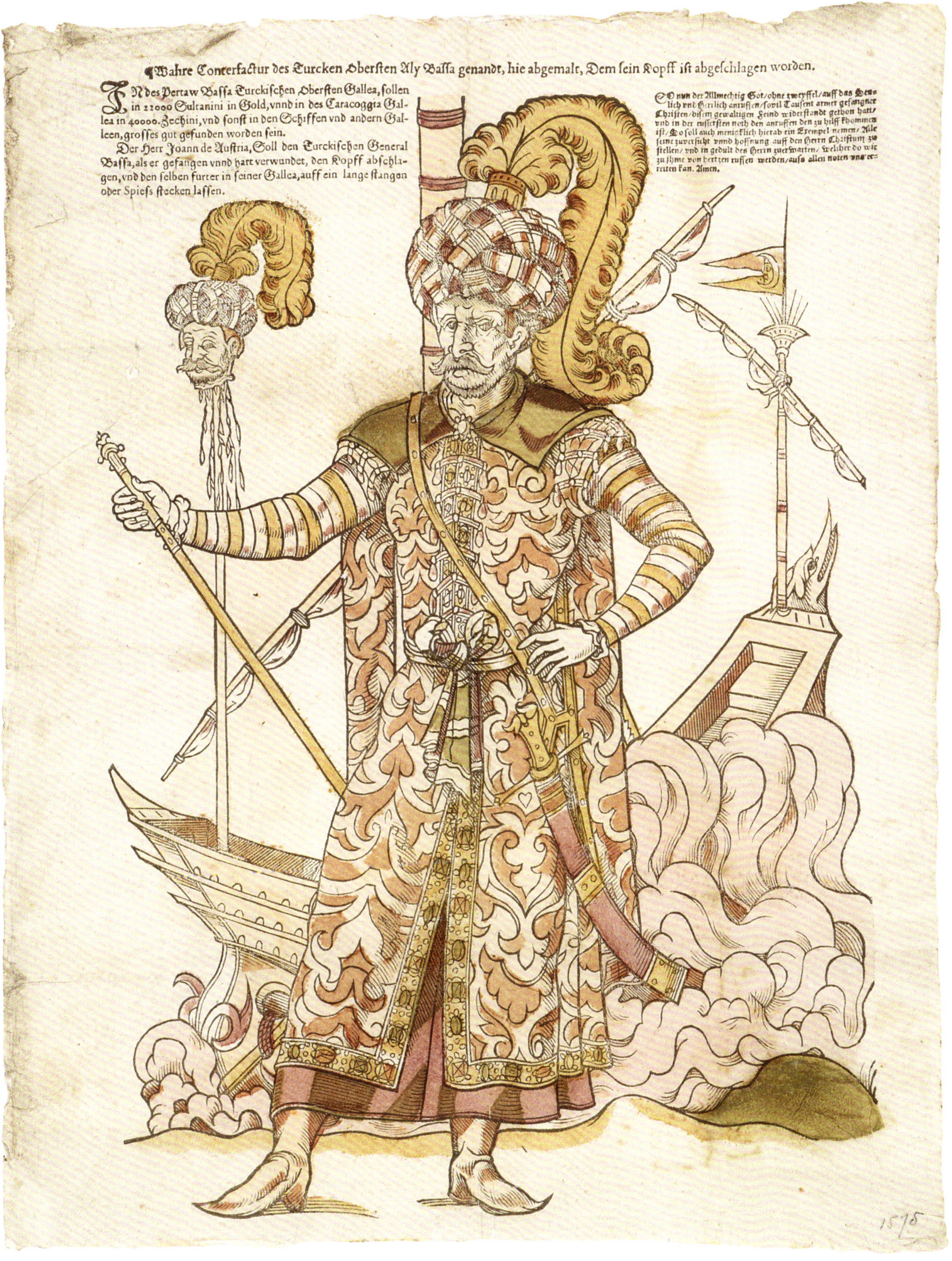
Wahre Conterfactur des Turcken Obersten Aly Bassa genandt, hie abgemalt, Dem sein Kopff ist abgeschlagen worden.

IN des Pertaw Bassa Turckischen Obersten Gallea, sollen in 22000 Sultanini in Gold, vnnd in des Caracoggia Gallea in 40000. Zechini, vnd sonst in den Schiffen vnd andern Galleen, grosses gut gefunden worden sein.
Der Herr Joann de Austria, Soll den Turckischen General Bassa, als er gefangen vnnd hart verwundet, den Kopff abschlagen, vnd den selben furter in seiner Gallea, auff ein lange stangen ober Spiess stecken lassen.

SO nun der Allmechtig Got, ohne zweyffel, auff das Hertzlich vnd Herrlich anruffen, sovil Tausent armer gefangner Christen, disem gewaltigen Feind widerstandt gethon hatt, vnd in der eussersten noth den anruffen den zu hilff khommen ist, So soll auch meniglich hierab ein Exempel nemen, Alle seine zuversicht vnnd hoffnung auff den Herrn Christum zu stellen, vnd in gedult des Herrn zuerwarten, welcher do wie zu jhme von hertzen ruffen werden, aus allen noten vnd erreiten kan. Amen.

1571

Crispijn de Passe the Younger
(*c.*1594–1670)
*Scene from the Parable of Lazarus
and the Rich Man,* Utrecht, *c.*1616
Engraving
27.8 x 33.2 cm
V&A: E.345–2003
Purchased through the Julie and
Robert Breckman Print Fund

This print is one of a set of four
illustrating the parable of Lazarus
and the rich man from Luke's Gospel.
The parable contrasts the fortunes of
a rich man and a pauper, Lazarus,
before and after their deaths. In life,
the rich man lives in great luxury,
but refuses to give Lazarus even the
crumbs from his table. After they
both die, as the rich man suffers the
torments of Hell, he looks up to see
Lazarus in Heaven.

The engraver has set the parable in
his own time, at the beginning of the
seventeenth century. The rich man is
the bearded figure in the upper left
corner. He wears a fur-trimmed robe
and has a goblet of wine in his hand.
He is seated next to a stepped buffet
or sideboard, where his formidable
wealth is on display in the form of
magnificent cups and dishes made
of gold and silver. In the room with
him are six couples, each dancing
or flirting. The amorous atmosphere is
underlined by the statue of a naked
Venus and Cupid in the niche on
the right. This is a night-time scene,
and de Passe shows off his skill by

suggesting the shadows cast from
the three light sources in the room:
the candelabra hanging from the
ceiling, a single candle on the
sideboard, and another held up
by the man on the right so that the
singer next to him can see his music.

This print depicts many types of
objects found in the V&A: furniture,
precious metalwork, lighting, historical
dress and musical instruments. More
importantly, it suggests how such
items were used by their owners
and what impact they had on their
behaviour. Prints play an important
role as visual evidence for the
manners and morals of the past,
illustrating interiors, costume and
other aspects of material culture.
This example has been selected
for display in the Museum's new
permanent galleries covering Europe
in the period 1600–1815.

LM

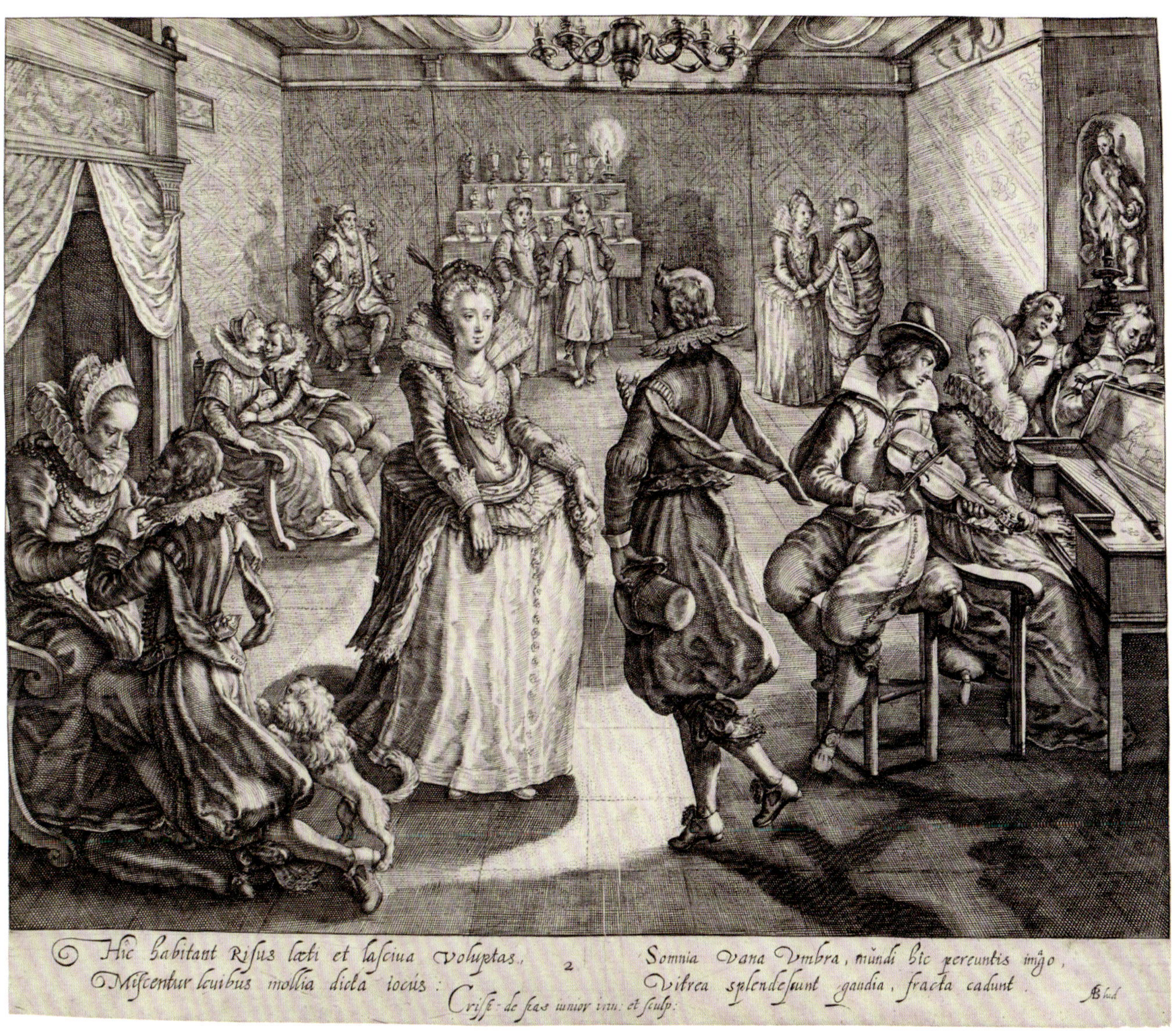

Hic habitant Risus laeti et lasciua voluptas,
Miscentur leuibus mollia dicta iocis:
2
Somnia vana Vmbra, mundi hic pereuntis imâgo,
Vitrea splendescunt gaudia, fracta cadunt.
Criss· de seas iunior inu: et sculp:

Anonymous
The Royall Oake of Brittayne, 1649
Etching and engraving
Size of sheet 19.2 x 26 cm
V&A: E.217–2002
Purchased through the Julie and
Robert Breckman Print Fund

This satirical print depicts Oliver
Cromwell (1599–1658) ordering
the felling of the Royal Oak of
Britain, symbol of the English
monarchy. It was made in 1649
during the English Civil War, in the
year of the execution of Charles I
(1600–49). The image is believed
to have been the frontispiece to
the book *Anarchia Anglicana, or
the history of independency: The
second part*, by Clement Walker
(1595–1651), a pamphleteer and
Member of Parliament writing under
the pseudonym Theodorus Verax.
Although initially sympathetic to
Parliament during the Civil War, Walker
became disillusioned with Cromwell
and believed he had become a
religious radical and despot whose
actions had led Britain into anarchy.
This print expresses Walker's unease at
developments during this period.

The image is full of references to Oliver
Cromwell's dismantling of the regime
of Charles I. Cromwell is shown
to the left of the image, standing
on a sphere suspended over the
mouth of Hell, from which he draws
diabolical inspiration. The sphere is
inscribed in Latin *Locus Lubricus* or

'slippery place', indicating Cromwell's
precarious position. The print
portrays him as a hypocrite, driven
by ambition and greed, and various
quotes from the Bible link him to
notorious biblical figures. Suspended
in the branches of the tree are the
royal crown, sceptre and coat of
arms, with the Bible and Magna
Carta and a copy of *Eikon Basilike*
(Greek, meaning 'Royal Portrait'), a
book supposedly written by Charles
I in the days before his execution.
The tree is being felled by republican
soldiers and its branches gathered by
the ignorant multitude. The references
are clear: if Cromwell was allowed to
continue in his rise to power, his rule
would result in lawless tyranny.

Clement Walker was arrested for
writing *Anarchia Anglicana* and
charged with high treason. However,
his case never came to trial and he
died in the Tower of London in 1651.

This print was acquired as an
addition to the V&A's important
holdings of political satires, and
complements other printed material
in the collection relating to the
Civil War.

FR

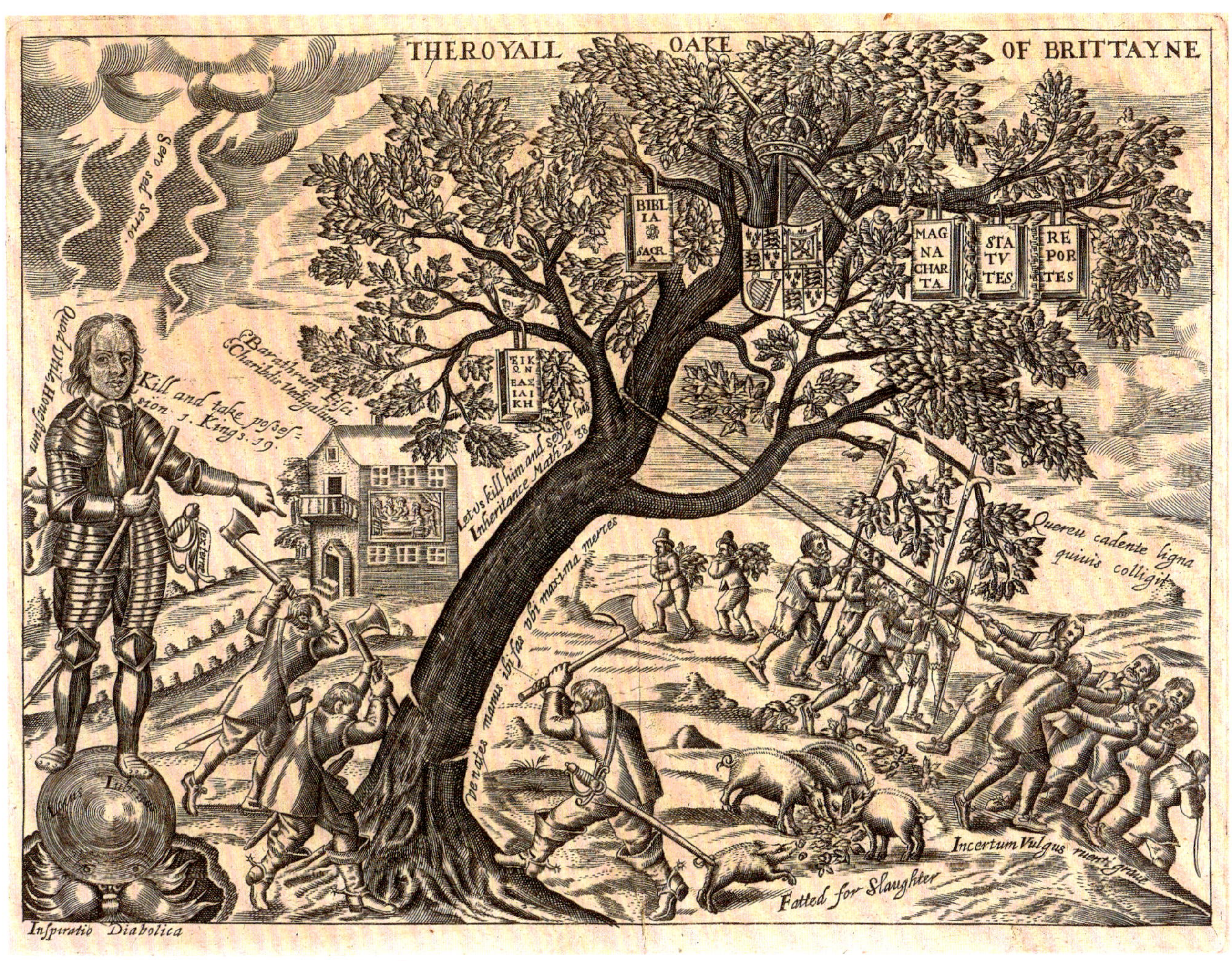

THE ROYALL OAKE OF BRITTAYNE
Sero sed Serio
Quod Diabt: Hortatum
BIBLIA SACR
EIKΩN BAΣIΛIKH
MAGNA CHARTA
STATVTES
REPORTES
Barathrum Legis &Charibdis Vectigalium
Kill and take posses=sion 1 Kings 19
lex terrae
Let us kill him and seise his Inheritance Math 21 38
Venales manus ubi fas ubi maxima merces
Quercu cadente ligna quivis colligit
Incertum Vulgus ruunt fruunt
Fatted for Slaughter
Inspiratio Diabolica
Leges Liberas

Unused sheet of wallpaper in the
chinoiserie style
English, *c*.1780–1800
Etching, coloured by hand
63 x 92 cm
V&A: E.937–2000
Purchased through the Julie and
Robert Breckman Print Fund

The chinoiserie style – stimulated
by exports from China that included
lacquer work, silks and panels of
Chinese wallpaper – was one of
the most enduring fashions in British
interior decoration. The Chinese
papers and their designs were
much imitated. So-called 'single
sheet' papers such as this, with
fanciful interpretations of Chinese
motifs, were produced by British
manufacturers from the 1760s
onwards. With printed outlines and
colours added by stencil, or by
hand (as here), they were intended
as cheaper alternatives to the
fashionable but expensive hand-
painted Chinese papers that were
imported by the East India Company
to satisfy a seemingly insatiable
demand for chinoiserie decoration,
which continued into the early
decades of the nineteenth century.

This is an unusual design, and a
rare survival, with its bold, unfaded
colours. The caged songbird and
the 'Chinese' musical instruments
are motifs that feature in genuine
Chinese wallpapers, but the object
on the right-hand side is tantalizing.

No one has yet been able to identify
it, but the best guesses are that it is
a drum, a tambourine or a cymbal,
with coloured silk bands attached.
This theory is supported by the fact
that there is a pair of sticks – for
beating or striking perhaps? – tied
with ribbon and suspended next to it.

The composition – with the
decorative hexagonal frames, which
are cut in half at each end of the
sheet, and the birdcage seen from
below – suggests that the paper
was designed to be joined end-to-
end with identical sheets, to create
a frieze-like decoration high on the
wall. The motifs themselves imply
that it was perhaps intended as
decoration for a music room or a
space for entertaining.

GS

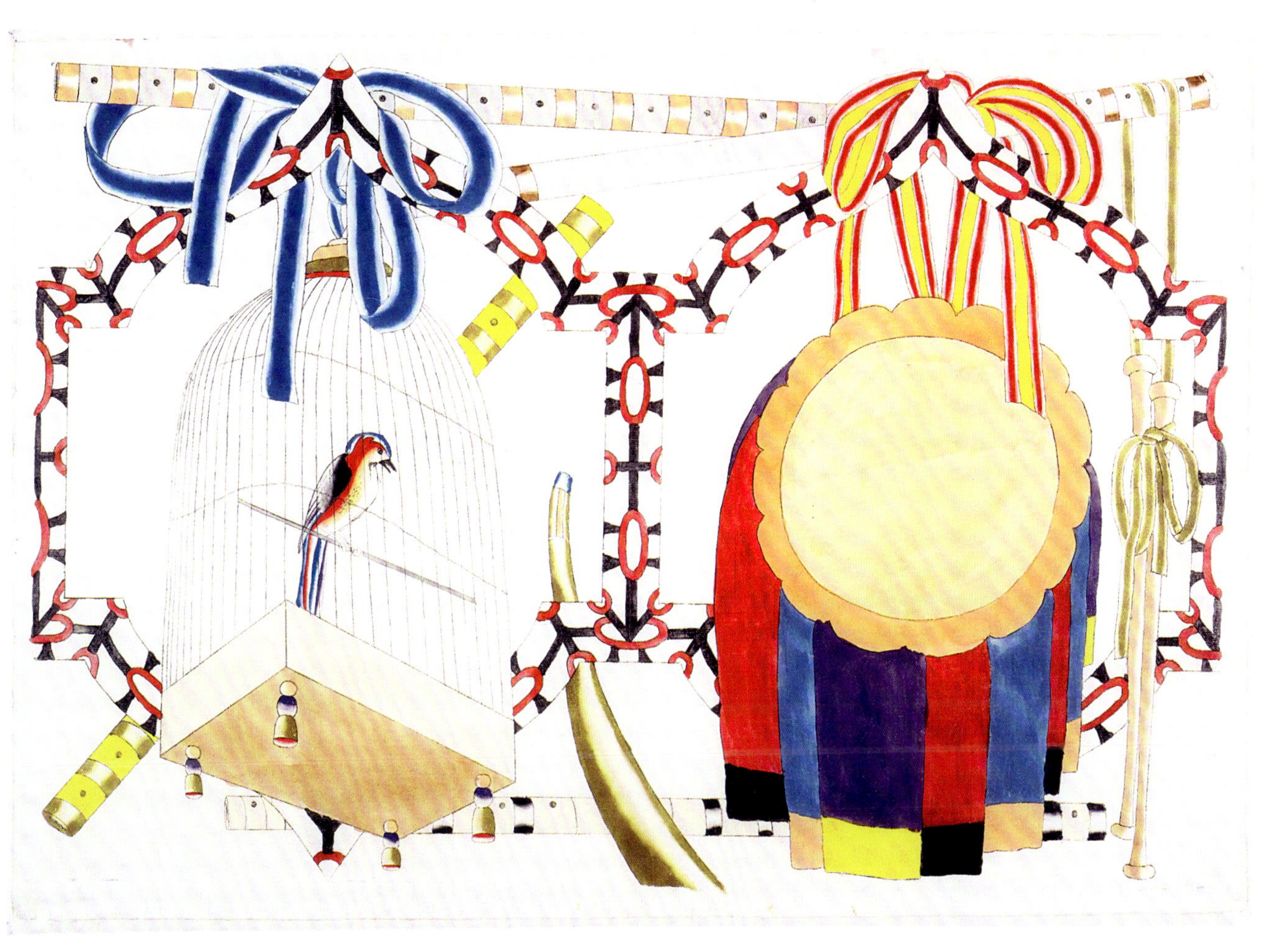

Probably designed by Jacques
Coissieux (1740–1801)
Advertisement for *Nouvelles Cartes
de la République Française* (French
revolutionary playing cards),
published by Urbain Jaume and
Jean-Désmosthène Dugourc, Paris, 1793
Woodcut with stencil colouring
Size of sheet 38.5 x 24.4 cm
V&A: E.409–2005
Purchased through the Julie and
Robert Breckman Print Fund

This advertisement for a sheet of
French playing cards of 1793 is a
remarkable survival documenting an
intriguing interface between politics,
social history and design in the crucial
years of the French Revolution. It is a
proof-sheet or sample, as submitted to
secure official approval and copyright
(*brevet d'invention*), and has the
four-page printed description and
explanation to accompany it.

The year 1789 saw the outbreak of
revolution in France, in which the
ancien régime (literally the 'old rule')
was being challenged by those
eager to replace the unlimited royal
power of an absolute monarchy
with a new constitution. The country
became immersed in revolutionary
politics. The ideals of the new
order were disseminated through
newspapers and pamphlets, political
clubs and public festivals, and by a
wealth of novel imagery and visual
symbolism intended to reinforce the
revolutionary message and eliminate

any reference to the old regime. This
extended to items used in everyday
life, such as playing cards bearing
revolutionary and, later, Napoleonic
imagery. In this advertisement the
traditional representations of kings,
queens and knaves, emblematic
of royal rule, have been replaced
with classically inspired figures – the
Revolution identified strongly with
the democratic ideals of the Roman
Republic. The kings have become
Geniuses, the queens Liberty and
the knaves Equality. The aces are the
Law of the French Republic and are
represented by Roman republican
fasces (bundles of wooden rods)
lashed together. The red Phrygian or
liberty cap – symbol of the freed slave
– appears on many of the cards. While
some of the attributes may have been
understood only by an educated
minority, the overall message is clear,
and playing cards would have
been an effective way of circulating
revolutionary ideals and ideas.

Cards of this type are extremely
rare and this object, with a
provenance from the distinguished
later nineteenth-century Laterade
collection, is a significant addition to
the Museum's holdings of playing
cards. It is currently on display in
the newly devised galleries devoted
to Europe in the period 1600–1815,
where it features in the section
devoted to art and design spawned
by the French Revolution.

FR

NOUVELLES CARTES DE LA RÉPUBLIQUE FRANÇAISE.

PLUS DE ROIS, DE DAMES, DE VALETS; LE GÉNIE, LA LIBERTÉ, L'ÉGALITÉ LES REMPLACENT;

LA LOI SEULE EST AU-DESSUS D'EUX.

SI les vrais amis de la philosophie et de l'humanité ont remarqués avec plaisir, parmi les types de l'Égalité, *le Sant-Culotte* et *le Nègre* ; ils aimeront sur-tout à voir LA LOI, SEULE SOUVERAINE D'UN PEUPLE LIBRE, environner L'As de sa suprême puissance, dont les faisseaux sent l'image, et lui donner son nom.

On doit donc dire, Quatorze DE LOI, DE GÉNIE, DE LIBERTÉ ou D'ÉGALITÉ ; au lieu de Quatorze d'As, de Rois, de Dames ou de Valets ; et Dix-septième, Seixième, Quinte, Quatrième ou Tierce au GÉNIE, à LA LIBERTÉ ou à L'ÉGALITÉ ; au lieu de les nommer au Roi, à la Dame ou au Valet : LA LOI donne seule la dénomination de MAJEURE.

Aux Jeux où les Valets de Trefle ou de Cœur ont une valeur particulière, comme au *Reversy* ou à *la Mouche*, il faut substituer L'ÉGALITÉ DE DEVOIRS ou celle DE DROITS.

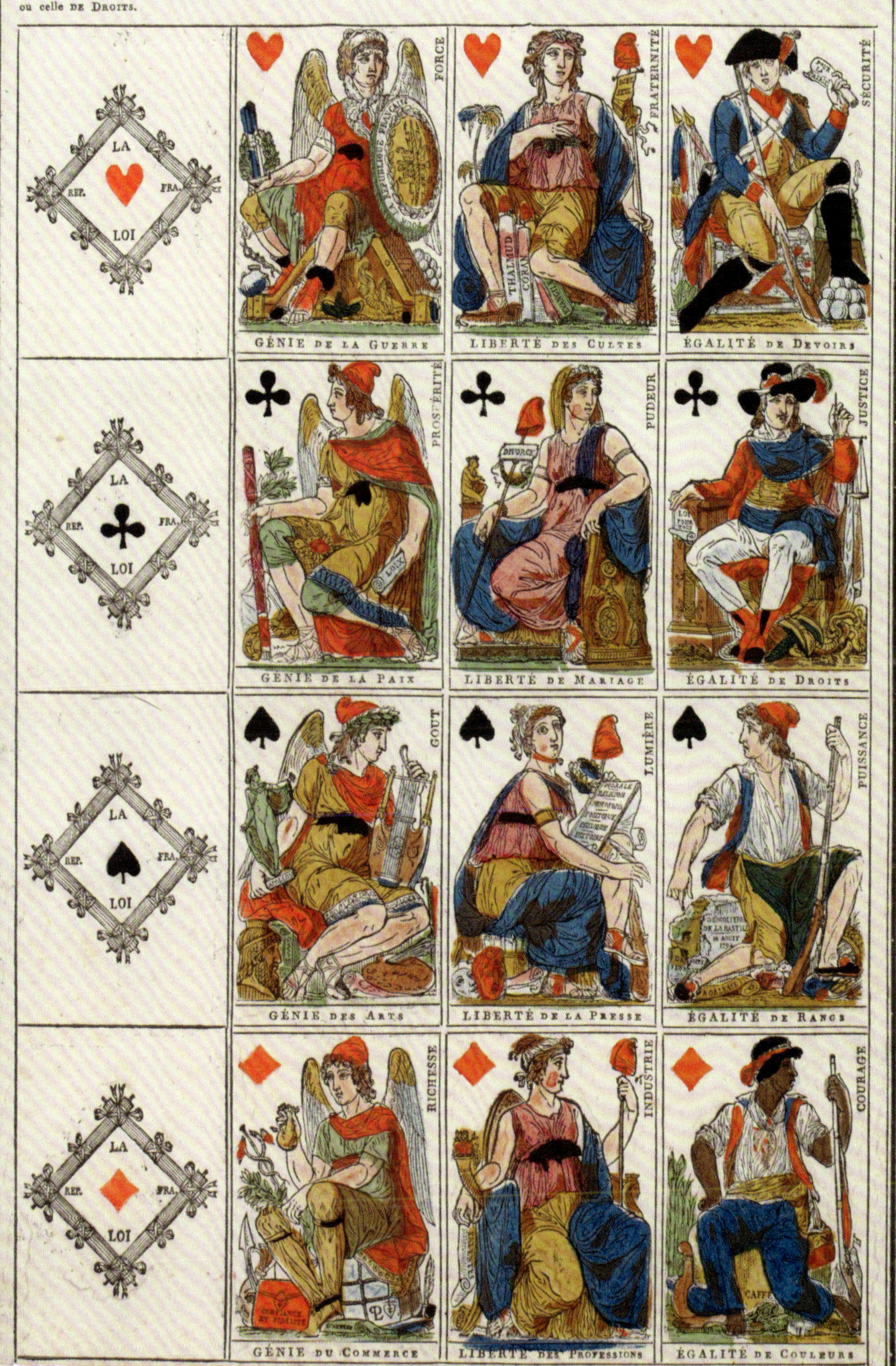

James Hitchcock
'Hitchcock's Metamorphosis', or transfigurative print, *c.27 February 1793*
Containing Pietro Antonio Leone Bettelini (Swiss, 1763–1829) after Angelica Kauffmann (1741–1807), *Laura*, 1780–92, stipple and etching in brown; and Gavriil Skorodumov (Russian, 1754–1992) after Angelica Kauffmann, *Artemisia*, 1775–82; printed 1775–92
Stipple in red, in a deal (probably) and mahogany frame, with *verre églomisé* decoration
27.5 x 24.6 cm (framed)
V&A: E.832–2002
Purchased through the Julie and Robert Breckman Print Fund

This is an example of a transfigurative (or transformation) print of a kind that became popular in the late eighteenth century. The process involved combining two (sometimes three) prints in one frame, in such a way that the viewer could switch between them. The method of producing such novelties was patented by James Hitchcock, of 31 Wellclose Square, London, on 26 March 1793. This example has operating instructions on the back, dated a month earlier and contemporary with the frame, suggesting how to hang and view the piece. Hitchcock's method could display two or more prints or drawings, as follows: strips forming the topmost image were fixed onto a 'slider' backboard by their lower halves, each overlapping the strip above. With the slider board sitting within the frame, strips forming a second image were fixed at their edges onto the frame's raised sides, while interleaved with the first set. Additional sliders could be inserted. Loop screws enabled sliders to move up or down, revealing the other images. The method worked best with blank paper strips, which could then be printed or drawn on, once they were fixed in place. Pencil ruling and wider backing strips show that in this instance pre-existing prints were used.

Besides having novelty value, this object, with its elaborate decorative frame, was intended for display in a fashionable interior. 'Furniture prints' were a growing part of print-sellers' business from the 1750s, as more people could afford such luxuries. This example displays stipple engravings reproducing work by Angelica Kauffmann, who was celebrated as a portrait and history painter, and who also painted ceiling and fireplace panels incorporated by the Adam brothers into their Neoclassical interiors. An astute businesswoman, she had her drawings and paintings reproduced as prints, which were hung in frames, pasted onto walls and fireplaces and reproduced on textiles and ceramics. Her popularity led the artist Gottlob Schönborn (1737–1817) to write in 1781: 'the world has gone angelicamad'.

Kauffmann favoured the technique of stipple engraving. Involving patterns of dots or flicks, this became popular from about 1773, when roulette wheels with spikes or flat-headed spiked tools called mattoirs (*opus mallei*) made it easier. Its delicate tonal effects and ability to print in colours made it particularly suitable for decorative purposes. The size, shape and distribution of the dots could be varied to imitate drawings in different media, such as wash, pastel or chalk.

AB

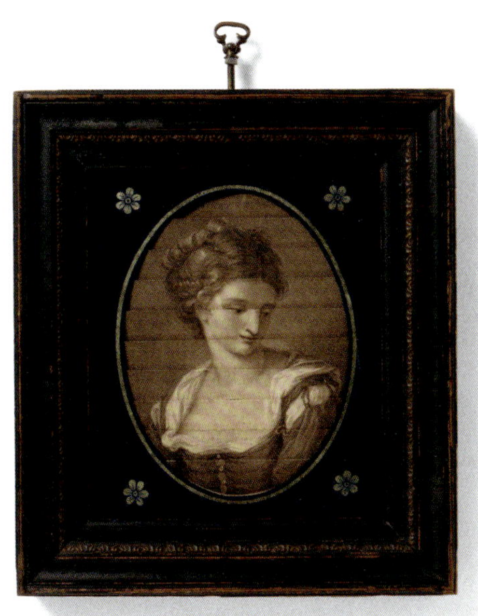

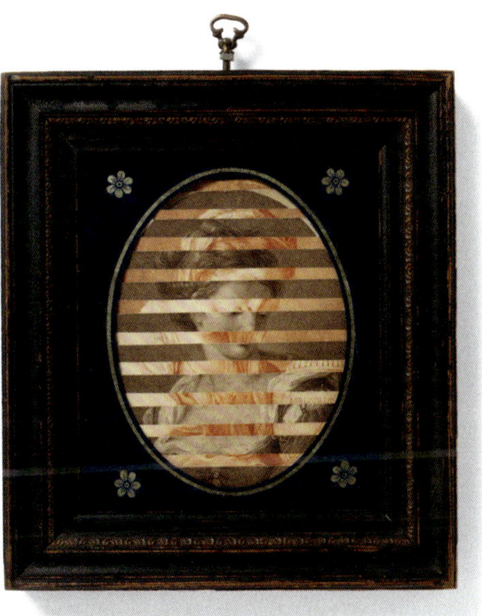

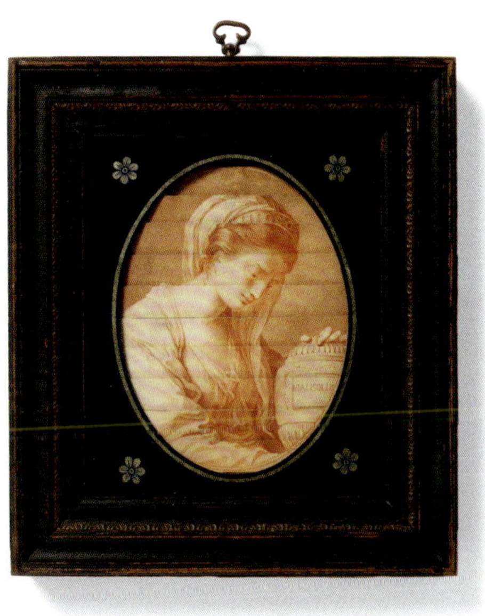

Fire grate, stove, balcony and fencing designs

Metalware pattern book issued by
M. & G. Skidmore, London, *c*.1794
Engraving, bound in boards covered
with blue marbled paper
Size of volume 20.5 x 25 cm
V&A: E.444:1 to 44–2003
Purchased through the Julie and
Robert Breckman Print Fund

This pattern book shows a selection
of designs for grates, fencing and
balconies from the late eighteenth
century (two of the pages are of
paper watermarked 1794). It was
produced by M. & G. Skidmore,
Founders and Stove Grate
Manufacturers of High Holborn
and Clerkenwell.

Recent research suggests this is
probably the earliest trade catalogue
issued by a founder to assist retailers
in ordering such metalwares, a
distinction previously accorded to
a volume dated 1811, also issued
by Skidmore, in the V&A's National
Art Library. Such publications
marked a significant shift in the
way manufacturers promoted and
marketed their products. The V&A
has important collections of pattern
books for various trades, ranging
from ceramics, printed textiles and
wallpapers, to jewellery, furniture,
cruets and cutlery, and this early
example of the genre was a significant
addition to existing holdings.

Illustrated with boldly incised
engravings, the volume is a
fascinating record of changing tastes
in interior design and furnishing,
with many of the designs reflecting
the then-fashionable styles such as
Neoclassicism, with ornament in a
watered-down version of the so-called
'Adam style' – after the architect
brothers Robert (1728–92) and James
Adam (1732–94) – characterized by
urns, vases, swags and medallions.

GS

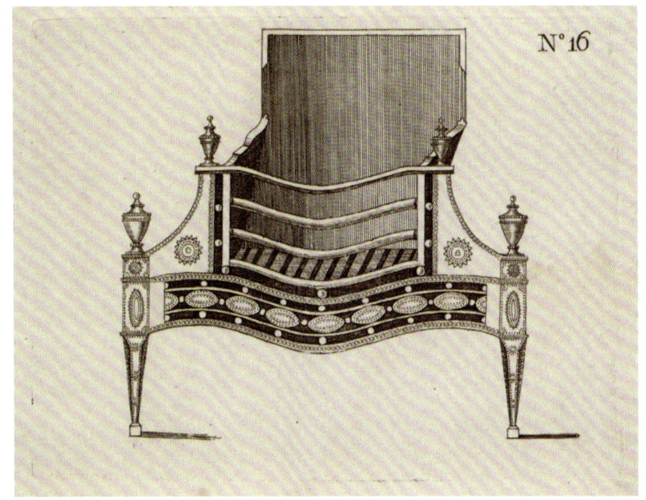

N° 16

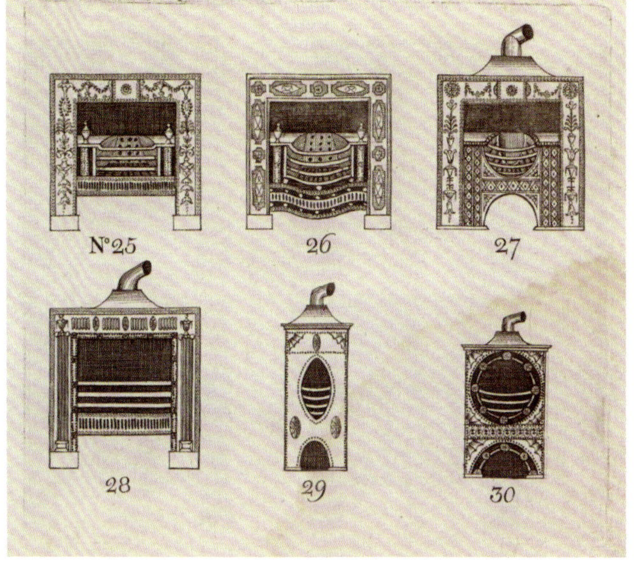

N° 25
26
27
28
29
30

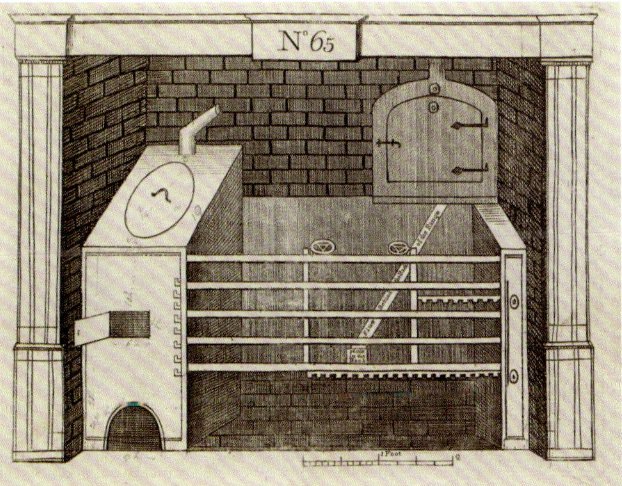

N° 65

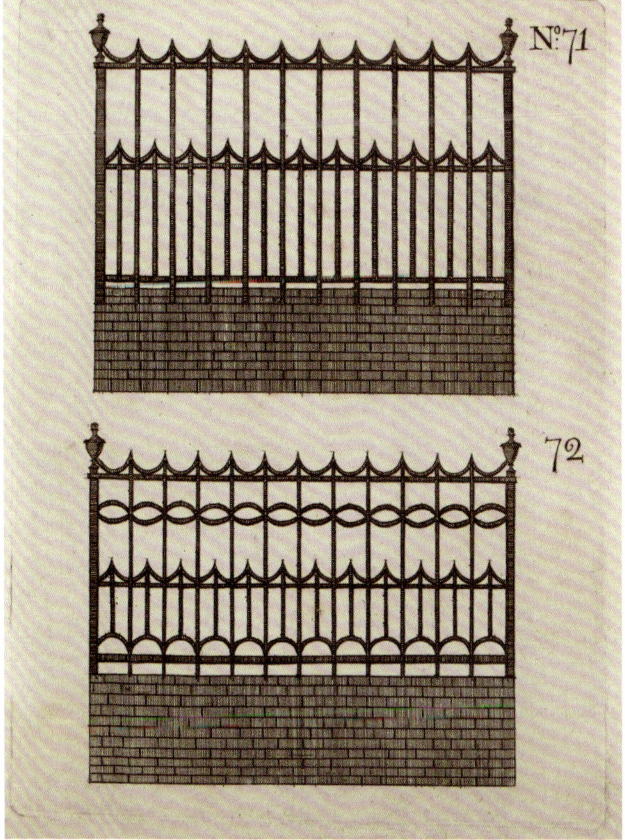

N.° 71
72

Honoré Daumier (1808–79)
Robert Macaire Dentiste
Plate 57 from *Caricaturana* (printer's proof for 1839 album of hand-coloured reissues), dated 1838
Hand-coloured lithograph
21.5 x 23 cm
V&A: E.831–2000
Purchased through the Julie and Robert Breckman Print Fund

Although he was an able painter and sculptor, Honoré Daumier is known chiefly today as a printmaker, and rightly so: in his lifetime the artist executed a staggering 5,000 prints – 4,000 of which were lithographs, as is this example. A speedy, economical and expressive technique, lithography was the great medium of the nineteenth century. Most of Daumier's lithographs, which took contemporary society and politics as their focus, were satirical in nature and were produced for publication in a handful of urbane Paris journals. Thanks to their barbed messages, the young artist was briefly imprisoned in 1833–4.

The series *Caricaturana*, from which this plate is drawn, featured more than 100 lithographs starring the fictional character Robert Macaire, a tall, curly-haired and sideburned Parisian, whose exploits reveal him to be an unscrupulous and opportunistic businessman, thereby embodying the city's prevailing politics of avarice and corruption. Macaire assumes a number of different professions (restaurateur, professor, doctor, banker) and appears in countless contexts in the series, including a self-portrait of the artist, where he compliments Daumier, shown seated working at his desk, on his accurate portrayal of 'the thieves of our time'. In this particular print, however, originally published in *Le Charivari* in 1837, Macaire assumes the role of a dentist who has mistakenly pulled two of his patient's good teeth, leaving the offending decaying teeth behind. The crooked Macaire rebuffs his patient's complaints with the justification that his healthy teeth would have gone rotten eventually as well.

The V&A has a large collection of Daumier's printed caricatures. This particular example was acquired because it illuminates the processes that lie behind print-publishing. This impression was printed and hand-coloured in 1838 for a special edition of all 100 Macaire caricatures, which was sold to collectors in 1839. It bears the instructions of the printer, Edouard Bouvenne (1811–67), who also added the watercolour wash so that this proof could serve as a model for the workshop's colourists to copy. His colouring brings out the detail of the domed glass vase of flowers on the mantelpiece and Macaire's splendid patterned dressing gown with its velvet collar – details that served to underline the bourgeois pretensions of the ambitious protagonist.

SG

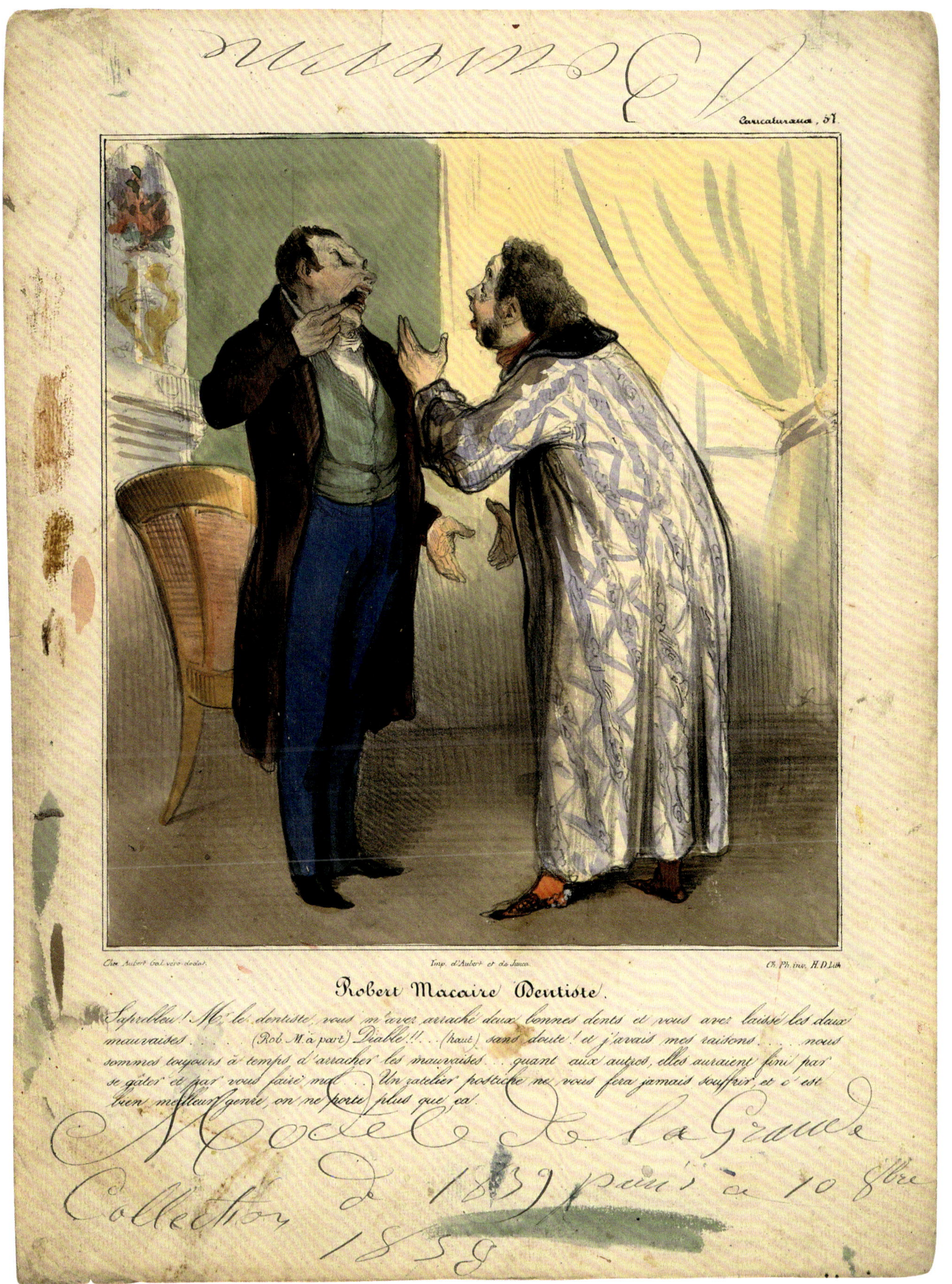

Cher. Aubert Gal. vero-dodat. Imp. d'Aubert et de Junca. Ch. Ph. inv. H. D. Lith.

Robert Macaire Dentiste.

Sapreblleu! M.° le dentiste, vous m'avez arraché deux bonnes dents et vous avez laissé les deux mauvaises ..... (Rob. M. à part) Diable!!.. (haut) sans doute! et j'avais mes raisons ..... nous sommes toujours à temps d'arracher les mauvaises ... quant aux autres, elles auraient fini par se gâter et par vous faire mal ... Un ratelier postiche ne vous fera jamais souffrir, et c'est bien meilleur genre, on ne porte plus que ça.

Volume of 44 fashion plates from
the fashion magazines *La Novita*
and *Margherita,* Milan, 1879–82
Hand-coloured lithographs
Each 37 x 24 cm
V&A: E.151:1 to 44–2003
Purchased through the Julie and
Robert Breckman Print Fund

For more than 150 years, from the
late eighteenth century until the
early twentieth century when they
were finally unseated by fashion
photography, fashion plates were
the key means of communicating
fashionable dress and deportment
to an enthusiastic reading public.
Although they showed men and
women of fashion at their most
idealized, they tell us how historical
dress and all its accoutrements
were intended to be worn, and
in what context. They provide a
comprehensive overview of the
evolution of western dress and are a
fascinating guide to contemporary
ideals of beauty and propriety; their
suggested narratives also provide
valuable and nuanced insights into
social customs and mores, and
evidence of contemporary interiors,
furniture and furnishings.

Most of these plates are taken
from the Italian women's monthly
magazine *Margherita* (Daisy), with a
handful from *La Novita* (The News),
both of which were published in
Milan at a time when the city was
second only to Rome in population

and importance. The city already
enjoyed a reputation as a centre for
fashion and shopping, a legacy that
endures visibly today in Milan Fashion
Week, and in its famous fashion
houses and department stores.

In arrangement and conception,
Margherita's plates followed – as
did the fashions themselves – the
vogues set by and disseminated
from Paris. However, the magazine
gave its plates a discernibly Italianate
aesthetic: the mannequins are
mostly depicted as brunette with
dark colouring, as they are here;
and the dresses they model, while
fashionable, are singularly demure
and correct and the palette
subdued, reflecting the conservative
taste of the Milanese. These two
friends in their summer day-dresses
wear the new close-fitted bodice of
the 1880s, which gave a streamlined
silhouette and would have made it
very difficult indeed to enter with
any great gusto into their game
of croquet.

Such fanciful scenarios, with their
veneer of gentility, were beloved of
fashion-plate designers, who used
aspirational settings to imbue the
fashions depicted with even greater
glamour and appeal. These included
train stations (which suggested
foreign travel), opera houses and
seaside resorts. Another plate from
Margherita shows two women in a
well-appointed interior engaged in
amateur artistic practice – one holds

a palette and brush as she attends
to a painting on an easel, while her
companion arranges drawings or
prints in a portfolio – a setting and
an activity chosen for their perceived
refinement (see pl.25).

SG

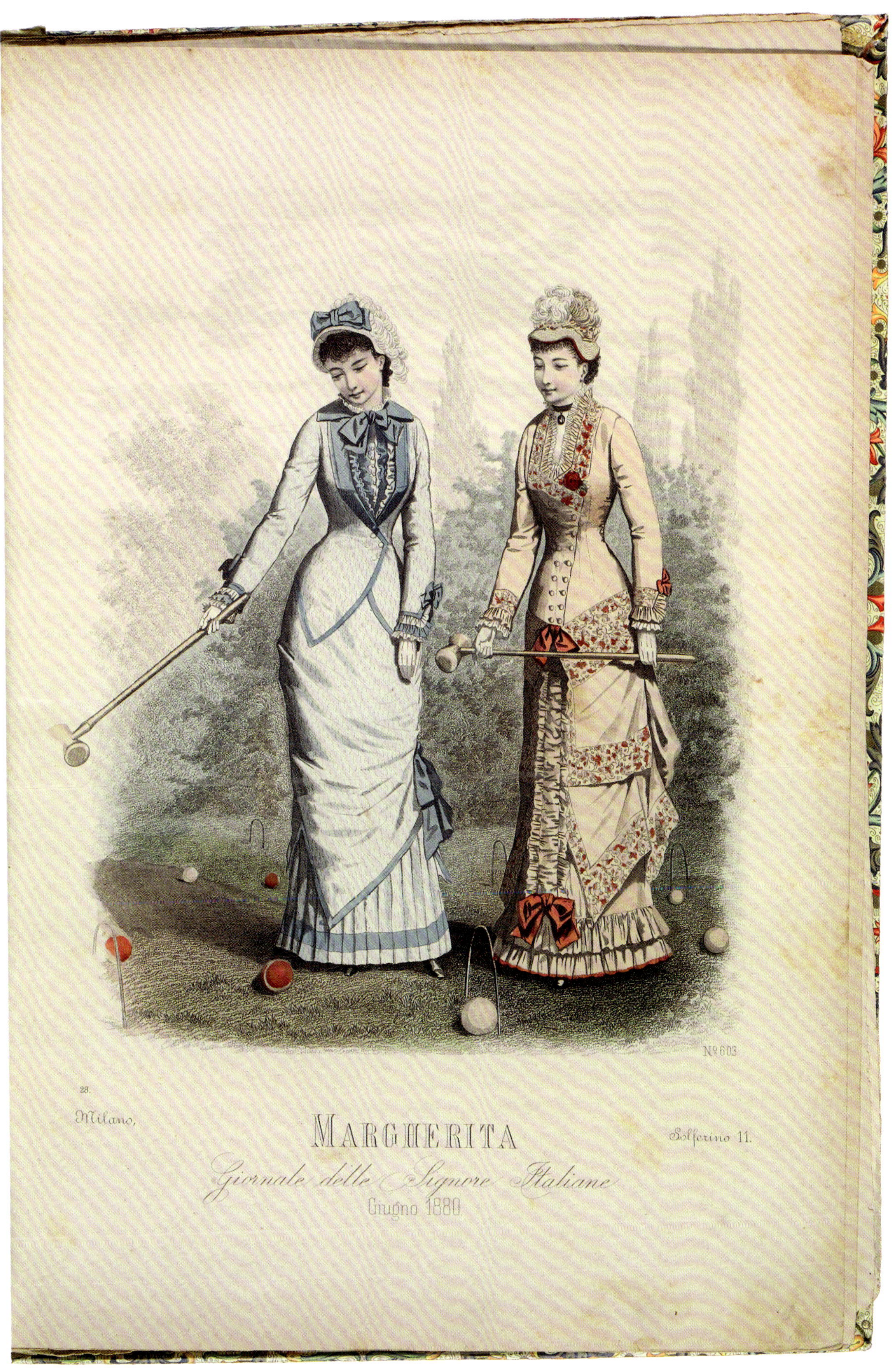

MARGHERITA

Giornale delle Signore Italiane

Giugno 1880

Willi Baumeister (1889–1955)
Poster advertising the exhibition *Die Wohnung* (The Dwelling), held in Stuttgart in 1927
Lithograph printed in black and red
115.1 x 82.9 cm
V&A: E.266–2005
Purchased through the Julie and Robert Breckman Print Fund

This poster by Willi Baumeister publicized *Die Wohnung*, a housing exhibition organized by the Deutscher Werkbund (the German association of artists, designers and architects) in Stuttgart, from July to September 1927. With architects such as Mies van der Rohe (1886–1969), Walter Gropius (1883–1969) and Le Corbusier (1887–1965) taking part, it marked an important moment in the development of Modernist architecture and its promotion to a wide international audience. *Die Wohnung* presented solutions for living arrangements for the modern city-dweller, also demonstrating the use and implementation of new building materials and construction methods. It featured the Weissenhof Siedlung, a housing development that, through its individual designs for dwellings, showcased the Neues Bauen (New Building) movement.

In cursive script, the poster (in whose concept van der Rohe and graphic artist Werner Graeff (1901–78) were probably involved) poses the question 'Wie wohnen?' ('How should we live?'). Its visual language communicates a key intention of the exhibition: the rejection of an out-of-date, highly decorative interior style in favour of a bold Modernist agenda. A photograph of a cluttered and ornate turn-of the-century interior is cancelled out by a fiercely drawn red cross. The use of crosses to signify repudiation was current in avant-garde design journals. Here, the diagonal red slashes lead the eye into the surrounding L-shaped 'frame', on which the exhibition details are proclaimed in bold typography. The poster was one of three of identical format, each featuring a different ornate interior to emphasize the message. Art critic Fritz Stahl (1864–1928) criticized the depiction of a long-outmoded interior, rather than of a more typical recent example, as posing a false choice in favour of Modernism.

Stuttgart-born Baumeister was a significant figure in both German and European art, respected as a painter, theatre designer, commercial artist, art professor and typographer. A member of the Novembergruppe collective of Expressionist artists, and a founder of the Stuttgart artist group Üecht, he was also closely associated with architectural circles, being familiar with members of the Bauhaus, and a friend of Le Corbusier. In 1927 he joined Der Ring, a circle of new commercial artists to which Kurt Schwitters (1887–1948) and other important German typographers belonged. In Baumeister's oeuvre, *Die Wohnung* was highly significant – he not only designed many printed graphics, but also furnished a number of rooms with his artworks.

This poster was acquired for the V&A exhibition *Modernism: Designing a new world 1914–1939*, held in 2006.

MT

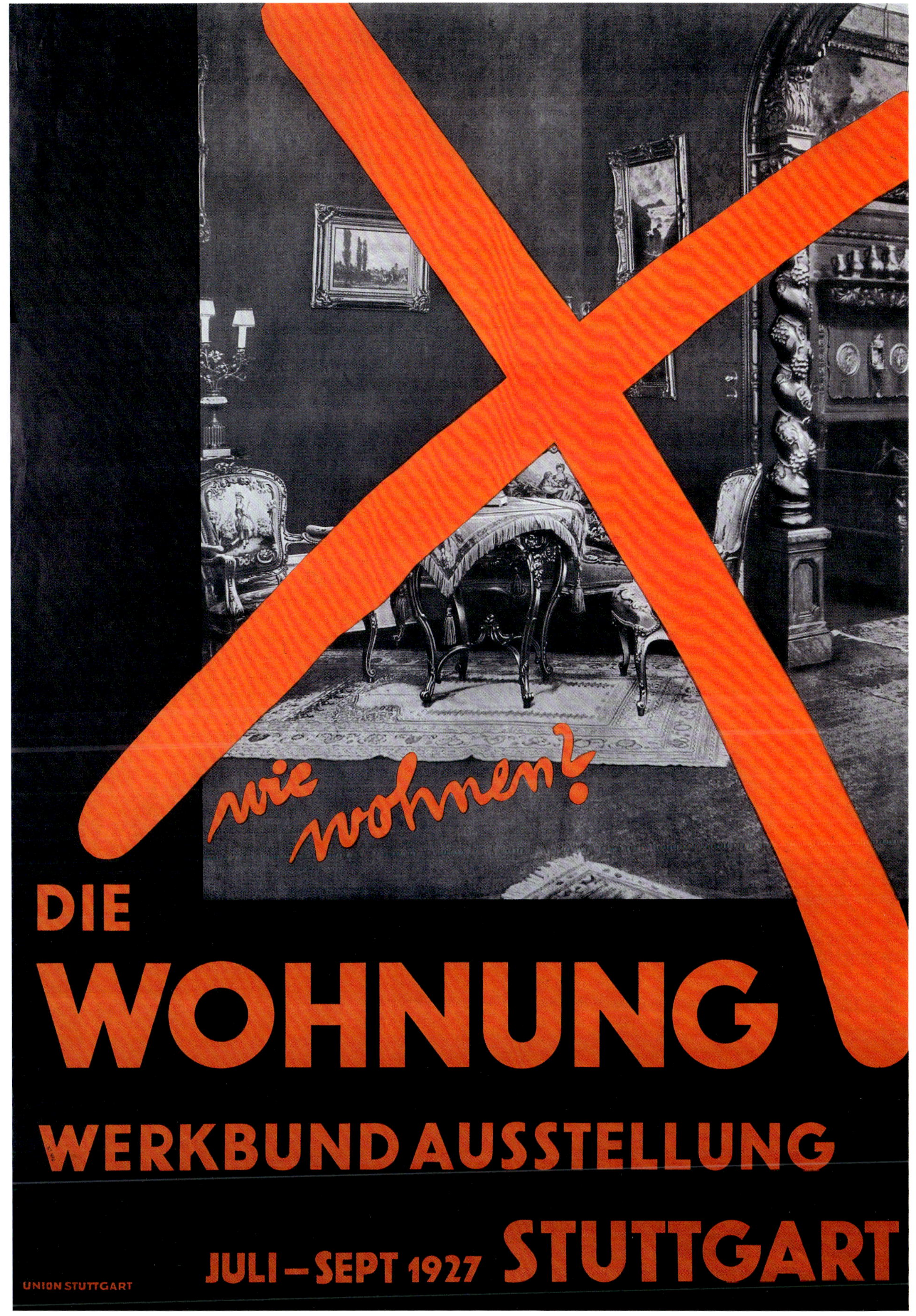

wie wohnen?
DIE
WOHNUNG
WERKBUND AUSSTELLUNG
JULI – SEPT 1927 STUTTGART
UNION STUTTGART

Ernst Mumenthaler (1901–78)
Typenmöbel (Standardized-Type
Furniture)
Swiss poster advertising an exhibition
at the Gewerbemuseum, Basel,
2 June–7 July 1929, printed by
Wassermann A.G., Basel
Lithograph printed in black and
dark pink
127.7 x 90.8 cm
V&A: E.267–2005
Purchased with the support of the
Julie and Robert Breckman Print Fund

This poster by the Swiss designer
and architect Ernst Mumenthaler
advertises *Typenmöbel*, an exhibition
of standardized-type furniture
held at the Gewerbemuseum
(Applied Arts Museum) in Basel
in 1929. The exhibition aimed to
demonstrate that contemporary
furniture should be functional and
flexible; it promoted designs that
were rational, undecorated and
industrially produced (for economy
of production and assembly), rather
than monumental, ornate and
individually made. It presented a
series of uniform rooms containing
examples of basic furniture by
different designers (including chairs
by Marcel Breuer, 1902–81): the
pieces were not specific to the
rooms, being adaptable to different
interiors and sometimes to alternative
uses. This approach met Modernist
aspirations for functional neutrality,
social purpose and aesthetic rigour,
in keeping with contemporary

movements for housing reform
(see Willi Baumeister's poster for
Die Wohnung on p.123).

Mumenthaler and Otto Meier
(1901–82) were partners in a leading
progressive architectural practice
in Basel. In 1927 they won a Swiss
competition for 'Contemporary
Simple Furniture' with their designs
for a *Typenmöbel* system. For the
exhibition at the Gewerbemuseum,
they showed various costed designs
for furniture, including a living room
for 460 Swiss francs that included
modular bookshelves and chairs,
as well as a folding day-bed.
Mumenthaler's poster, a fine
example of the contemporary Swiss
graphic-design school, expresses the
simplified Constructivist style of 1920s
Bauhaus. It presents an axonometric
view of a wardrobe, whose obliquely
angled planes are delineated with
the precision of an architectural
drawing. The composition's formalized
geometry makes clear that
standardized furniture offers logical
spatial and structural solutions, while
the cropping of the design indicates
that the image is intended to be read
as a piece of information, not merely
as a pictorial illustration.

There is a dynamic interplay between
the poster's angular imagery and
its horizontal text. The latter, lettered
in lower-case Modernist typography,
extends to the very edge of the sheet,
to emphasize the idea of a rational
continuum. The style of the lettering

is similar to that developed by Theo
Ballmer (1902–65), an advocate of
precise geometry (his letters were
drawn with ruler and compasses on
a grid), who worked as a graphic
designer in Basel, sometimes in
collaboration with Mumenthaler
and Meier.

The poster was acquired for the V&A
exhibition *Modernism: Designing a
new world 1914–1939*, held in 2006.

MT

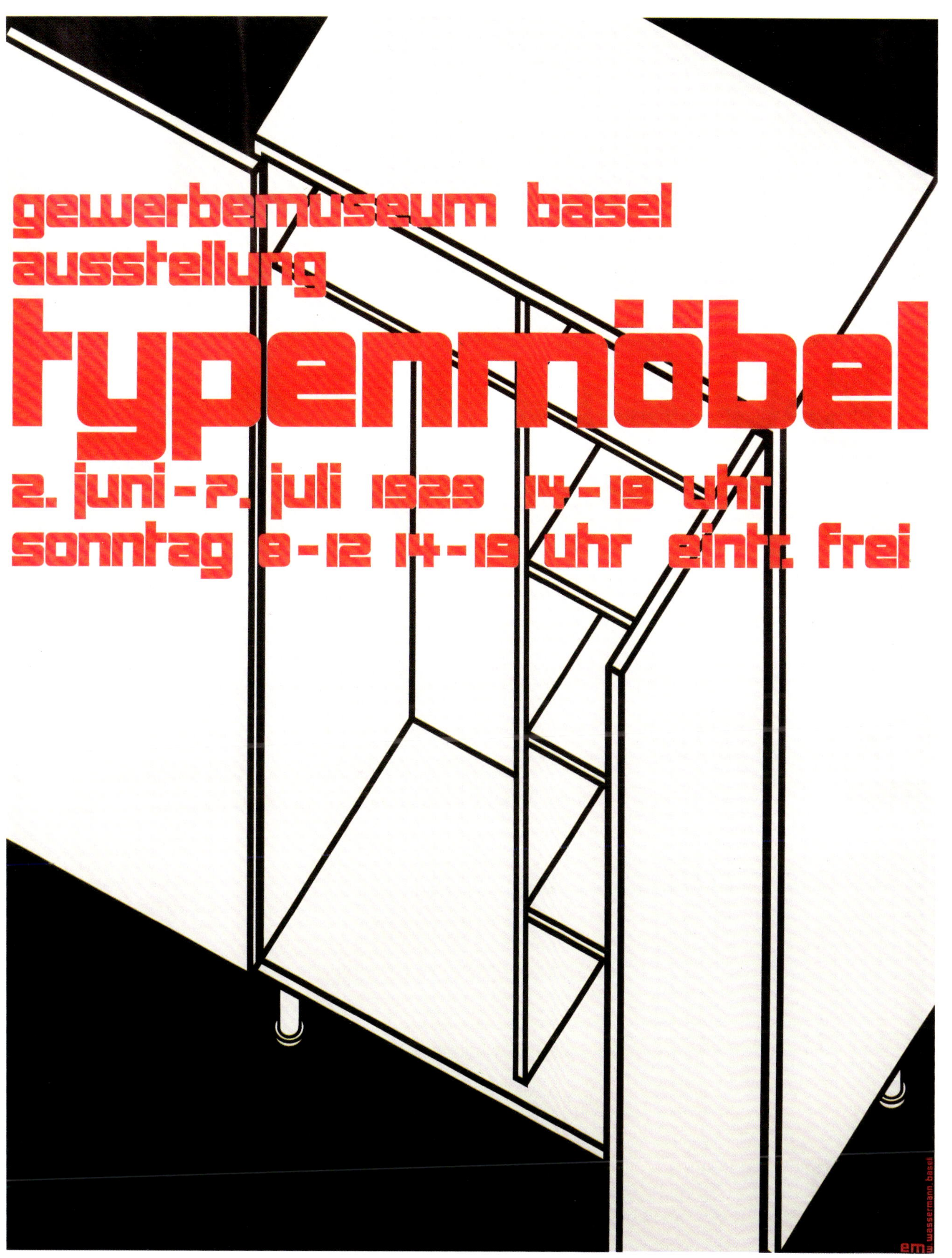

gewerbemuseum basel
ausstellung
typenmöbel
2. juni – 7. juli 1929 14–19 uhr
sonntag 8–12 14–19 uhr eintr. frei
wassermann basel
 em

Lester Beall (1903–69)

Light
Poster issued by the Rural
Electrification Administration, USA,
1937
Colour screen print
Size of sheet 101 x 76.2 cm
V&A: E.265–2005
Purchased through the Julie and
Robert Breckman Print Fund

Light was one of the first set of three
series of posters designed by the
American graphic designer Lester
Beall for the Rural Electrification
Administration (REA) between 1937
and 1941. The REA was created in
1936 as part of the programme for
relief, recovery and reform, known as
the 'New Deal', of President Franklin
Delano Roosevelt (1882–1945). It
was responsible for bringing cheap
electrical power to rural America
at a time when electricity was
commonplace in cities, but largely
unavailable in farms, ranches and
other remote areas. It was believed
that rural electrification would
improve the standard of living and
the economic competitiveness
of the family farm. Through REA
co-operatives, a transmission and
distribution network was established
to provide long runs of power lines,
to which rural households could
connect by having domestic
transformers and wiring installed.

Beall's propagandist message for
the REA is a bold composition in red,
white and blue. The central motif is a
monumental light bulb (a universal
symbol for electric light), while in the
background rays emanate from the
illuminated windows of an isolated
dwelling. The sky and the word 'Light'
are an intense electric-blue; the bulb
is white, bright and bold; and the
foreground is an earthy red, evoking
the soil of country farmsteads. Beall's
use of a simplified pictographic style,
combined with clear and concise
typography, was effective in reaching
out to a rural audience in which there
was a high degree of illiteracy.

Lester Beall was a key proponent of
Modernist graphic design in America.
Largely self-taught as a designer, he
had nevertheless studied art history
at Chicago University and taken
classes at the Art Institute of Chicago.
When he moved to New York City
in 1935 he became a member of a
progressive group that included well-
known European émigré artists and
designers, such as photographer
Alexey Brodovitch (1898–1971),
graphic designers Erik Nitsche
(1908–98) and Joseph Binder
(1898–1972), and artist and
theoretician Josef Albers (1888–1976).
He absorbed many influences
from European avant-garde art
movements, which he synthesized
into his own distinctively American
Modernist aesthetic. The artistic
significance of Beall's posters was
recognized when he was invited to
exhibit six of his REA posters at the
Museum of Modern Art in 1937.

Here they were heralded for their
vigorous design, modern style and
bold symbolism.

This particular poster was acquired
for the V&A exhibition *Modernism:
Designing a new world 1914–1939*,
held in 2006.

MT

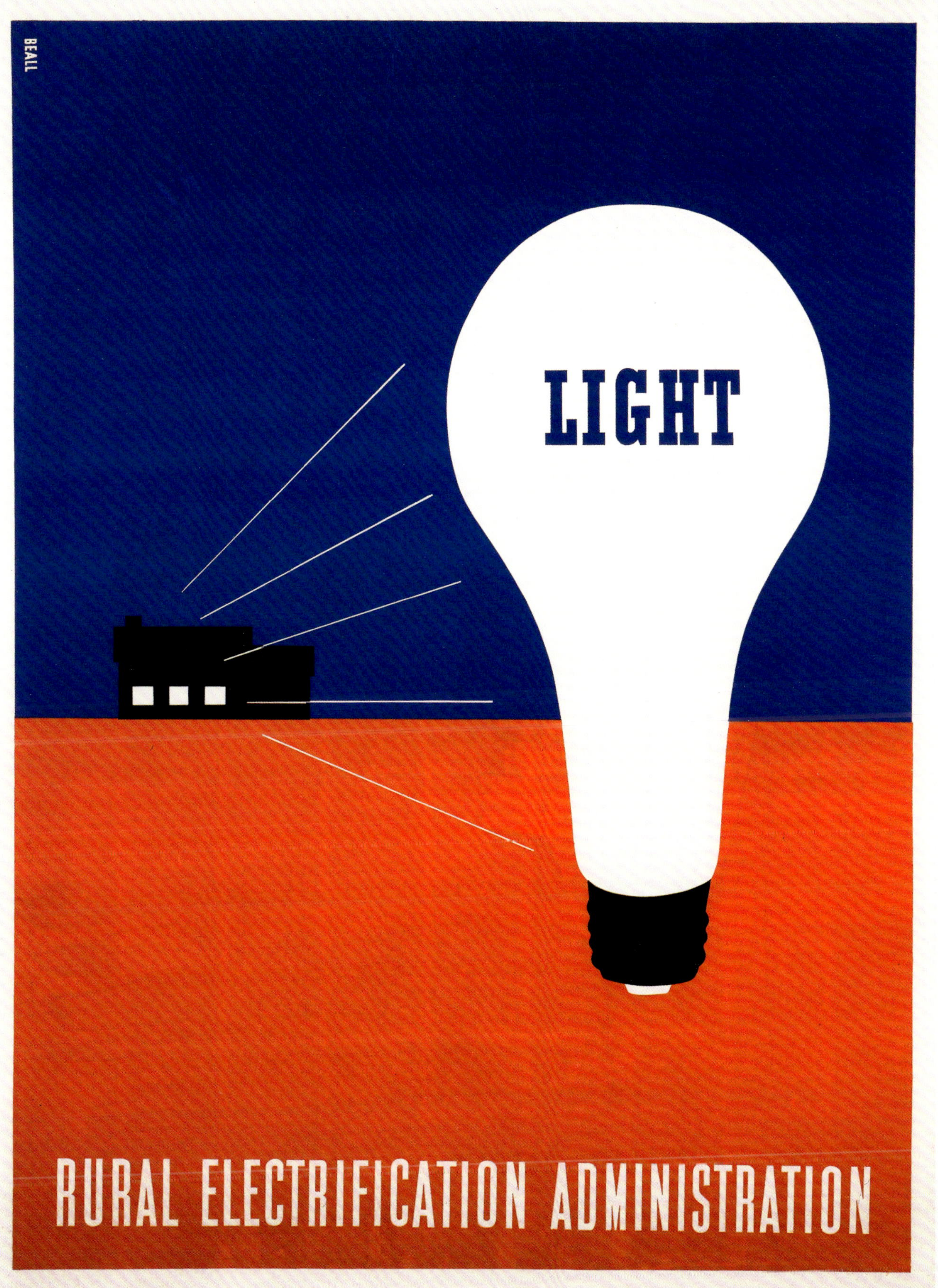

BEALL
LIGHT
RURAL ELECTRIFICATION ADMINISTRATION

José Bardasano Baos (1910–79)
Propaganda poster issued by the
Spanish Communist Party during the
Spanish Civil War, 1937
Colour lithograph
Size of sheet 97 x 66.4 cm
V&A: E.361–2003
Purchased through the Julie and
Robert Breckman Print Fund

This poster is the fourth (indicated
by the number 4 in the upper right
corner) of an eight-part poster series
created by José Bardasano for the
Partido Comunista de España (PCE),
the Spanish Communist Party, during
the Spanish Civil War. Each in the
series illustrated one of the points
listed in the PCE's document entitled
Condiciones Para Ganar La Guerra
(Conditions for Winning the War),
published by the Comite Central
del Partido Comunista de España
(the Central Committee of the PCE)
on 18 December 1936. The fourth
Condition stated: *That it nationalizes
and reorganizes our basic industries
beginning with the industries of war.*
This precept is symbolized by the
image of a worker's arm powerfully
striking a hammer against an anvil,
while in the background images of
battleships and aeroplanes represent
the industrial products that were vital
to victory against the Nationalists. The
shape of the anvil even suggests that
of a ship's hull and of aircraft wings.

The Conditions and the posters
that accompanied them were

promulgated at a time when there
was disagreement among the
Republican side (broadly made up
of socialists, communists, anarchists
and republicans) over how the war
could be used as an opportunity
to reorganize Spanish society.
Some argued that the war needed
to be won before radical social
change could begin. However,
many communist groups pushed
for economic reforms to come first:
they believed that the nationalization
and reorganization of industry could
increase armament production, and
thus their side's chances of winning.
This poster, a powerful piece of visual
propaganda reaching out to a
largely illiterate audience, reinforces
that link between the war effort at
home and success on the front line.

Bardasano made a significant and
prolific contribution to the creation of
propaganda on the Republican side.
He was a member of the Communist
Party and in 1936, at the outbreak of
the Civil War, formed a group of artists
and writers known as 'La Gallofa'
in Madrid. This studio, which also
included Bardasano's wife, Juana
Francisca, was transformed into
the Fine Arts Section of the Unified
Socialist Youth (JSU) and devised
propaganda such as posters and
brochures. Posters were made
collectively, avoiding an emphasis
on the individuality of the artist.
Nevertheless, Bardasano's style of
expressive realism became one of
the most distinctive, during a war

in which art was such a powerful
instrument of persuasion for the
competing ideologies.

MT

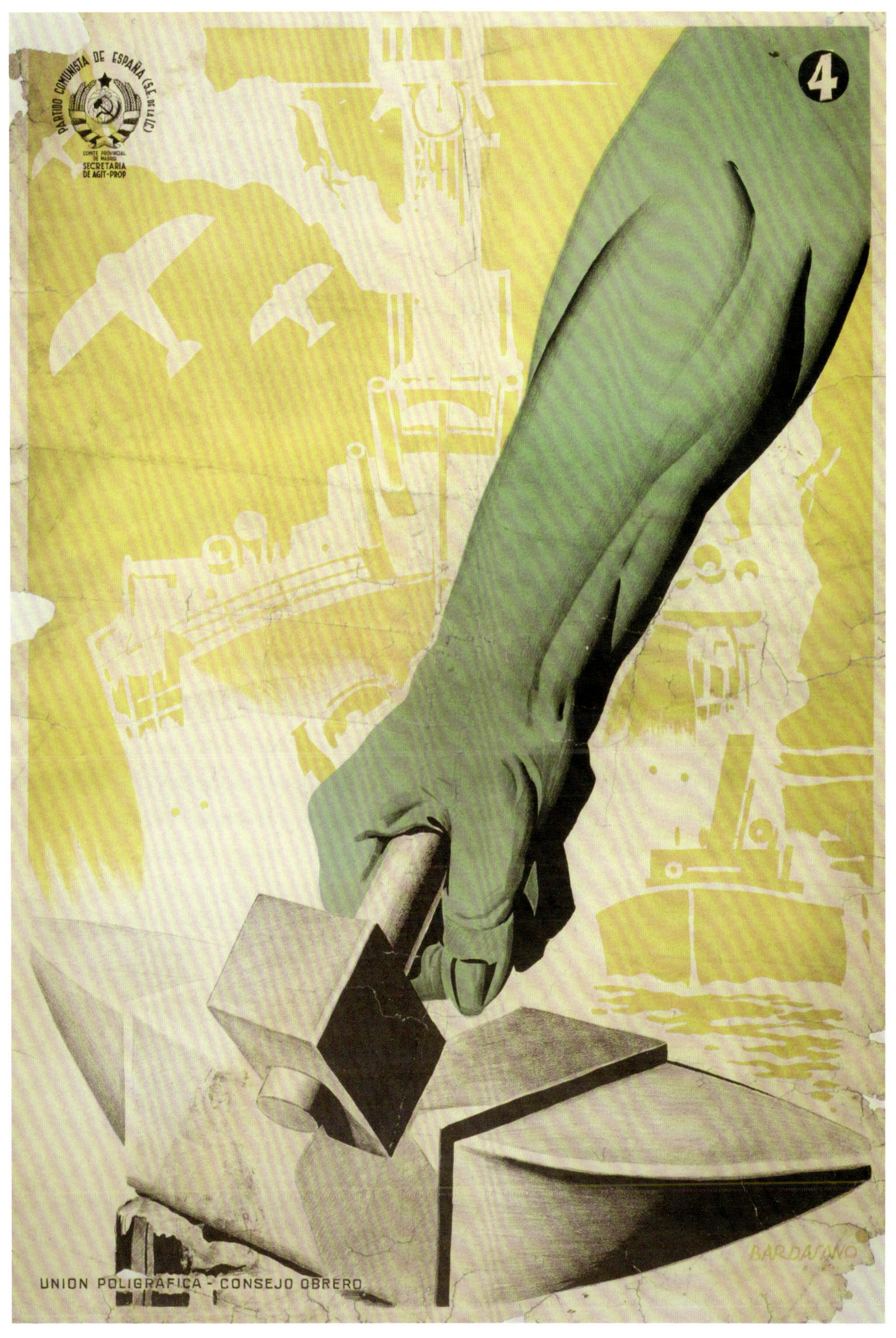

PARTIDO COMUNISTA DE ESPAÑA (S.E. DE L.I.C.)
COMITÉ PROVINCIAL DE MADRID
SECRETARIA DE AGIT-PROP
4
BARDASANO
UNION POLIGRAFICA - CONSEJO OBRERO

Abram Games (1914–96)

BEA Olympic Games. London.
July 29–Aug 14 1948, 1948
Printed by the Baynard Press and
bearing the BEA logo
Colour offset lithograph
Size of sheet 102 x 63.5 cm
V&A: E.296–2006
Purchased through the Julie and
Robert Breckman Print Fund

In 1948 London hosted the Games
of the XIV Olympiad, the first Olympic
Games following the Nazi-dominated
Games of Berlin 1936 and the
shattering events of the Second
World War, which had caused a
twelve-year hiatus in the competition.
Although the city was scarred by war
damage, and a climate of post-war
austerity and rationing prevailed,
many sporting facilities remained
functioning, and the Empire Stadium
at Wembley was chosen as the
principal venue. Here the Games
were declared open by King George
VI (1895–1952) on 29 July 1948.

As was customary, the spin-off
opportunities offered by the Games
were seized upon by the travel
industry, whose transport systems
provided the means by which
participants and spectators could
reach the venues. Abram Games'
surrealist poster for British European
Airways (BEA) wittily associates
the airline with the Games, in the
viewer's mind. Evoking sensations of
speed, air and flight, he depicts an
airborne sprinter with wing-like shapes
racing along the nose of an aircraft
that has metamorphosed into the
curve of a race track; the aircraft's
wheel, too, echoes the shape of a
stadium. The imagery is enhanced
by the deployment of the artist's
consummate airbrush skills, while
the sloping lettering increases the
dynamism of the composition.

Abram Games was a pioneer of
twentieth-century graphic design. He
was influenced by Edward McKnight
Kauffer (1890–1954), whose Modernist
style of visual communication helped
to inspire Games' own aesthetic
of 'Maximum Meaning, Minimum
Means'. He also acknowledged his
debt to other great poster artists,
such as the Frenchmen Jean Carlu
(1900–97) and A.M. Cassandre
(1901–68) and the German Ludwig
Hohlwein (1874–1949), whose style
integrated text and image into
powerfully unified designs. As Official
War Office Poster Artist during the
Second World War, Games became
famous for many memorable posters.

His success continued afterwards:
he designed a stamp for London
1948, thereby earning himself the
nickname 'Olympic Games'; created
the emblem for the Festival of Britain
(1951), which made him a household
name; and conceived the first BBC
moving ident (1953). BEA was one
of a large number of commercial
clients – including London Transport,
Guinness, BOAC, Orient Line, *The
Times* and *Financial Times* – that
commissioned his work. Throughout
his career he retained his fierce belief
in the individuality of the graphic
designer, and his sense of artistic
purpose was matched by
an original vision and by sheer
technical accomplishment.

MT

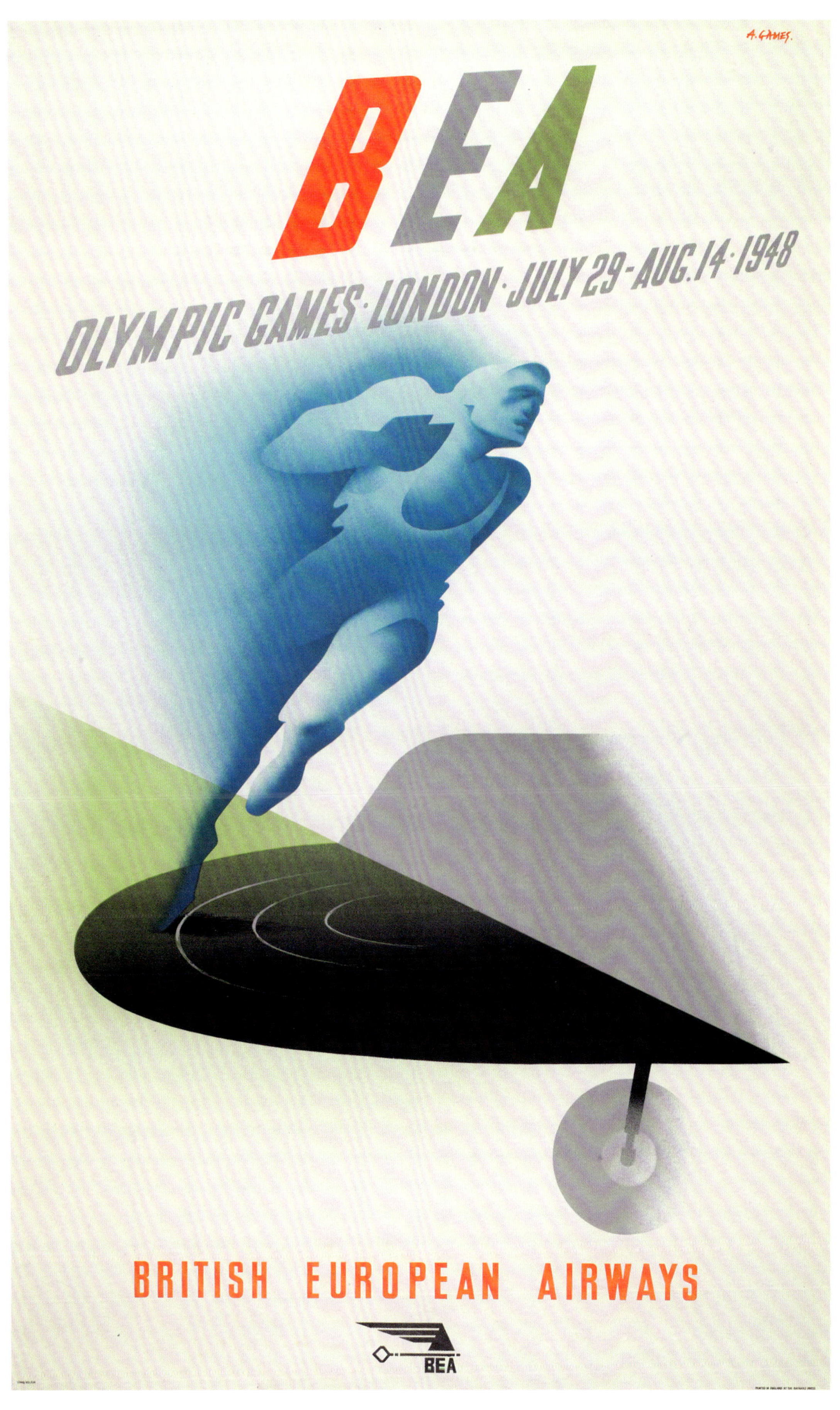

A. GAMES.
BEA
OLYMPIC GAMES · LONDON · JULY 29 · AUG. 14 · 1948
BRITISH EUROPEAN AIRWAYS
BEA

Waldemar Świerzy (1931–2013)
Rzeczywistość (Reality)
Polish film poster, 1961, produced by
CWF (Centrala Wynajmu Filmow =
Central Film Hire)
Lithograph printed in black and pink
Size of sheet 85.2 x 60.1 cm
V&A: E.352–2003
Purchased through the Julie and
Robert Breckman Print Fund

Waldemar Świerzy's poster advertises
the 1960 film *Rzeczywistość* (Reality), a
Polish political drama starring Henryk
Boukołowski (b.1937), Pola Raksa
(b.1941) and Leon Pietraszkiewicz
(1907–87), which premiered in
1961. It was directed by Antoni
Bohdziewicz (1906–70), with a script
by Bohdziewicz and Tadeusz Byrski
(1906–87), and produced by Zespół
Filmowy Droga.

The drama was based on a first
novel, *Reality*, by Jerzy Putrament
(1910–86), the Polish writer, poet,
editor, publicist and politician who
worked as a journalist during the
1930s, when he was arrested and
tried for communist activism under
an authoritarian nationalistic regime.
Published in 1947, the novel drew on
his experiences of this trial. In the film,
the police try to force Julek Szulc, a
young lawyer who has contributed
a powerful article about a strike to
the magazine *Reality*, to implicate
co-journalists on the publication,
who are also suspected of seditious
political activities. Their links with the

illegal communist party Kompartia
are unproven, and the trial ends
in a moral victory against state
authority and the misuse of power.
Soon afterwards, however, Szulc is
rearrested and murdered in police
custody. This proved to be a key film
in the evolution and understanding
of Polish cinema.

Świerzy's poster acts as a metaphor
for the film. His deconstructed image
of Szulc focuses on the man's moral
dilemma. A crumpled news-sheet
suggests both Szulc's journalism and
his silhouette likeness, while a cut-out
'eye' evokes his haunting experience.
The jagged tear symbolizes his
divided self and the rending effects of
his trial and persecution.

Świerzy graduated in 1952 from the
Katowice Graphics Department of
Cracow ASP, where he was taught
by Józef Mroszczak (1910–75),
the acclaimed Polish poster artist
and graphic designer. In his early
work Świerzy developed his own
conceptual style, often featuring
the human figure as a starting
point. He became famous for his
posters, graphics and publishing,
illustration and exhibitions, and was
a co-founder of the Polish School
of Posters. He is best known for his
posters for the performing arts –
theatre, film, circus and music. These
were areas of publicity where, from
the mid-1950s onwards, communist
state patronage in Poland allowed
an unusual degree of artistic

freedom and experimentation. Polish
film posters became a particularly
powerful genre.

MT

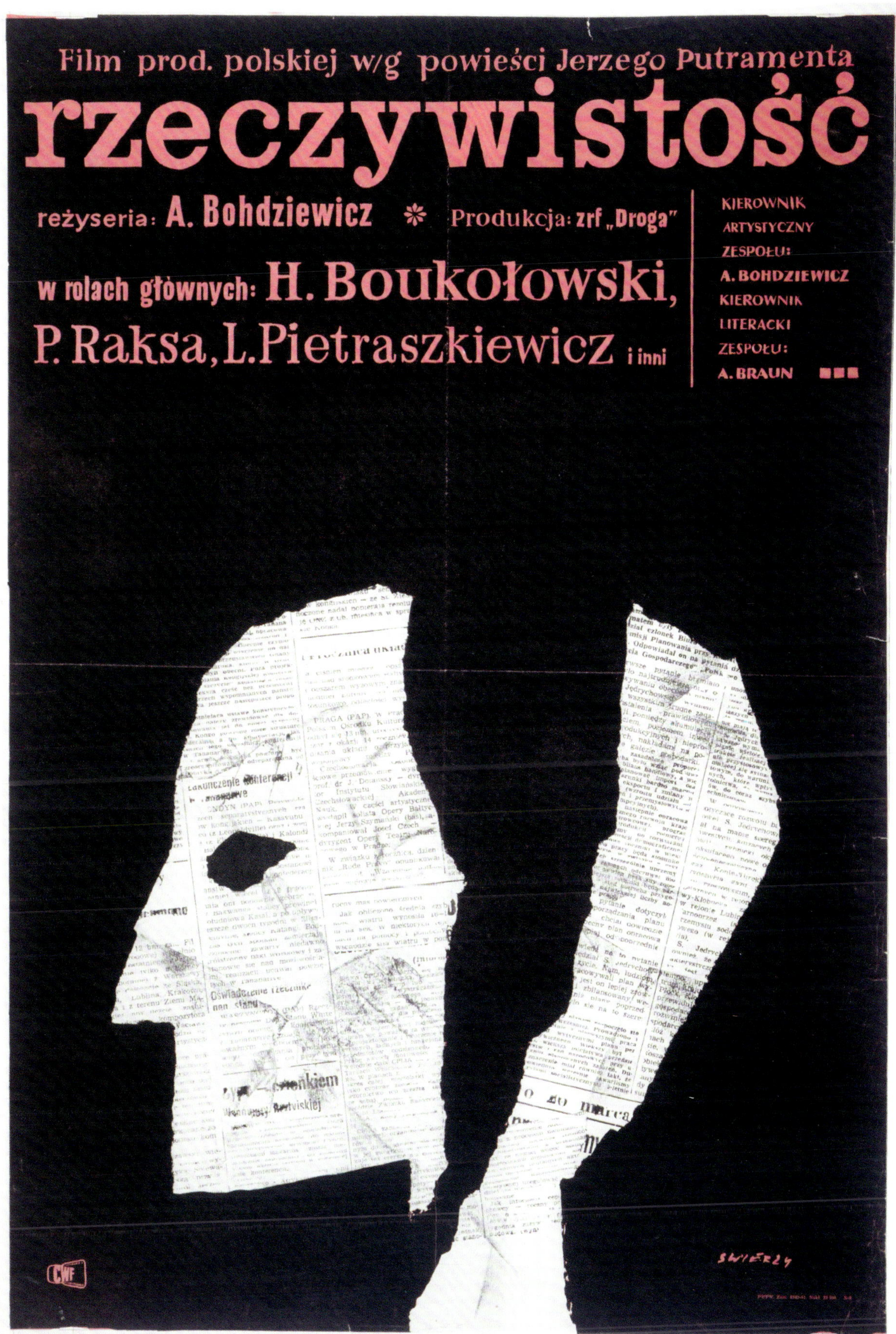

Film prod. polskiej w/g powieści Jerzego Putramenta
rzeczywistość
reżyseria: A. Bohdziewicz ✳ Produkcja: zrf „Droga"
w rolach głównych: H. Boukołowski,
P. Raksa, L. Pietraszkiewicz i inni
KIEROWNIK ARTYSTYCZNY ZESPOŁU:
A. BOHDZIEWICZ
KIEROWNIK LITERACKI ZESPOŁU:
A. BRAUN

Atelier Populaire

Les Beaux-Arts Sont Fermés, Mais L'Art Revolutionaire Est Né (The Fine Arts Are Over, But Revolutionary Art Is Born)
Poster supporting anti-government strikes and demonstrations in Paris;
Paris, 1968
Screen print
63 x 30 cm
V&A: E.762–2008
Purchased through the Julie and Robert Breckman Print Fund

In May 1968 the art students and staff of the Ecole des Beaux-Arts in Paris occupied their college building and set up the Atelier Populaire (People's Workshop). Using basic screen-printing equipment and requisitioning a giant roll of newsprint paper, they began printing posters in support of a wave of strikes and demonstrations in Paris against rising poverty, unemployment and the conservative policies of the government of Charles de Gaulle (1890–1970). Over a number of months they produced a continuous stream of posters characterized by bold, quick-to-print monochrome images and sharp, often poetic, slogans.

The Atelier Populaire was a collective that worked by consensus. Each day a general assembly met to debate the unfolding political situation on the streets, and to agree the next designs and slogans to be printed. Participants were inspired by Marxist philosophy and revolutionary groups, such as the Situationist International. The intention in setting up the press was not simply to produce propaganda materials, but also to experiment with a new kind of anti-capitalist and anti-consumerist culture, in which art was produced to serve a social struggle, rather than being valued for its own sake. In a statement the Atelier Populaire wrote that:

> The posters produced by the ATELIER POPULAIRE are weapons in the service of the struggle and are an inseparable part of it…these works should not be taken as the final outcome of an experience, but as an inducement for finding, through contact with the masses, new levels of action, both on the cultural and the political plane.

This poster depicting Marianne (the allegorical figure of France) wielding a palette knife and emblazoned with the slogan 'The Fine Arts Are Over, But Revolutionary Art Is Born' is particularly interesting because it makes explicit the intention to use art as a form of direct action.

The example of self-initiated guerrilla poster-making, established by the Atelier Populaire, was immediately followed by artists and activists around the world, from Mexico City to Belfast.

CF

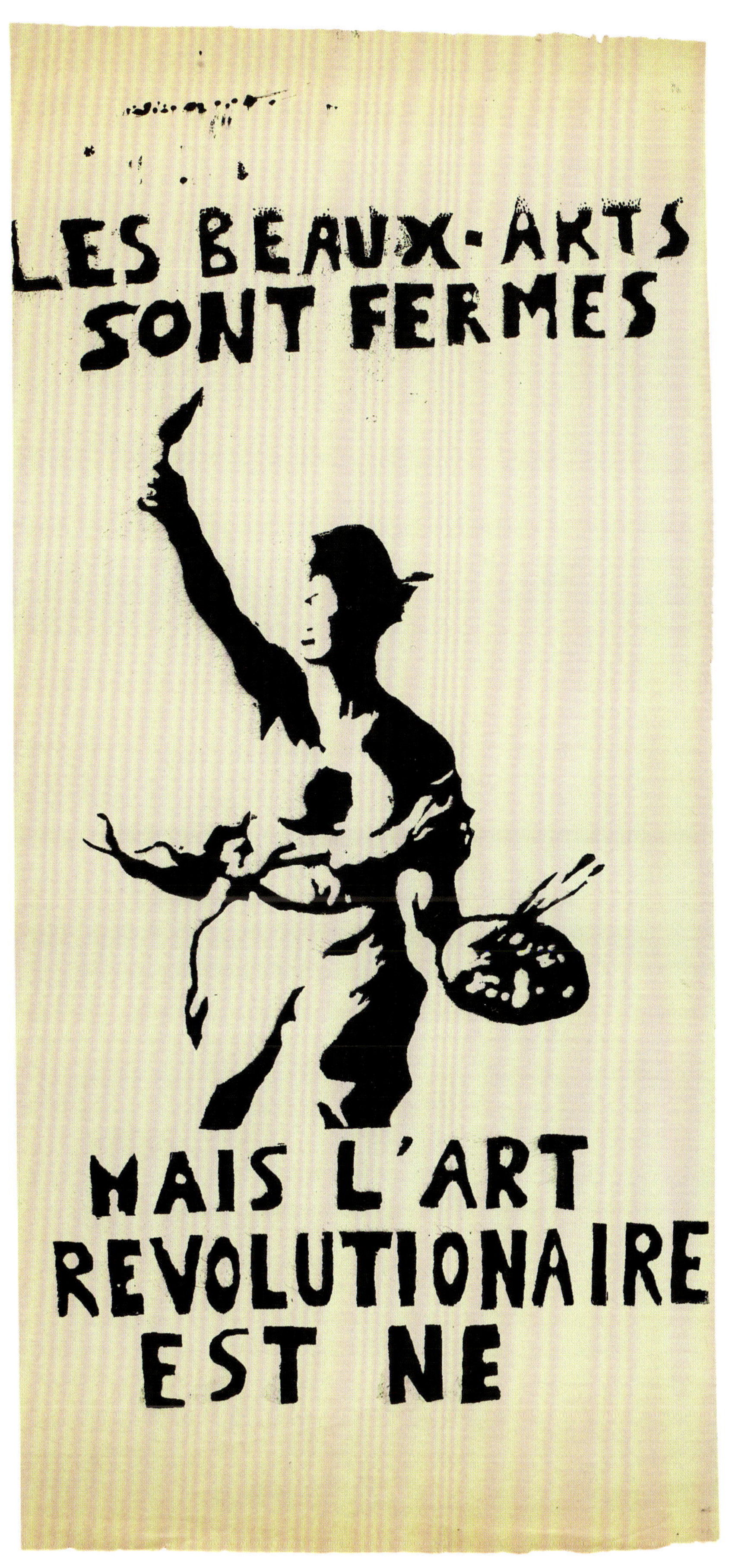

LES BEAUX-ARTS
SONT FERMES
MAIS L'ART
REVOLUTIONAIRE
EST NE

Badges

Produced in Britain and America,
1960s–1980s
Offset lithographs on paper, mounted
on metal and coated with plastic
Various sizes
V&A: E.300 to 782–2002
Purchased through the Julie and
Robert Breckman Print Fund

The first 'button' badges were made
in the 1890s by the American firm
of Whitehead and Hoag Company.
Except for one or two technical
refinements, their form has not
changed significantly since the end
of the nineteenth century. From the
outset they were used to announce
political affiliation or to drum up
support for election candidates.

They first appeared in Britain during
the Boer War (1899–1902) and were
adorned with patriotic slogans, such
as 'We hold a vaster empire than
has ever been.' Ironically, at this time
they were imported from America
– a former colony. Throughout the
twentieth century they continued
to be produced in vast numbers,
being sold or given away to advance
political causes, promote bands,
advertise products or simply express
the wearer's personality through eye-
catching imagery or witty slogans.

The counterculture of the 1960s
quickly adopted badges as a
cheap and cheerful medium of
propaganda for (usually left-wing)
political positions on issues like the
Vietnam War, nuclear disarmament,
workers' rights, race, gender and
sexuality, turning them into a fashion
accessory in the process. This
collection of nearly 500 badges was
amassed by Barry Miles, a key figure
on the London 'alternative' scene in
the 1960s. He was a founder of the
Indica Bookshop and the Marxist
newspaper *International Times*,
and was involved in setting up the
underground nightclub UFO.

This collection of badges
complements the V&A's important
holdings of posters that supported,
promoted or protested against similar
causes over the same period.

TT

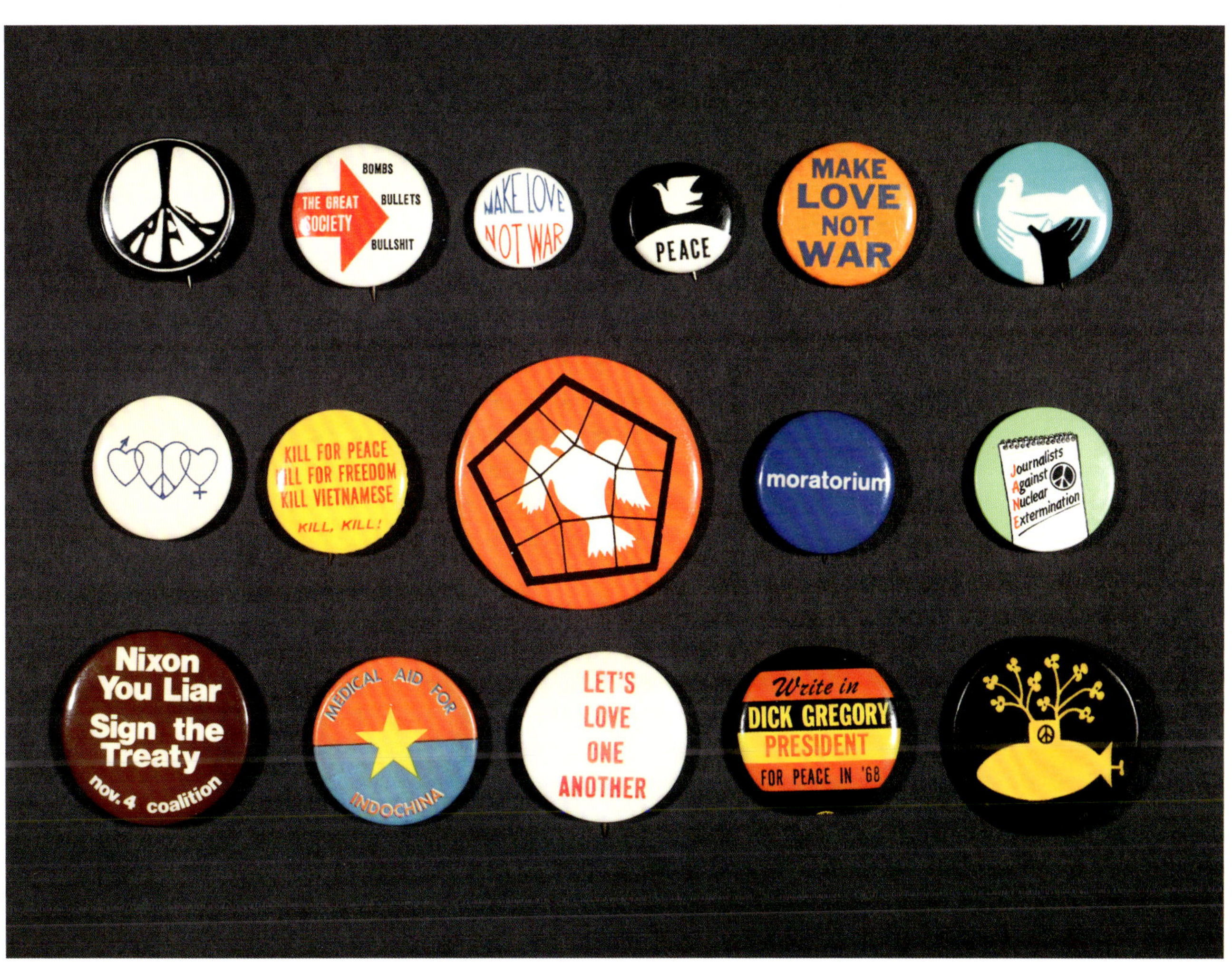
THE GREAT SOCIETY
BOMBS
BULLETS
BULLSHIT
MAKE LOVE NOT WAR
PEACE
MAKE LOVE NOT WAR
KILL FOR PEACE
KILL FOR FREEDOM
KILL VIETNAMESE
KILL, KILL!
moratorium
Journalists Against Nuclear Extermination
Nixon You Liar Sign the Treaty
nov. 4 coalition
MEDICAL AID FOR INDOCHINA
LET'S LOVE ONE ANOTHER
Write in DICK GREGORY PRESIDENT FOR PEACE IN '68

Sara Fanelli (b.1969)

Paris Fluctuat nec Mergitur, 2001
Collage of printed papers
28 x 22.5 cm
V&A: E.347–2003
Purchased through the Julie and
Robert Breckman Print Fund

Italian-born Sara Fanelli, artist
and illustrator, is a graduate of
Camberwell School of Art and the
Royal College of Art. This collage was
made for an exhibition at the Alliance
Graphique Internationale (AGI)
meeting in Paris in 2001. Fanelli had
become a member of the AGI a year
earlier. '*Fluctuat nec Mergitur*' (which
translates as 'It floats, it does not sink')
is the motto of the city of Paris and
appears on the city's coat of arms.
Inspired by this, Fanelli shows the Eiffel
Tower, a popular emblem of Paris, as
a creature with wings and eyes, flying
through the air.

This image exemplifies Fanelli's
distinctive visual style and her
use of simple colourful elements,
combined with a slightly surreal,
naïve edge. Puns and playful
allusions abound in her work; here,
she makes a subtle reference to
flight by including some patterned
papers that appear to have been
cut from envelopes – possibly airmail
envelopes. Her composition also
draws inspiration from the Cubist
tradition of paper collage. Here, in a
manner reminiscent of Pablo Picasso
(1881–1973), she has used fragments

of paper printed with text, including a
reference to Buttes-Chaumont, a park
in northern Paris.

The quirky humour apparent here
is also characteristic of her book
illustrations, especially those for
children. Fanelli has written and
illustrated a number of books, in
which winged creatures often feature,
and in 2004 she was the winner of the
V&A Illustration Awards.

GS

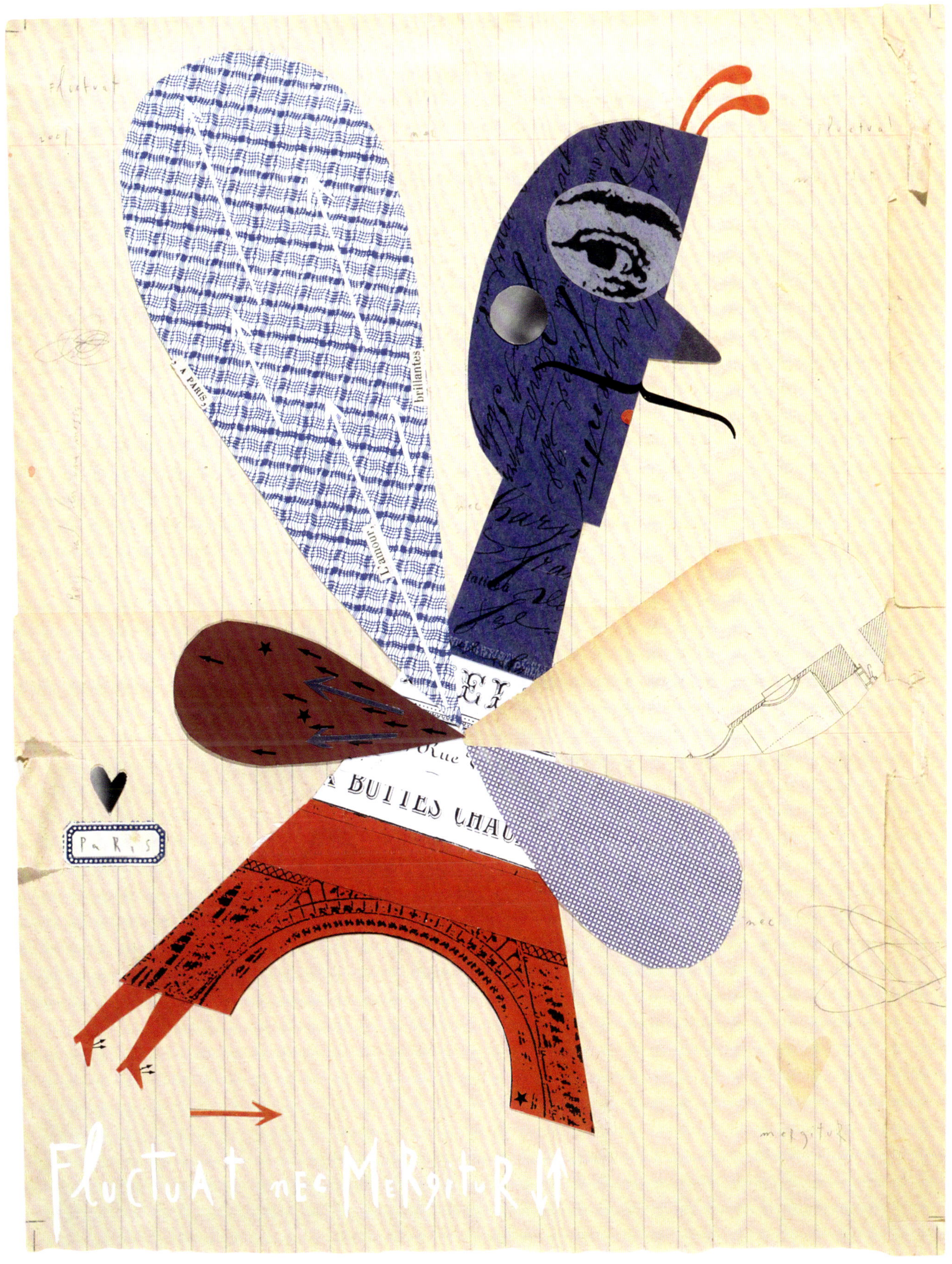
PARIS
BUTTES CHAU
FLUCTUAT NEC MERGITUR

David Gentleman (b.1930)
NO
Limited-edition print of a placard
designed for the Stop the War
Coalition, 2003, published by the
Stop the War Coalition in the poster
portfolio *Art Against War*
Offset lithograph in black and red;
edition no. 41/100
59.5 x 42 cm
V&A: E.1047–2003
Purchased through the Julie and
Robert Breckman Print Fund

David Gentleman is one of Britain's
leading artists and designers, whose
work has ranged from the design of
postage stamps and book covers
to the 100-metre mural on the walls
of Charing Cross Tube station. As
a young man, he took part in the
first CND marches from London
to the Atomic Weapons Research
Establishment at Aldermaston. In
1987 his anger at the US military's
use of British airfields to bomb Libya
prompted him to produce a book of
acerbic illustrations denouncing the
'special relationship' between Britain
and America. In 2003, when Britain
was about to invade Iraq, Gentleman
felt compelled to react and sent an
idea for a placard to the Stop the War
Coalition. The design was a simple,
bold 'No' in the clear Helvetica
typeface, blood-splattered with red ink.

Gentleman felt that the essential
message was not coming across
strongly enough in media images
of the first Stop the War marches.
His 'No' placard was designed
to create a unified statement
repeated throughout a crowd of
demonstrators, which would be
clearly legible in news footage and
newspaper photographs. He tested
whether his design would have the
necessary impact by superimposing
thumbnail-sized versions of it over
photographs of previous marches.
The placard was mass-printed by
Stop the War and handed to people
in London marching against the Iraq
war on 15 February 2003 – the largest
demonstration ever seen in the UK,
with more than one million protestors.

This began an ongoing relationship .
between Stop the War and David
Gentleman, who has designed many
subsequent placards and posters
for the organization, including *BLIAR*
(a reference to Tony Blair, b.1953)
and, most recently, *Don't Bomb Syria*.
By repeating the striking formula of
bold type and red blood-spots, these
graphics have built a strong visual
identity for Stop the War.

Gentleman's *NO* design was also
sold as a limited-edition print in a
portfolio entitled *Art Against War*
that was published by Stop the War
to raise funds for the campaign.
This comprised prints by 20 artists,
including one of the iconic
caricatures of George W. Bush
(b.1946) and Tony Blair by
cartoonist Steve Bell (b.1951),
and a photomontage by the
well-known political artist Peter
Kennard. In reference to the so-called
'Dodgy Dossier' on which politicians
based the case for war, the *Art
Against War* portfolio presented a
body of visual documents arguing
against it.

CF

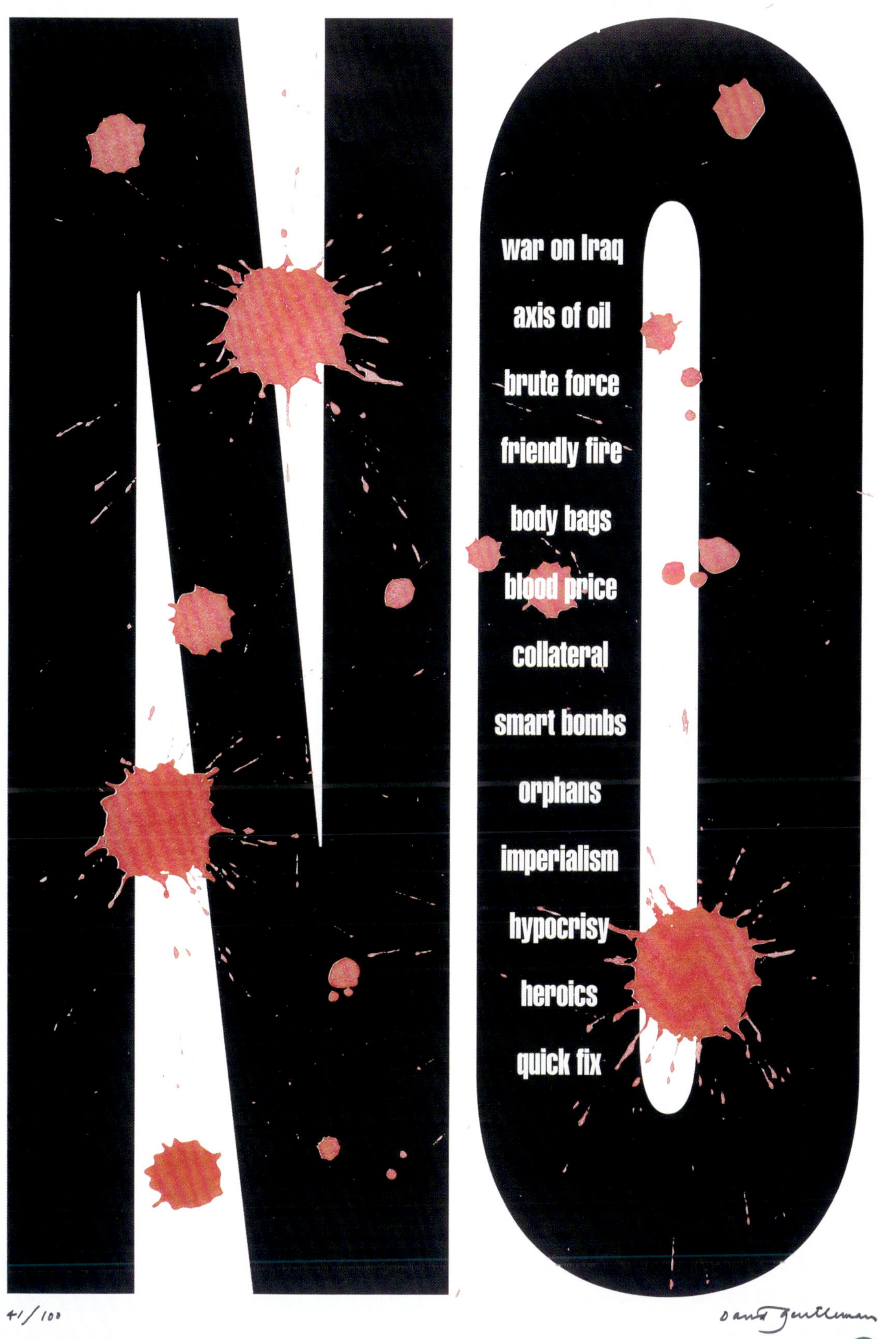

NO
war on Iraq
axis of oil
brute force
friendly fire
body bags
blood price
collateral
smart bombs
orphans
imperialism
hypocrisy
heroics
quick fix
41/100
Stop the War Coalition www.stopwar.org.uk Poster number 3 by David Gentleman 2003

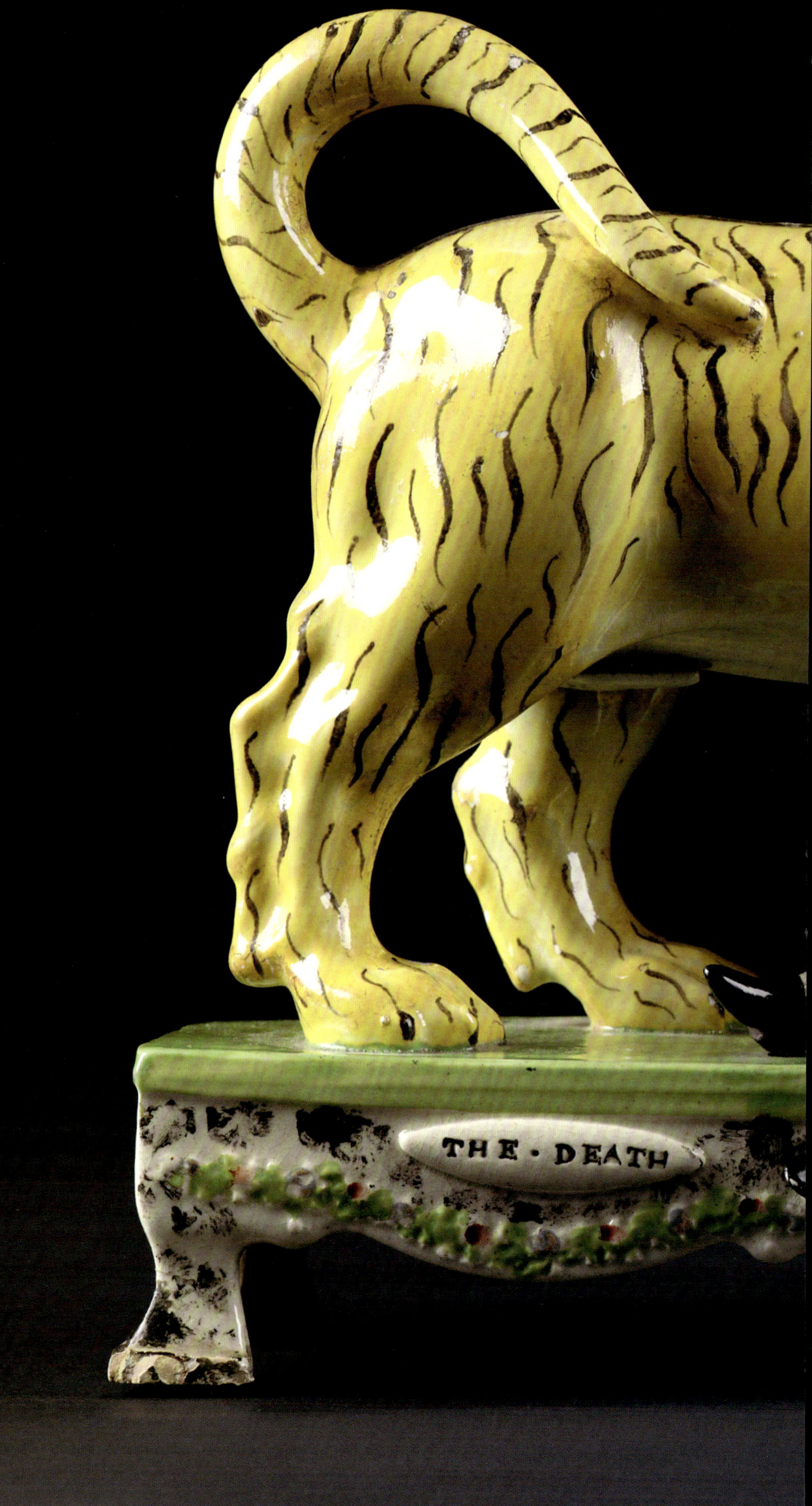
THE · DEATH

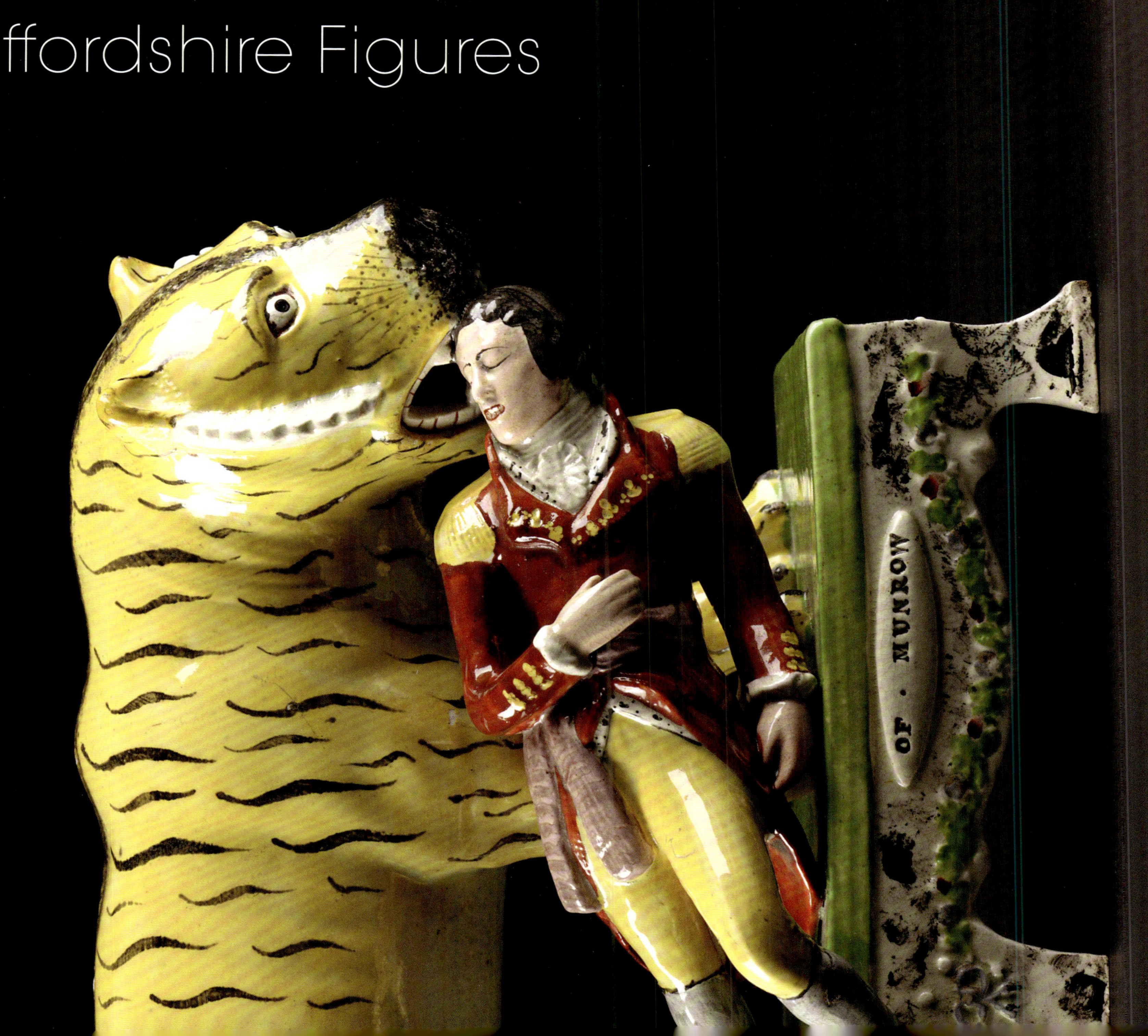

OF · MUNROW

Staffordshire Figures

Rebecca Wallis

The Staffordshire figures on display at the V&A often bring a smile to visitors' faces. These joyful, naïve figures are boldly decorated in what is now considered a traditional British style and stand proudly among the rich ceramics collections in the Museum. Made from the eighteenth century onwards in North Staffordshire, primarily in the potteries around Stoke-on-Trent, some of the best examples in the collection have been acquired thanks to the generosity of Julie and Robert Breckman. Thirty-seven of the figures were gifts from an impressive collection formed over 30 years by Julie, who travelled around the world with Robert to find new additions. Important figures have also been acquired for the Museum thanks to the Julie and Robert Breckman Staffordshire Fund, and many of these are dedicated in memory of Julie.

The development of Staffordshire figures was relatively slow, despite the introduction of imported porcelain figures to Britain from the seventeenth century. Inventories from around 1700 list 'Images on the Chimney', and these ceramics are likely to have been the popular 'Dehua' or 'Blanc-de-Chine' figures imported from China and South-East Asia (pl.52). Although ceramic sculptural modelling was technically possible in England from the 1600s, it was not until the following century that the porcelain table figures from Meissen and other European factories were imitated in England by new factories at Chelsea, Bow, Derby and elsewhere. Such figures, made with expensive materials by skilled artists and technicians, were aimed at an elite market, being so costly and desirable that even aristocrats would hire them for entertaining.[1]

The establishment of these first English porcelain factories in the 1740s occurred around the start of rapid expansion in North Staffordshire, and

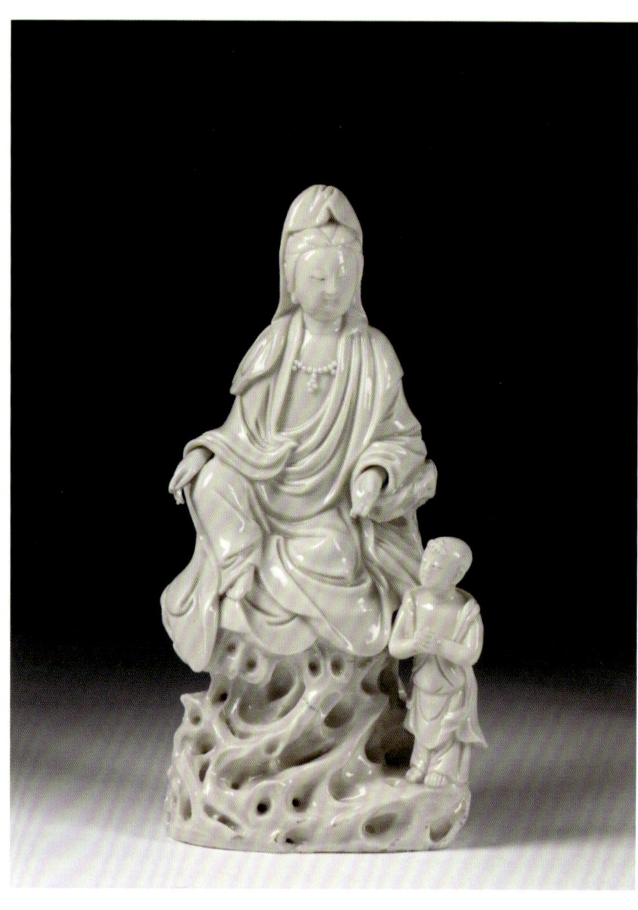

52. Figure of Guanyin, c.1620–70
Moulded porcelain with clear glaze, Dehua ware of the type imported to Britain
V&A: 1123–1875

ultimately the area became the centre of Britain's pottery industry. The six towns of Burslem, Fenton, Tunstall, Hanley, Longton and Stoke, which comprise Stoke-on-Trent, were ideally located for producing ceramics. They were an area of low wages and low land costs, with a ready supply of coal (for firing the kilns) and local brick clays, and the finer materials were also easily imported, thanks to the development of canals and, from the 1850s, rail networks, which also allowed for the transport of the final products. Major ceramics factories such as Wedgwood

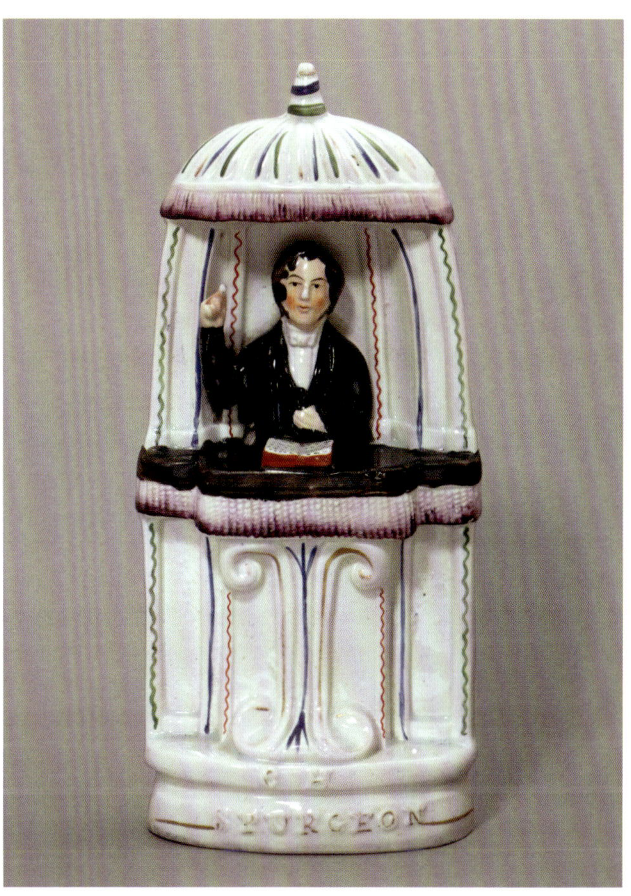

54. Figure of the preacher *The Reverend Charles Haddon Spurgeon*, in an arched pulpit, c.1855
Moulded glazed earthenware, Staffordshire
V&A: C.78–2001
Given by Julie and Robert Breckman

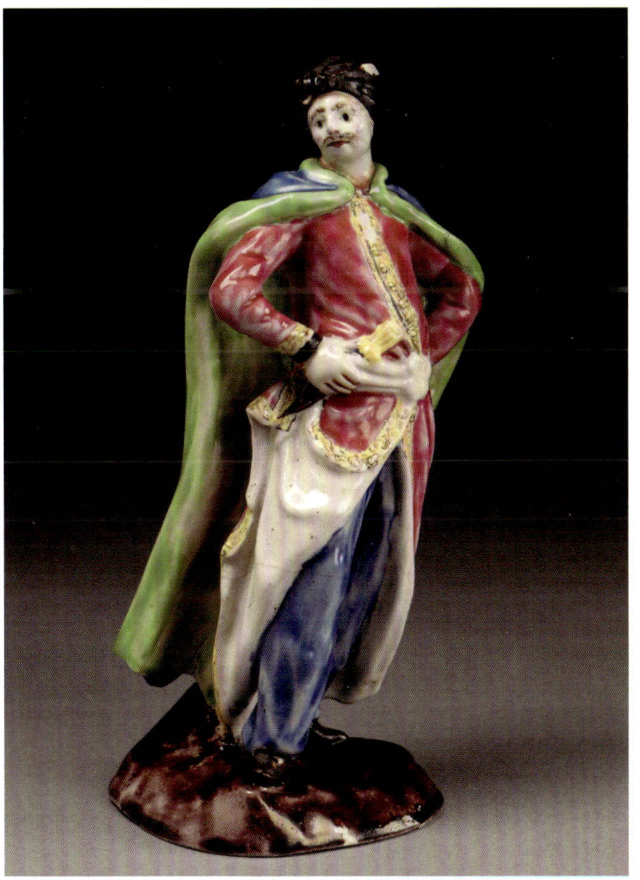

53. Figure in salt-glazed stoneware and painted with enamels of a Turkish man, c.1760
Made in Staffordshire, probably decorated in London
V&A: 414:858–1885
Given by Lady Charlotte Schreiber

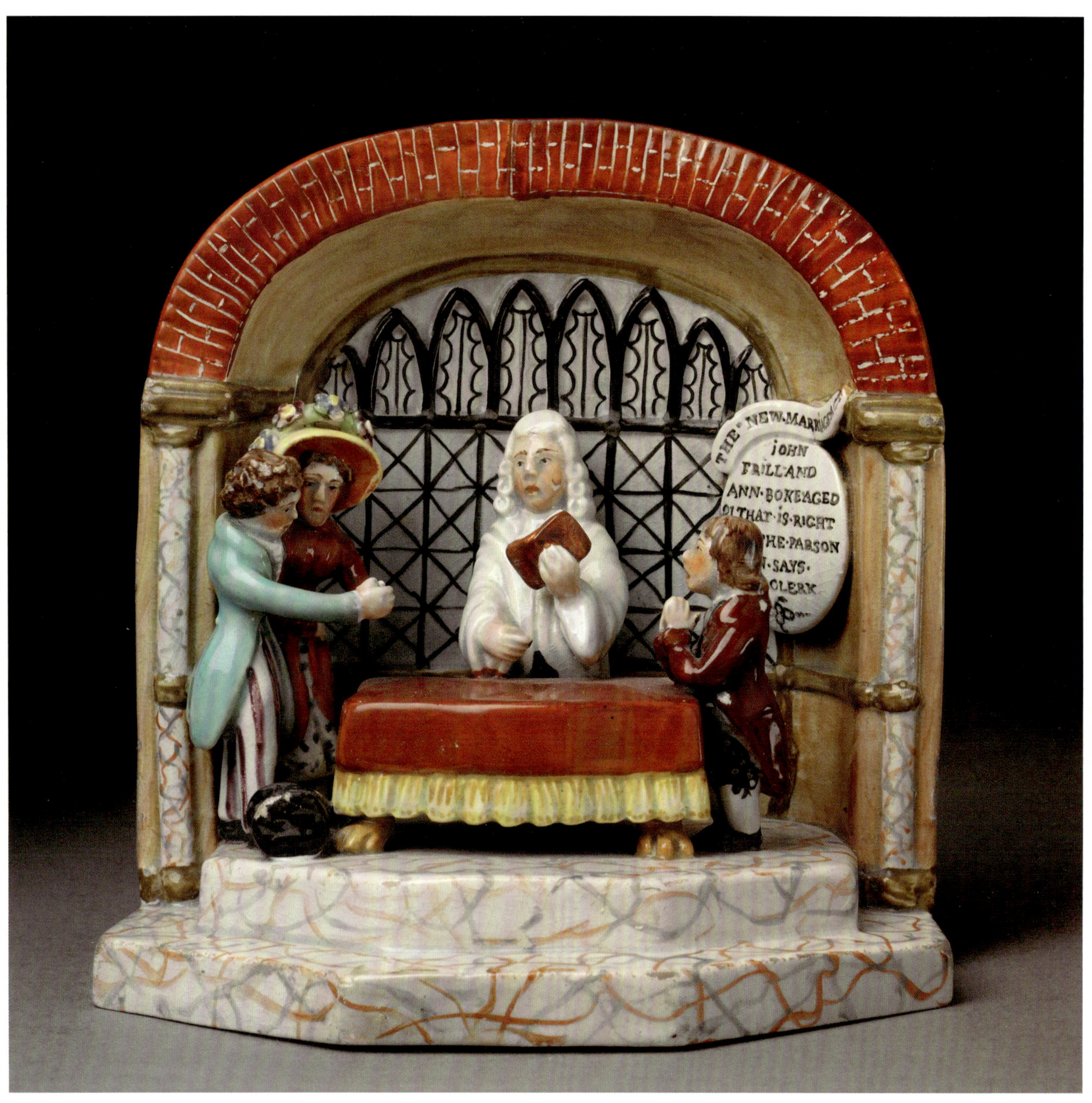

55. Figure group, *The New Marriage Act*, c.1823
Moulded lead-glazed earthenware, Staffordshire
V&A: C.4–2002
Purchased through the Julie and Robert Breckman Staffordshire Fund

and Spode pushed developments in technical innovation, design and trade within a region that grew to accommodate an estimated 4,000 bottle kilns by the nineteenth century. The production of figures was, however, just one aspect of the wider ceramics trade. Although larger factories made figures alongside the main output of table and ornamental wares, it was a production generally undertaken by smaller potteries, often using just two kilns – for the main firings and for enamelling. By 1796 the first specialist figure-maker was recorded in *The Staffordshire Pottery Directory*, and over the next 50 years more than 70 were listed.[2]

White stoneware, sometimes enhanced by freelance enamelling studios (pl.53), was at first used by some Staffordshire potters to make cheaper versions of popular porcelain models, but lead-glazed cream-coloured earthenware became the preferred clay due to its other advantages. With earthenware, the extra cost of biscuit and glaze firing ('biscuit' refers to wares that have had only a single firing and remain porous until glazed) was offset by the wide range of colours that could be used to decorate the figures, which could be fired at lower, cheaper temperatures. Besides a rich vein of native Staffordshire modelling skills, notably from many members of the Wood family of potters, plaster models from London shops such as John Cheere or Hoskins & Grant also enabled the Staffordshire potters to emulate the latest porcelains in fine earthenware at competitive prices. The average cost was 10d for a plain figure, 1s 3d for coloured glaze, 1s 9d for plain and gilt, 2s 3d for coloured glaze and gilt, and 2s 6d for enamel-painted.[3]

Generally the attribution of figures to individual potteries is rarely possible, and at the time was probably considered unimportant. By creating anonymous products, the potters widened their

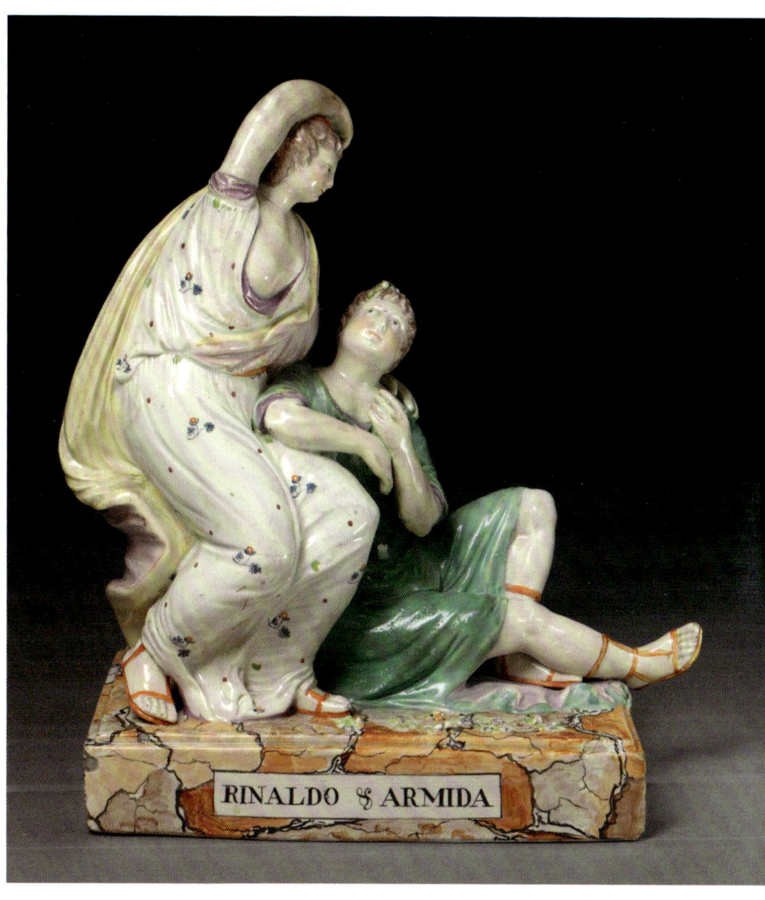

56. Figure group, *Rinaldo and Armida*, 1791–5
Moulded lead-glazed earthenware painted in enamel colours,
Lakin & Poole, Staffordshire
V&A: C.61–2001
Given by Julie and Robert Breckman

trade for sale by various merchants and by the London 'Staffordshire Warehouses'. It is often by style and decoration that we can attribute figures to a particular period of production. Figures produced from about the 1770s included relief-modelled examples painted with translucent coloured lead-glazes, followed in around 1780–1810 by fine creamware figures with muted overglaze coloured enamels. As the fashion for English Rococo porcelain groups waned, and as earthenware became acceptable at every social level, thanks in particular to Wedgwood's 'Queen's Ware', it was found that these styles and cool colours well suited the new craze for Neoclassicism inspired by the fashionable Grand Tour and a growing middle-class audience for history, arts and culture. Produced, among others, by the Wood family and Lakin & Poole potteries, subjects included philosophers and heroes of the ancient world (pl.56), along with British poets and writers. Around the same time, high-temperature underglaze decoration was developed, using a limited range of earthy metallic oxide colours painted onto the dry biscuit body, along with an attractive complementary bluish pearlware glaze (see p.153). It is, however, the bright painted overglaze enamel decoration of about 1810 onwards that we most associate with Staffordshire figures today (see p.155).

In a period when literacy levels were low and news was sometimes hard to come by, outside the main towns and cities, Staffordshire figures became a form of visual literacy depicting key personalities and events of the day, from politics, royalty, sport, literature and entertainment. By the 1820s the popularity of figures led to inspired new designs, such as the celebration of the 'New Marriage Act' (pl.55) or charismatic folk heroes such as the Baptist preacher, Reverend Charles Haddon Spurgeon (1834–92) (pl.54).

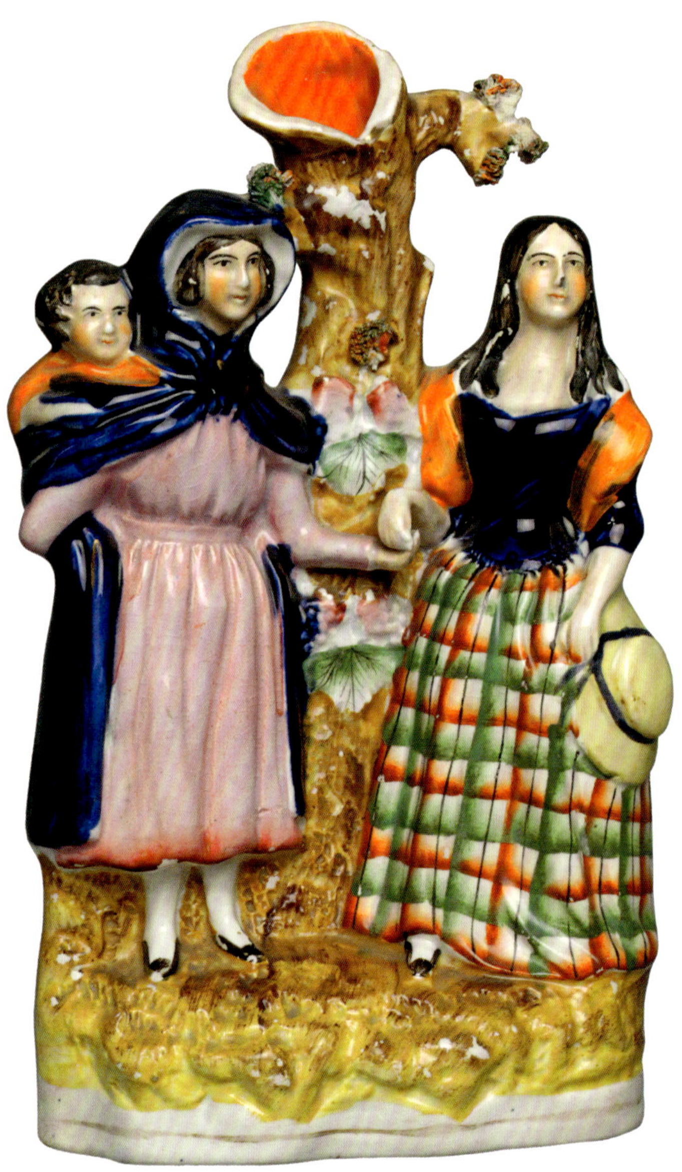

57. Figure group, *The Fortune Teller*, 1840s
Moulded earthenware, painted in enamel colours and gilded.
Staffordshire
V&A: C.55–2013
Given by Julie and Robert Breckman

The most ambitious Staffordshire figures are larger
ensemble pieces, usually on table-shaped base-
plinths and often made as complementary pairs
for larger mantelpieces. None are marked, and
it is unlikely that one pottery could have made
every group, given the variations in modelling
and decoration. These figure groups ranged from
simple, bold large subjects such as *The Death
of Munrow* (see p.157) to elaborate menageries
with multipart modelling requiring assembly and
detailed decoration (see p.159).

The development of these figures was also led
by the change in the way people lived in their
homes. From the late seventeenth century,
mantelpieces and shelves start appearing over
fireplaces. The fire as the heart of the home and
place of conversation became a prime location
to display a household's prized possessions, to
demonstrate taste, social standing and political
allegiances. By the nineteenth century the raised
cast-iron coal-burning hob grate framed by a
neat fire surround, with wood or painted slate
mantelpiece, was in general use, providing the
perfect setting for candlesticks, spill vases and
figures (pl.58). Until about the 1840s figures were
usually fully modelled and moulded in the round,
latterly with scrolled pedestals and leafy *bocage*
harking back to Rococo porcelain models of
the 1760s; and then in the second half of the
nineteenth century it was the flat-back that
came to dominate the market (pl.57). Designed
specifically to sit on a shallow mantelpiece, and
cheaply made with plain undecorated backs,
these figures were affordable by the working
classes. In many cases the quality of figures
deteriorated as demand grew and the subjects
became increasingly topical, selling as souvenirs
outside theatres, music halls, at holiday resorts
or fairs. Later figures are quite distinct from
early types, particularly as new colours were

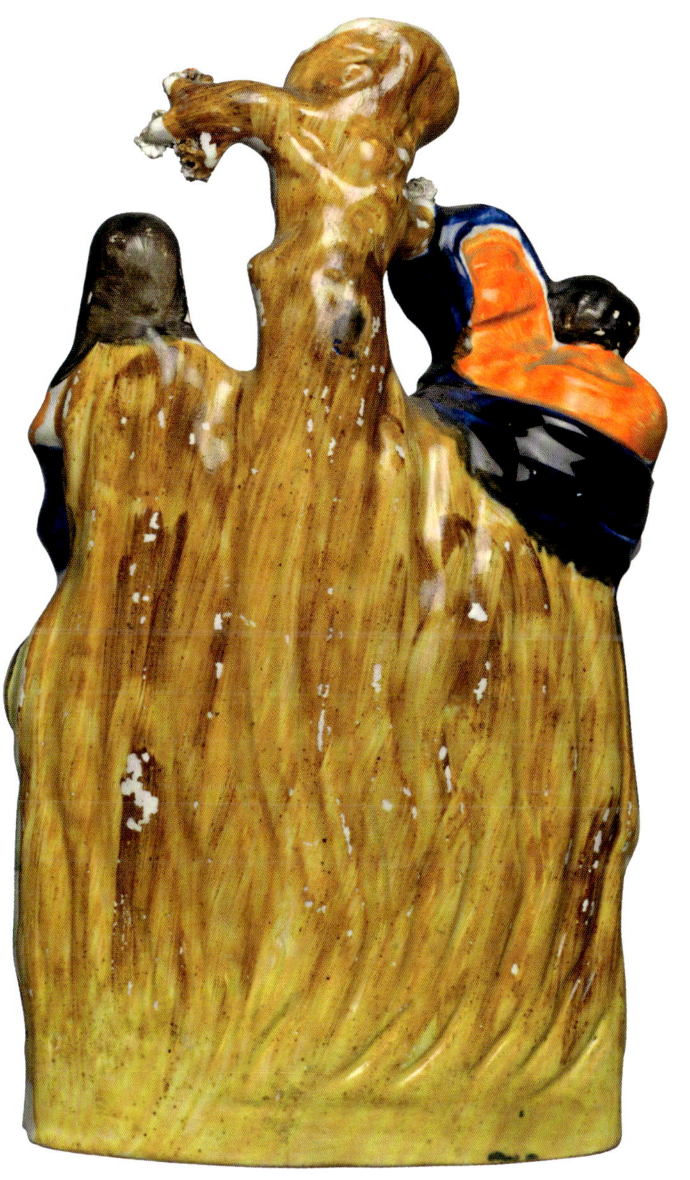

introduced, derived from chrome oxide: bright pinks, apple-greens and canary-yellows (see p.161). These were generally press-moulded, but the increased use of slip-casting produced lighter, cheaper examples.

Already by the second half of the nineteenth century Staffordshire figures had become synonymous with a Victorian style bordering on the kitsch. In an 1868 edition of *Punch* concerning 'Aesthetics', the main character Fadsby implores his landlady to remove what he considers these 'Fictile Abominations' from his rooms.[4] Staffordshire figures may have become unfashionable and out of step with contemporary design, but they were still produced – often derived from the original moulds – well into the twentieth century. There was a continued market appeal to these figures, being strongly associated with a sense of tradition and Britishness (pl. 59). A catalogue of about 1920 for the William Kent factory lists figures with nostalgic names such as *Wellington on a Horse* and they continued to make new 'Old Staffordshire' into the 1960s.[5] As early as the 1900s the original Staffordshire figures were already being treasured as family heirlooms, and by the 1920s were being referenced by artists such as the Bloomsbury Group.[6] The enduring appeal of these characterful figures, as minor but very affordable examples of English folk art, contributed to their ongoing production and reappraisal by ceramic factories, artists and designers. The iconic 1940s Zodiac Bull design by Arnold Machin (1911–99) for Wedgwood (pl.60) clearly references the earlier large animal types, and more recently Staffordshire figures have been the prime source material for a number of contemporary artists, including Carole Windham (b.1949), Rob Ryan (b.1962) and Stephen Bowers (b.1952).

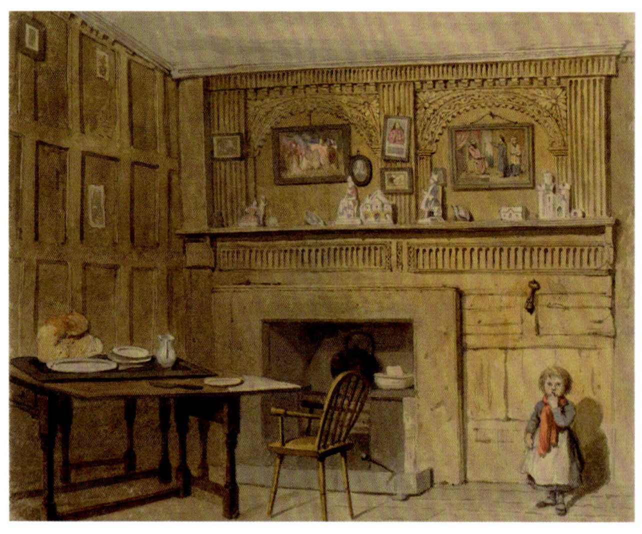

58. *Upper Room in Fulwood's Rents, Holborn*, 1852, by John Wykeham Archer
Watercolour with bodycolour over pencil
British Museum 1874,0314.364

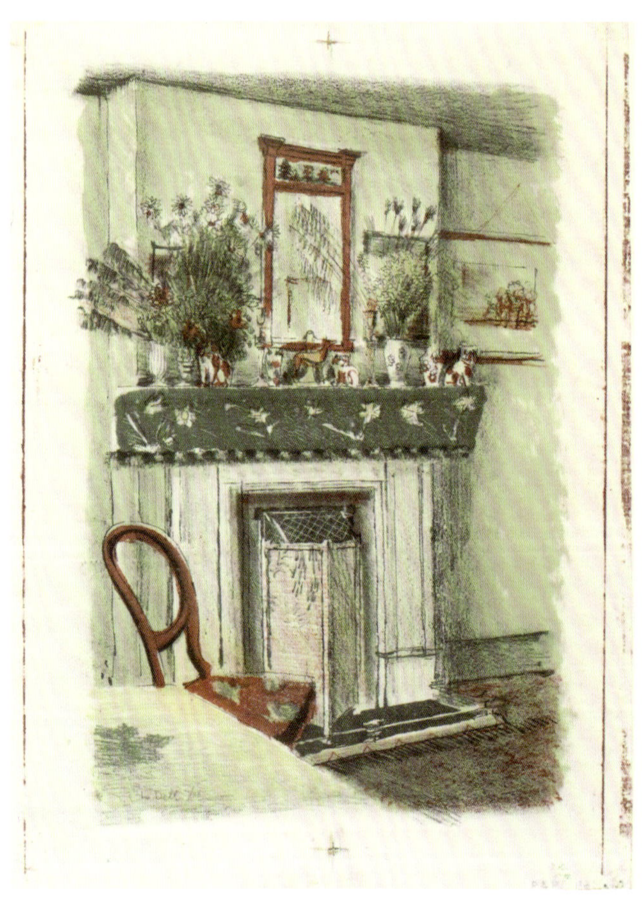

59. *Victorian Mantelpiece*, 1938, by Edwin Ladell
Colour lithograph
V&A: Circ.164–1939

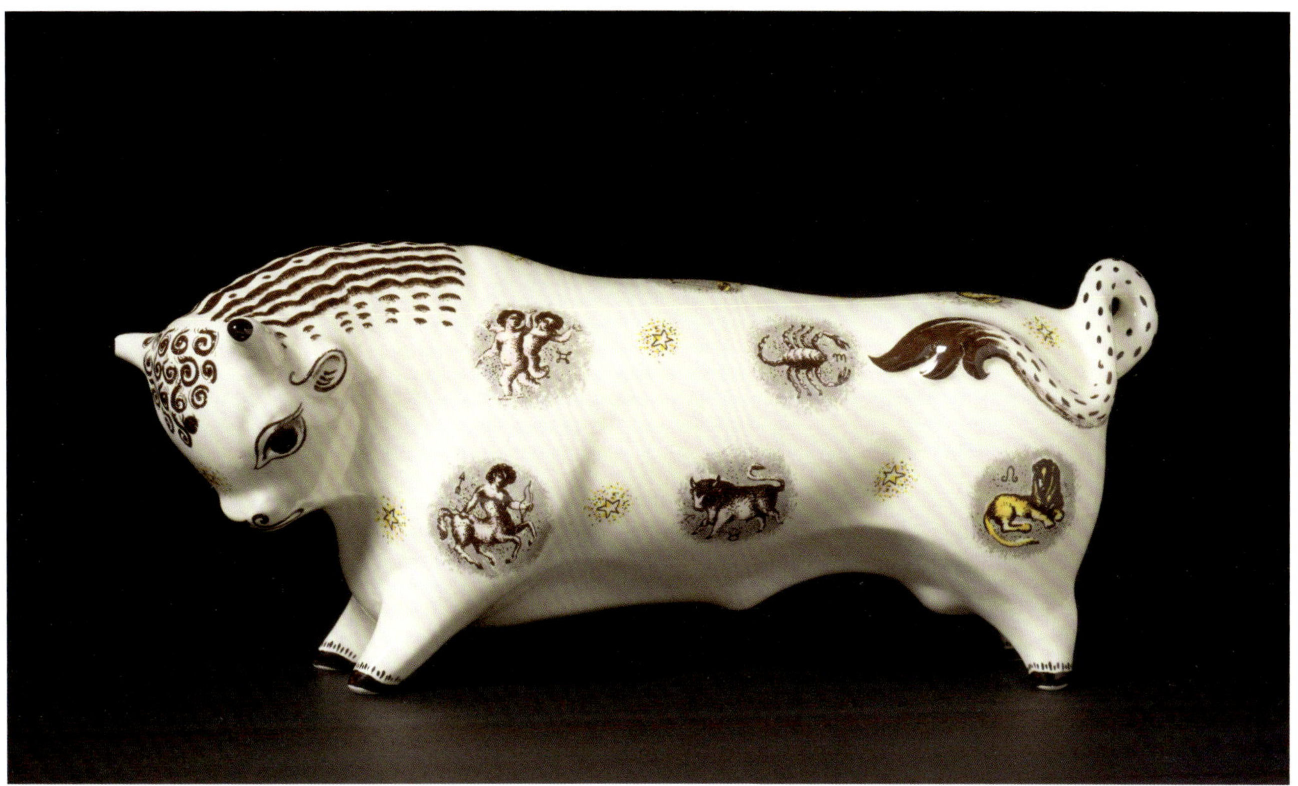

60. Figure of Zodiac Bull, 1950, designed by Arnold Machin c.1945, produced by Josiah Wedgwood & Sons
Earthenware, transfer-printed
V&A: Circ.276-1951.

Staffordshire figures continue to be collected today, with a healthy trade and a number of clubs and publications on the subject. When Julie and Robert Breckman donated their collection to the V&A in 2000, they expressed their pride and emotion at seeing them in a museum.[7] These fascinating ceramics, originally made for a domestic environment, can now be enjoyed and studied by new audiences in displays, exhibitions and publications such as this.

1 Robin Hildyard, 'Figures: Images of Their Age', in *English Pottery 1620–1840* (London, 2005), pp.146–69.
2 Pat Halfpenny, *English Earthenware Figures 1740–1840* (Woodbridge, 1991), p.12.
3 Hildyard, p.163.
4 Anthony Oliver, *The Victorian Staffordshire Figure* (London, 1971), p.108.
5 Trade catalogue, *William Kent Manufacturer of Novelties and Earthenware, Novelty Works, Wellington Street, Burslem, c.1920*. Copy bound 1952, V&A Ceramics Library 2B18.
6 Sonia Solicari, 'From Cottage to Kitsch: The Enduring Appeal of the Staffordshire Figure', in *The Decorative Arts Society Journal* 35 (London, 2011), pp.136–9.
7 *The Kensington & Chelsea News* (5 October 2000), p.9.

Figure of a deer

Staffordshire, England, unknown
maker, *c.*1800
Moulded lead-glazed earthenware
painted in underglaze colours
Height: 20.3 cm
V&A: C.5–2002
Purchased through the Julie and
Robert Breckman Staffordshire Fund

This recumbent female deer is one
of a number of earthenware figures,
produced from the late eighteenth
century, that celebrate the noble
animal. In Britain when this example
was made, about 1800, deer hunting
was considered the 'sport of kings'
and prized herds were enclosed on
country estates. Nostalgia for a fast-
vanishing world also gave birth to the
ever-popular stoneware hunting jug
at this time. Here the aesthetic charm
of deer combined with their exclusivity
were factors in the creation of these
figures as desirable ornaments for a
fashionable middle-class home.

Seated on a grassy mound in
heraldic pose, this deer is framed by
an elaborate oak-leaf *bocage* (a
decorative motif of trees, branches
or foliage), originally added to
porcelain figures in the 1750s when
they graduated from dining-table
set-pieces to become ornaments for
mantelpiece or cabinet. This backing
also gave extra support for figures
and groups as they increased in size.[1]
The decorator of this piece, having
a limited range of colours that would

withstand the glaze firing (iron-brown,
cobalt-blue, antimony-yellow and
copper-green), has not attempted
naturalistic colouring. Instead the
earthy colours are used sparingly,
but to good effect in conveying
the essence of the subject, thereby
creating a minor masterpiece of folk
art. Such high-temperature colours,
further muted by a blue-tinted glaze,
admirably suited the austerity of
the time and remained popular
from the 1790s to the 1840s. Large
numbers of pairs of 'Stag & Hind'
figures, often destined for the London
market and retailing from as little as
1s 3d (about 7p), are recorded in
Staffordshire potters' sales ledgers
during the period 1785–1815.[2] The
style of this figure, particularly the
turned neck, is similar to examples
produced by other potteries, such as
those belonging to the Wood family
or Samuel Bourne (1834–1912).[3]
Design sources for these types of deer
figures may include English porcelain
examples of the 1750s and '60s, as
well as popular prints by Thomas
Bewick (1753–1828) or Samuel Howitt
(1760–1822).[4]

RW & RH

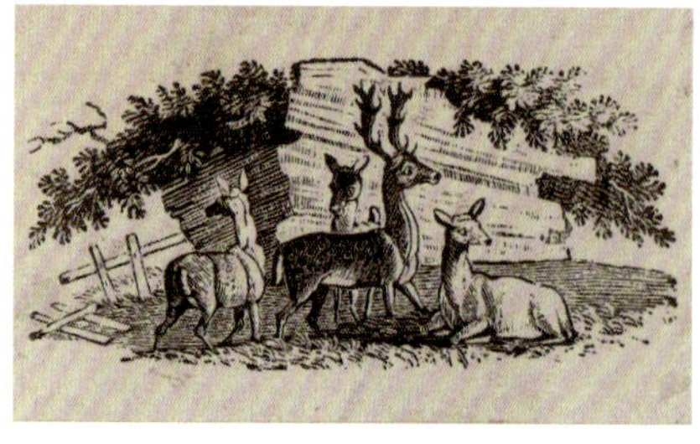

Tail-piece to *Robin Hood*, 1795,
by Thomas Bewick
Wood-engraving
British Museum 1882.0311.2866
Donated by Isabella Bewick

1 Pat Halfpenny, *English Earthenware Figures
1740–1840* (Woodbridge, 1991), p.215.
2 Halfpenny, pp.314–27.
3 Examples include an earthenware figure
of a recumbent doe with stained lead-
glazes, possibly Wood family, *c.*1770–80
(V&A: C.18–1930), and an earthenware
figure of a recumbent stag with stained lead-
glazes, marked for Samuel Bourne, *c.*1803–8
(Potteries Museum and Art Gallery Inv. 2941).
4 Pair of seated deer (stag and doe),
Bow Porcelain Factory, *c.*1755–6, Private
Collection; www.antique-porcelain.co.uk/
Archive.html, accessed 14 January 2016.
Print sources may include fallow deer by
Thomas Bewick (shown above) or *Does
& Fawns* by Samuel Howitt, 1798 (British
Museum, 1850, 1014.695).

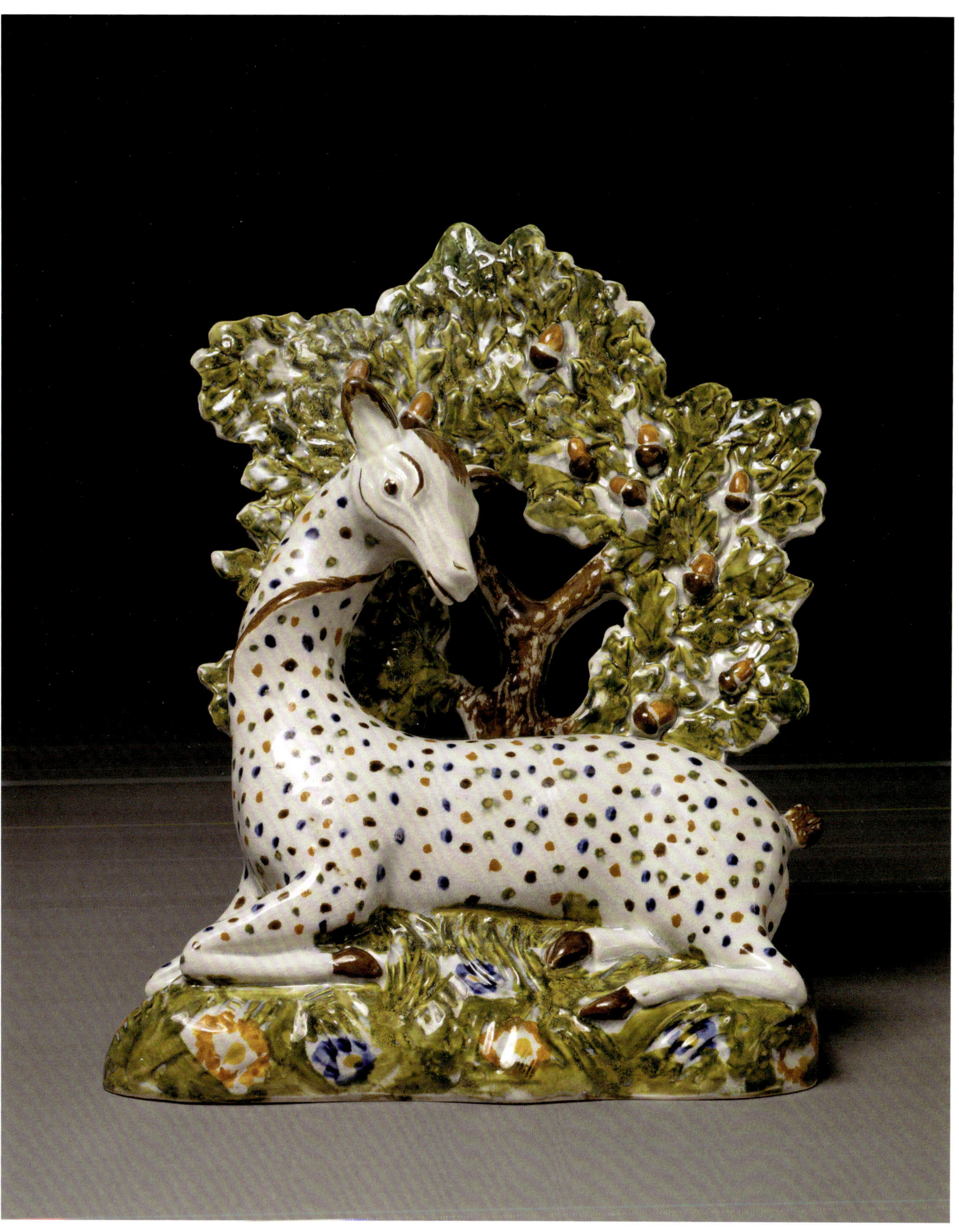

Figures of *Tom Molineaux* and *Tom Cribb*

Staffordshire, England, unknown
maker, *c*.1815
Moulded lead-glazed earthenware
painted with enamels
Height of each: 22.3 cm
V&A: C.130:1&2–2003
Purchased through the Julie and
Robert Breckman Staffordshire Fund

These boxing figures represent one
of the greatest sporting events of
the nineteenth century, a match
between Tom Cribb (1781–1848),
the most famous British bare-knuckle
fighter of his time, and his challenger,
Tom Molineaux (1784–1818), a former
Virginian slave. Molineaux was born
in 1784, the son of America's first
black boxer, Zachary Molineaux.
Winning his freedom, Molineaux
arrived in England in 1803 to become
a professional boxer. His second
match in England was against Cribb
at Copthorne, near East Grinstead, in
December 1810. It ran to 39 rounds,
during many of which the off-form
Cribb was physically supported by his
supporters, who feared his defeat by
a black man. Unfair play contributed
to Molineaux losing the match, and
he challenged Cribb to a follow-up
match at Thistleton Gap, Leicester, in
1811. This time the American, having
over-indulged in some of the rewards
of celebrity, was out of shape and
lost to Cribb, who then became
world champion.[1]

The owner of these figures in the
nineteenth century may have
attended the matches between
Molineaux and Cribb, but was most
likely one of the thousands who
attended boxing events in towns
and villages across the country.
As with many figures depicting
contemporary events, Staffordshire
potters have taken inspiration
from some of the well-known prints
published to celebrate the fight.
The painted decoration is in bold
on-glaze enamel, which is typical of
production in the early nineteenth
century when a wider market for
these ceramics was developed.
Quality often varied, but these figures
show proficient modelling and
decoration and, given the popular
sporting subject, they were most
likely retailed at a higher price than
plainer wares.

RW

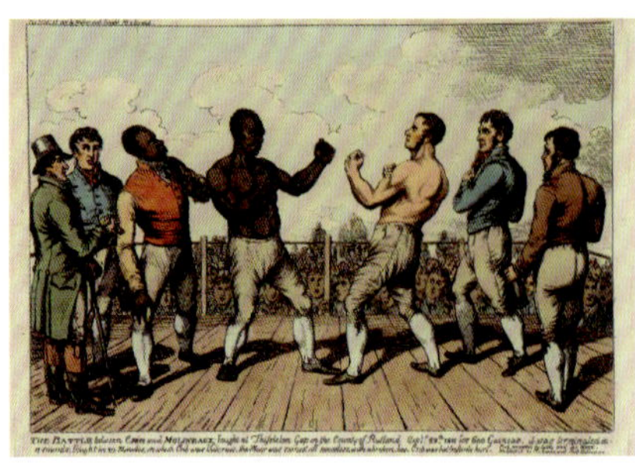

The Battle between Crib and Molineux, 1811,
by George Cruickshank.
Wood-engraving, coloured by hand
British Sporting Trust Inv. 2005.028

1 Prints published at the time include
The Battle between Crib and Molineux
(shown above); *Tom Molineaux*
('Molineaux'), hand-coloured etching, by
Robert Dighton (1747–1814), published
January 1812; and *Tom Cribb*, mezzotint,
by John Young (1755–1825), after Thomas
Douglas Guest (1781–active 1838),
published 1811, National Portrait Gallery
Inv. PG D13314 and D34310.

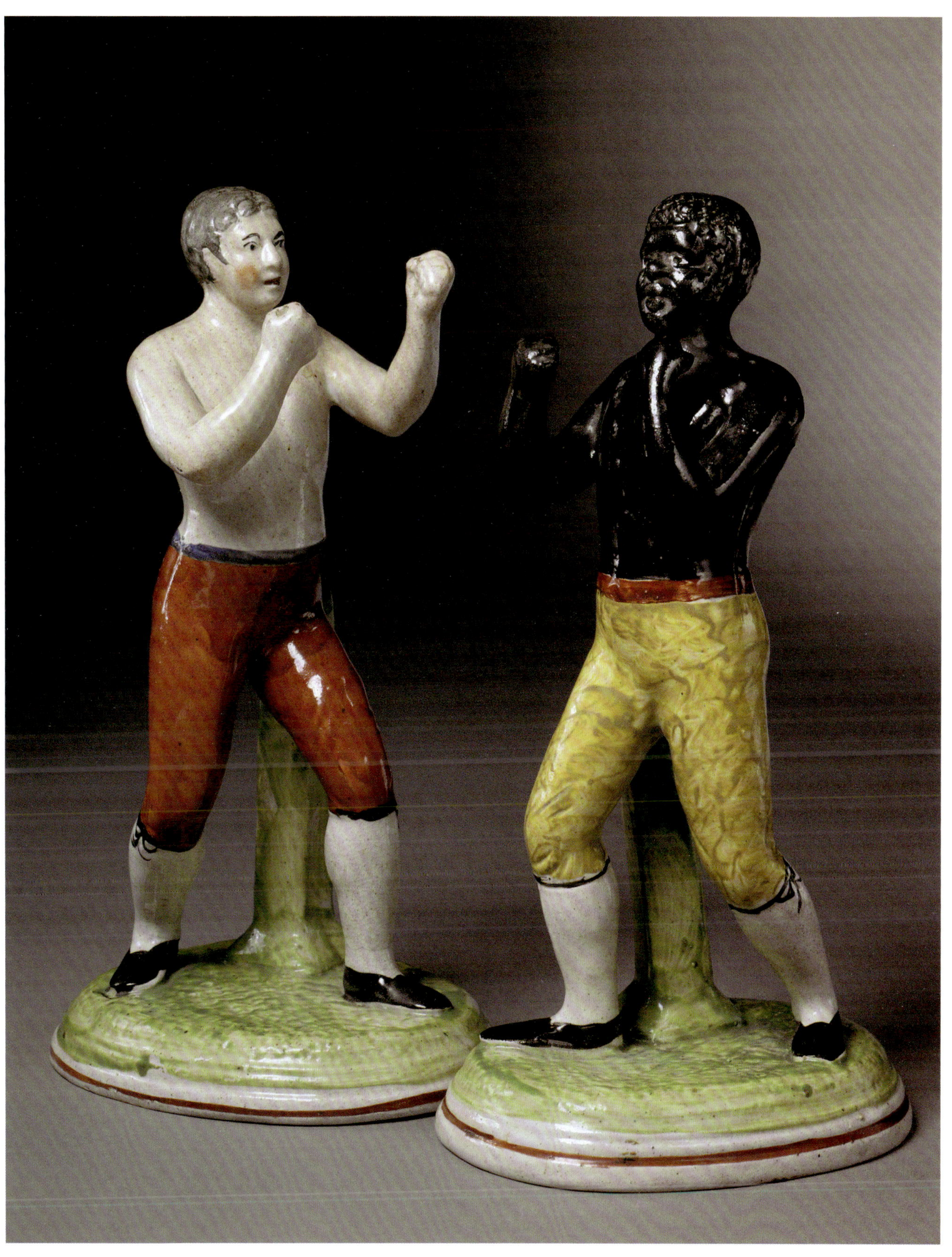

Figure, *The Death of Munrow*

Staffordshire, England, unknown
maker, *c.*1830
Lead-glazed earthenware, press-
moulded in sections and assembled
with title impressed with metal printer's
type, and painted in enamels
Length: 34.9 cm
V&A: C.1–2007
Donated by Robert Breckman in
memory of his wife Julie

This delightfully naïve ceramic
sculpture shows the death of
Lieutenant Hugh Munro, a young
British army officer serving in India,
who was mauled by a tiger while
picnicking on a hunting trip in 1792.
The incident became well known in
Britain and abroad through prints
and publications, partly because the
lieutenant was the son of General
Hector Munro (1726–1805), who
defeated Haider Ali (1722–82), ruler
of Mysore in South India, in 1781.
Lieutenant Munro's gruesome death
is erroneously said to have inspired
the creation of the automaton
and mechanical organ known as
Tippoo's Tiger (shown here). One
of the V&A's most popular exhibits,
the *Tiger* was made for Tipu Sultan,
Haider Ali's son, who reigned 1782–99.
The subject of a British military man
defeated by a tiger would have
appealed to Tipu Sultan, who fought
bitterly against British political and
territorial ambitions, forming an
allegiance with the French in 1798,
and who so identified with the power
and ruthlessness of the tiger that
he became known as the 'Tiger of
Mysore'. He is famously credited with
saying, 'In this world I would rather
live two days like a tiger, than two
hundred years like a sheep.'

The ceramic group echoes the
design of the automaton, and it is
possible that its modeller saw the
original, after it was seized by the
British who defeated Tipu Sultan in
1799. By 1808 the automaton was
formally listed as part of the collection
of the East India Library and Museum,
put on public display and published
in prints. Other sources may include
print illustrations of tigers by Thomas
Bewick, frequently referenced by
the Staffordshire potteries.[1] Pottery
groups of *The Death of Munrow*
were first made in Staffordshire in the
1810s and remained in production
until about 1830, when this version
with a 'table-top' base was made.
Munro is apparently blissfully unaware
of his fate and reclines stiffly at the
feet of the tiger – an effect that was
probably the result of the sculptor
having simply reused the model or
moulds for a standing military figure,
without adapting it in any way for
its new context. Examples can also
be found where the victim depicted
is a black man or boy, and both
forms are sometimes paired up with
the *Roring Lion* (*sic*) – an equally
monumental figure, but with no such
exciting story to tell.[2]

RW

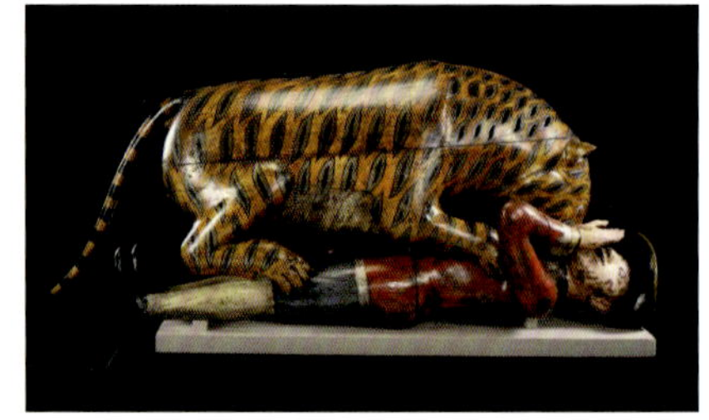

*Tippoo's Tiger, c.*1793, made in Mysore.
Painted wooden semi-automaton
V&A: 2545(IS)
Transferred from the Indian Museum in 1879

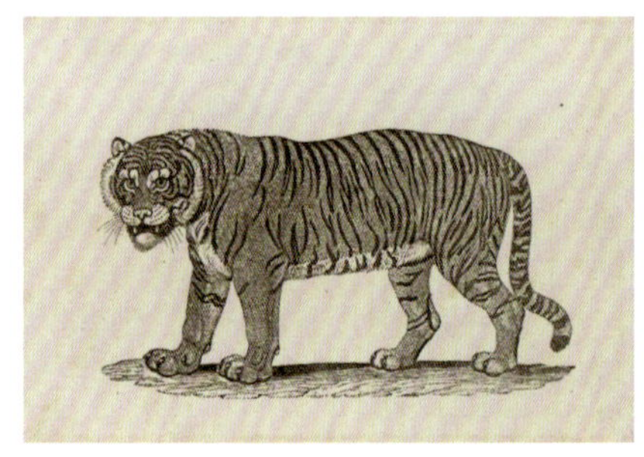

A tiger, from a series depicting Pidcock's Wild
Beasts, 1799, by Thomas Bewick
Wood-engraving
British Museum 1822,0311.2815

1 Examples include a print of a tiger from a
series depicting Pidcock's Wild Beasts
(shown above).
2 Examples include the same tiger form with
the dubious title *Death of a Negro*, as listed
in *Auction 19108: Fine British Pottery and
Porcelain*, Bonhams (London, 2 November
2011), Lot 31; and an earthenware figure
group of a tiger holding a black boy in its
mouth, *c.*1830, Potteries Museum and Art
Gallery Inv. 86P1964.

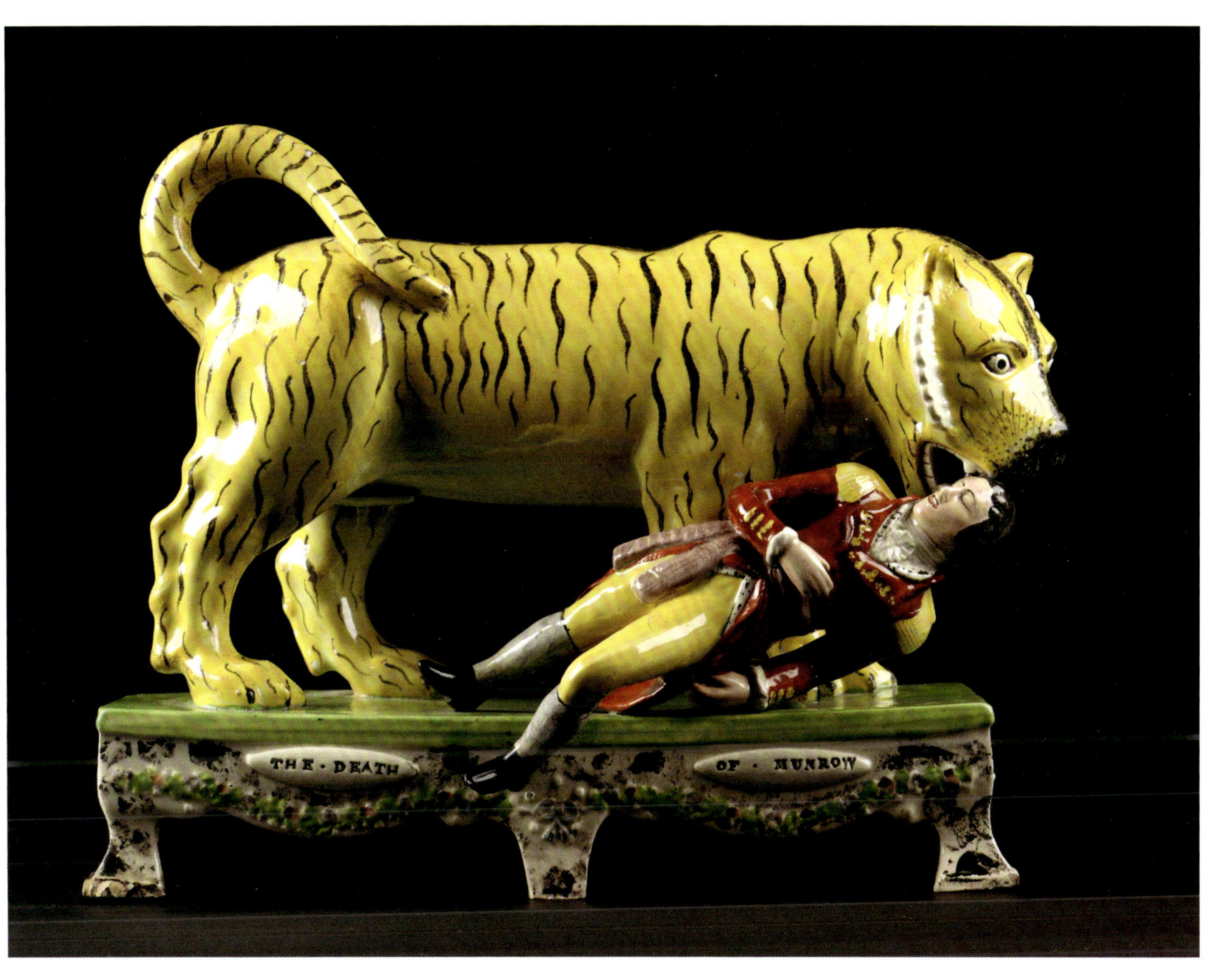
THE · DEATH
OF · MUNROW

Figure group, *Polito's Royal Menagerie*

Staffordshire, England, unknown maker, *c.*1830
Moulded lead-glazed earthenware, press-moulded in sections and assembled with title impressed with metal printer's type, 'POLITO'S / ROYAL / MENAGERIE OF THE / WONDERFULL BURDS / AND BEASTS FROM / THE WORLD / LIONS &C.' and painted in enamel colours
Height: 32 cm
V&A: C.128–2003
Purchased through the Julie and Robert Breckman Staffordshire Fund

This glorious mantelpiece ornament is one of the most celebrated, and certainly the most elaborate, of early nineteenth-century Staffordshire figure groups. Constructed on a stage with a detailed backdrop, the subject is the entrance of one of the famous travelling menageries, or animal exhibitions, of Stephen Polito (1763/4–1814). Polito was briefly the owner – between 1810 and 1814 – of Britain's most celebrated menagerie, which had been established by the self-styled 'modern Noah', Gilbert Pidcock (1743–1810), in the Strand, London. Polito's family continued to tour and exhibit animals under the Polito name during the 1820s and '30s, chiefly abroad.[1]

'A Splendid Band in Attendance', as advertised and depicted here, would welcome audiences to the menagerie, and the decoration above the entrance would indicate what caged beasts, such as monkeys, parrots and lions, lay beyond.[2] The central banner may depict Pidcock and Polito's star attraction, Chunee, the Asian elephant admired by Lord Byron (1788–1824) in his diary entry of 1813: 'The elephant took and gave me my money again – took off my hat – opened a door – *trunked* a whip – and behaved so well, that I wish he was my butler.' Long-term captivity, perhaps unsurprisingly, did not suit Chunee; increased aggression and possible toothache led to the elephant killing his keeper and he was subsequently destroyed in 1826.[3]

Many smaller Staffordshire figures of exotic animals, such as elephants, lions and zebras, were also produced for an eager consumer market that viewed these creatures as being both educational and entertaining. Of these large figure groups, only Polito's and the equally famous George Wombwell's menageries survive. They represent a high point in quality and detailed execution of models made for a wide market, before makers increasingly concentrated on the very much cheaper 'flat-backs' (figures with only rudimentary details on the reverse, made using fewer and simpler moulds). Although made of earthenware, an inexpensive material, all the figures and architectural components would have been formed in separate two-part moulds, then carefully assembled by a 'repairer', before firing and decoration with painted and sponged enamels, so the group would have been relatively costly to produce. The larger size also indicates that a substantial mantelpiece, most likely in a wealthier home, would have been required for display.

RW

1 Stella Beddoe and Pat Halfpenny, *Circus and Sport: English Earthenware Figures, 1780–1840* (Kentucky, 1990), pp.7–8.
2 www.sheffield.ac.uk/nfa/projects/menagerieshistory, accessed 14 January 2016, and www.antiquetobyjugs.com/staffordshire-pottery-articles/menagerie-and-travelling-showmen-of-staffordshire.htm, accessed 14 January 2016.
3 Myrna Schkolne, *People, Passions, Pastimes and Pleasures, Staffordshire Figures, 1810–1835* (Winston Salem, NC, 2006), pp.102–5.

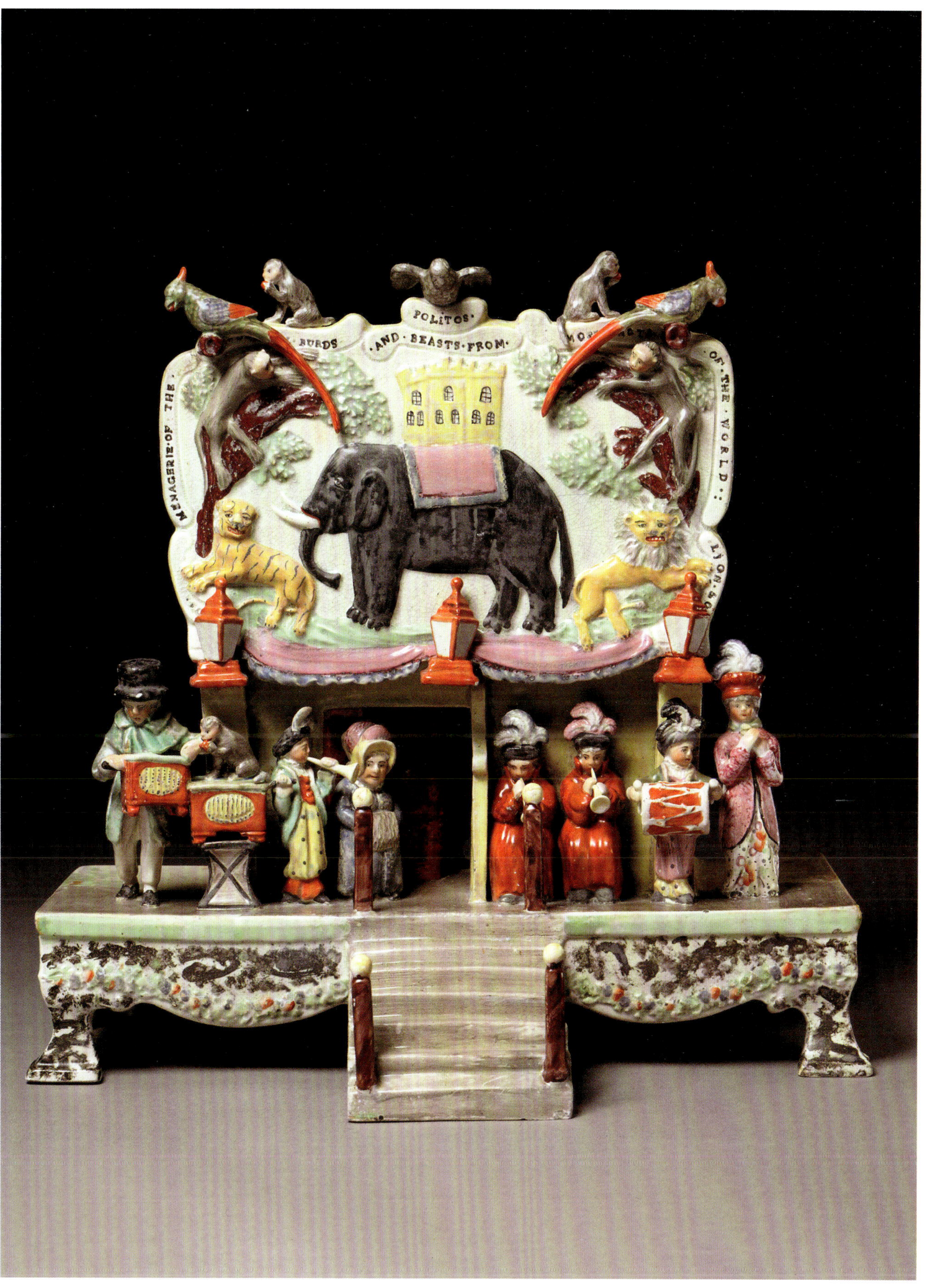

POLITOS
BIRDS AND BEASTS FROM
MENAGERIE OF THE
OF THE WORLD
LION &

Figures, Jules Perrot as 'Albrecht' and Carlotta Grisi as 'Giselle'

Staffordshire, unknown maker,
c.1842–5
Moulded earthenware, painted in
enamel colours and gilded
Height: 24 cm, width: 9.8 cm; and
height: 22.9 cm, width: 10.4 cm
V&A: C.52 and 53–2013
Given by Julie and Robert Breckman

These playful Staffordshire figures
represent the choreographer and
dancer Jules Perrot (1810–92) as
'Albrecht' and his partner Carlotta
Grisi (1819–99), who played 'Giselle'
in the ballet of the same name.
Giselle is arguably one of the most
famous Romantic ballets of all time,
and these figures were possibly
acquired as souvenirs outside the
stage door. Created by the French
writer, journalist and art critic,
Théophile Gautier, the ballet was
choreographed by Perrot and Jean
Coralli (1779–1854) for Grisi to take
the lead role, premiering at the
Théâtre de l'Académie Royale de
Musique in Paris in June 1841. The
Italian dancer was likened to 'a
tea-rose about to bloom' – perfect
casting for the role of a youthful,
innocent peasant girl. In the first
performance the role of Albrecht was
danced by Lucien Petipa (1815–98),
but Perrot later took on the role in
London, becoming Grisi's dancing
partner. *Giselle* was incredibly
popular and was staged throughout
the 1840s at venues across Europe.

The ballet was first performed in Britain
at Her Majesty's Theatre, London, on
12 March 1842, with Grisi and Perrot in
the lead roles.

The Staffordshire figure of 'Albrecht'
is based on a print used for a
frontispiece in the *Musical Bouquet*
sheet-music series.[1] In the nineteenth
century many households had
pianos for home entertainment,
and thousands of pieces of music
were produced and printed for
this market, many illustrated with
portraits of famous performers of the
day. In Britain, Perrot and Grisi were
most celebrated for introducing the
polka onto the London stage, which
caused an immediate sensation.
The female Staffordshire figure of
'Giselle' was almost certainly made
to accompany 'Albrecht' and has
the same moulded construction
and style of decoration. The dress
decoration is not from the same print
of Act 1, but possibly from another of
Grisi in the title role (shown above),
with similar floral patterns on her skirts.

RW

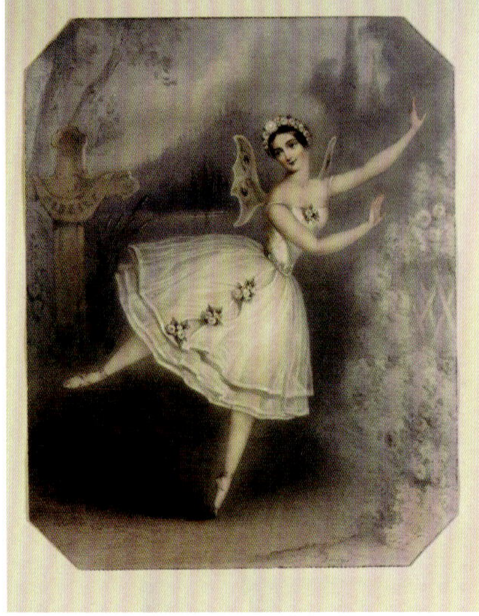

Carlotta Grisi in Act II of *Giselle*, 1840s, by
John Brandard
Tinted lithograph coloured by hand
V&A: E.5017–1968

1 Print of Perrot and Grisi in *Giselle* by
J. Bingley and W. Strange of London, used
in *Musical Bouquet* No. 24, to head the
unrelated sheet music for *Come Away to the
Glen* by Francis Lancelott, 1845.

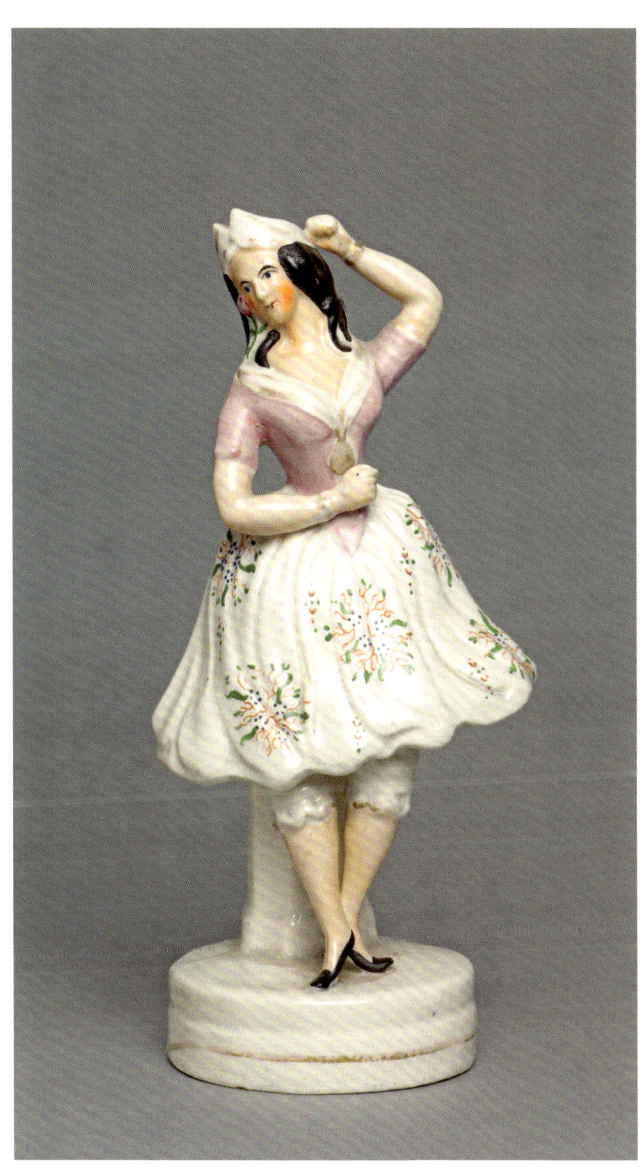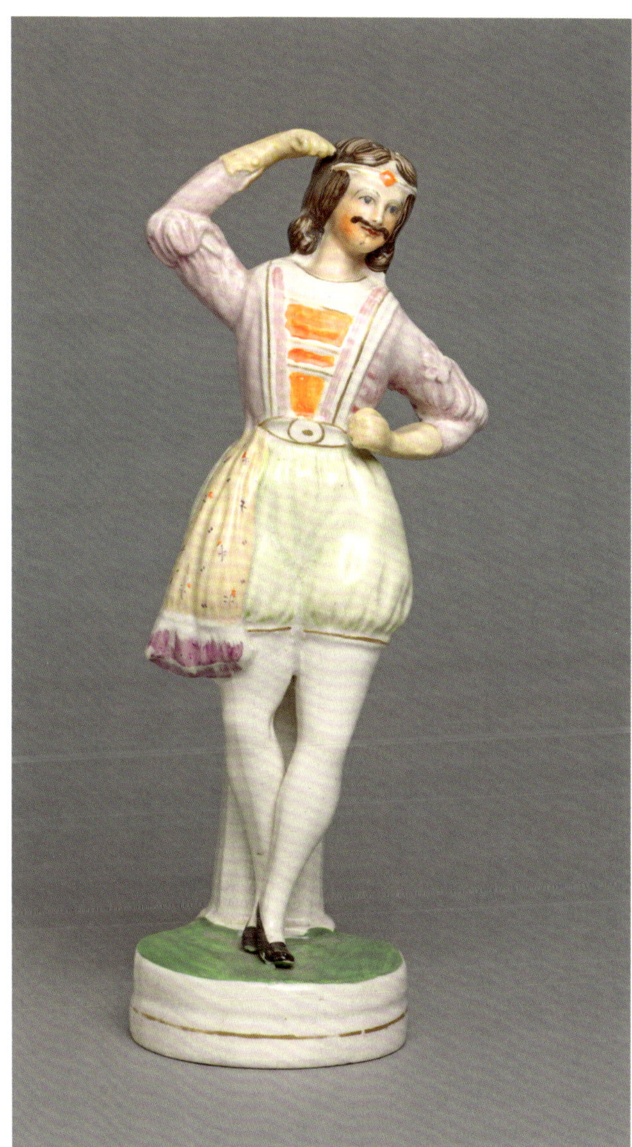

Flood, Catherine
British Posters: Advertising, Art & Activism (V&A, 2012)

Hildyard, Robin
English Pottery 1620–1840 (V&A, 2005)

Kuittinen, Riikka
Street Art: Contemporary Prints (V&A, 2011)

Lambert, Susan
Prints: Art and Techniques (V&A, 2001)

Miller, Elizabeth, and Young, Hilary
Arts of Living: Europe 1600–1815 (V&A, 2015)

Saunders, Gill
Wallpaper in Interior Decoration (V&A, 2002)

Saunders, Gill, and Miles, Rosie
Prints Now: Directions and Definitions (V&A, 2006)

Saunders, Gill, and Whitley, Zoe
In Black and White: Prints from Africa and the Diaspora
(V&A, 2013)

Timmers, Margaret
The Power of the Poster (V&A, 1998)

Timmers, Margaret
A Century of Olympic Posters (V&A, 2008; 2nd edition 2012)

Wilk, Christopher (ed.)
Modernism: Designing a New World: 1914–1939 (V&A, 2008)

ACKNOWLEDGEMENTS

I would like to extend my thanks to the many people who have contributed to the production and publication of this book. First of all I would like to thank all the contributors – V&A colleagues, past and present – who have shared their considerable expertise in the pithy texts highlighting 'star objects', and the essays. In addition to writing for the book, my colleagues Margaret Timmers and Liz Miller also read an early draft of the introductory essay and offered valuable corrections and revisions. Louise Taberer of the Development team has ably liaised between all the parties involved, and I have appreciated her practical advice and support. I am also most grateful to Tom Windross and his team in V&A Publishing for all their professional input, guidance and support, and in particular Rachel Daley who dealt so swiftly and efficiently with all the image rights and permissions, and Geoff Barlow for his advice on production issues. Thanks also to Richard Davies and Paul Robins for the new photography. It has been a pleasure to work with project manager Linda Schofield, who kept us all on track through a tight schedule, and with the excellent copy-editor Mandy Greenfield. The designer Clifford Richards has brought a lifetime of expertise and experience to the challenge of presenting these eclectic collections in all their marvellous diversity.

And thanks above all to Robert Breckman, who initiated and funded the project and has taken a keen and active interest in every aspect of the production from start to finish.

Gill Saunders

Andrew /   Brian /   Brian /   Cliff /   Colin /   Deirdre /

Ethan /   Frances /   Freda /   Geoffrey /   Gill /   Graham /

Graham /   Heather /   John /   Julie /   Keith /   Keith /

Keith /   Kevin /   Laurence /   Lin /   Liz /   Lou /

Louise /   Manix /   Margaret /   Marilyn /   Mel /   Pat /

Peter /   Raj /   Richard /   Robert /   Robin /   Sam /

Shirley /   Ted /   Thomas /   Tony /   Trilby /   Victor /

Robert Breckman

All objects purchased through the Julie and Robert Breckman Staffordshire Fund or the Julie and Robert Breckman Print Fund, unless otherwise noted. They are listed within each grouping in order of accession number.

CERAMICS

Figure group: *Contest*, c.1810, Staffordshire earthenware
V&A: C.57–2001
Given by Julie and Robert Breckman

Figure group: *The Tithe Pig*, c.1825, Staffordshire earthenware
V&A: C.58–2001
Given by Julie and Robert Breckman

Figure group: *Charity*, c.1795, Staffordshire earthenware
V&A: C.59–2001
Given by Julie and Robert Breckman

Figure: *Faith*, c.1800, Staffordshire earthenware
V&A: C.60–2001
Given by Julie and Robert Breckman

Figure group: *Rinaldo and Armida*, c.1791–5, Staffordshire earthenware
V&A: C.61–2001
Given by Julie and Robert Breckman

Figure: *William Macready in his role as James V of Scotland*, c.1846, Staffordshire earthenware
V&A: C.62–2001
Given by Julie and Robert Breckman

Figure: *Dick Swiveller* from Dickens' *Old Curiosity Shop*, c.1840–50, Staffordshire earthenware
V&A: C.63–2001
Given by Julie and Robert Breckman

Figure group: *Uncle Tom and Little Eva*, c.1853, Staffordshire earthenware painted in enamel colours
V&A: C.64–2001
Given by Julie and Robert Breckman

Figure group: *Independent Order of Good Templars*, c.1868, Staffordshire earthenware
V&A: C.65–2001
Given by Julie and Robert Breckman

Figure: *Duke of Wellington*, c.1840, Staffordshire earthenware
V&A: C.66–2001
Given by Julie and Robert Breckman

Figure: *Duke of Wellington* (in old age), c.1852, Staffordshire earthenware
V&A: C.67–2001
Given by Julie and Robert Breckman

Figure: *Camel*, c.1870, Staffordshire earthenware
V&A: C.68–2001
Given by Julie and Robert Breckman

Figure: *Camel*, c.1870, Staffordshire earthenware
V&A: C.69–2001
Given by Julie and Robert Breckman

Figure: *Elephant with howdah*, c.1880, Staffordshire earthenware
V&A: C.70–2001
Given by Julie and Robert Breckman

Figure: *Parakeet*, c.1840, Staffordshire earthenware
V&A: C.71–2001
Given by Julie and Robert Breckman

Figure group: *Lion Tamer*, c.1860, Staffordshire earthenware
V&A: C.72–2001
Given by Julie and Robert Breckman

Figure group: *Dog and child*, c.1835, Staffordshire earthenware
V&A: C.73–2001
Given by Julie and Robert Breckman

Figure group: *John Anderson, My Jo*, c.1850, Staffordshire earthenware
V&A: C.74–2001
Given by Julie and Robert Breckman

Figure: *D.W. Moody*, c.1873, Staffordshire earthenware
V&A: C.75–2001
Given by Julie and Robert Breckman

Figure: *I.D. Sankey*, c.1873, Staffordshire earthenware
V&A: C.76–2001
Given by Julie and Robert Breckman

Figure: *Rev. (Charles Haddon) Spurgeon*, c.1855, Staffordshire earthenware
V&A: C.77–2001
Given by Julie and Robert Breckman

Figure: *Rev. J. Bryan*, c.1855, Staffordshire earthenware
V&A: C.79–2001
Given by Julie and Robert Breckman

Figure: *Jemmy Wood*, c.1845, Staffordshire earthenware
V&A: C.80–2001
Given by Julie and Robert Breckman

Figure: *(W.E.) Gladstone*, c.1894, Staffordshire earthenware
V&A: C.81–2001
Given by Julie and Robert Breckman

Figure: *Mrs Gladstone*, c.1894, Staffordshire earthenware
V&A: C.82–2001
Given by Julie and Robert Breckman

Figure: *King Edward VII*, c.1902, Staffordshire earthenware
V&A: C.83–2001
Given by Julie and Robert Breckman

Figure: *Elijah*, c.1825, Staffordshire earthenware
V&A: C.84–2001
Given by Julie and Robert Breckman

Spill vase (?) in the form of a boot, c.1840, Staffordshire earthenware
V&A: C.85–2001
Given by Julie and Robert Breckman

Spill vase (?) in the form of a boot, c.1840, Staffordshire earthenware
V&A: C.86–2001
Given by Julie and Robert Breckman

Obelisk, c.1880, Gateshead: Sowerby, slag glass
V&A: C.87–2001
Given by Julie and Robert Breckman

Obelisk, c.1880, Gateshead: Sowerby, slag glass
V&A: C.88–2001
Given by Julie and Robert Breckman

Figure: *Sphinx*, c.1880, Gateshead: Sowerby, slag glass
V&A: C.89–2001
Given by Julie and Robert Breckman

Tobacco jar with lid: Wilhelm I (1797–1888), King of Prussia 1861, Emperor of Germany 1871, c.1880–90, Conta and Boehme of Poessneck, Germany
V&A: C.90:1–2001 and C.90:2–2001
Given by Julie and Robert Breckman

Tobacco jar with lid: Figure of a man of Oriental appearance, c.1880–90, Voigt factory, Sitzendorf, Germany
V&A: C.91:1–2001 and C.91:2–2001
Given by Julie and Robert Breckman

Tobacco jar with lid: Figure of a lady taking tea, c.1880–90, Conta and Boehme of Poessneck, Germany
V&A: C.92:1–2001 and C.92:2–2001
Given by Julie and Robert Breckman

Tobacco jar with lid: Figure of a man reading *The Times*, c.1880–90, Conta and Boehme of Poessneck, Germany
V&A: C.93:1–2001 and C.93:2–2001
Given by Julie and Robert Breckman

Inkstand with inkwells and a pounce pot inside, representing a lady with her maid, c.1870–80, German, unmarked
V&A: C.94:1 to 5–2001
Given by Julie and Robert Breckman

Tobacco jar and lid: Figure representing a German matriarch, c.1880–90, German
V&A: C.95:1–2001 and C.95:2–2001
Given by Julie and Robert Breckman

Tobacco jar and lid: Figure of a child in a pram with a Punch doll, c.1880–90, Conta and Boehme, Poessneck, Germany
V&A: C.96:1–2001 and C.96:2–2001
Given by Julie and Robert Breckman

Tobacco jar with lid: Figure of a boy on a turtle, c.1880–90, Conta and Boehme, Poessneck, Germany
V&A: C.97:1–2001 and C.97:2–2001
Given by Julie and Robert Breckman

Loving cup: Two-handled loving cup transfer-printed in green with romantic views and 'LOVE FEAST', c.1840, Staffordshire earthenware
V&A: C.1–2002

Figure group: *Teetotal*, c.1835, Staffordshire earthenware
V&A: C.2–2002

Figure group: *Ale Bench*, c.1835, Staffordshire earthenware
V&A: C.3–2002

Figure group: *The New Marriage Act*, c.1823, Staffordshire earthenware
V&A: C.4–2002

Figure of a deer, c.1800, Staffordshire earthenware
V&A: C.5–2002

Group: *Polito's Royal Menagerie*, c.1830, Staffordshire moulded lead-glazed earthenware, painted in enamel colours
V&A: C.128–2003

Figure: *Freed slave*, c.1833, Staffordshire moulded lead-glazed earthenware, painted in enamel colours
V&A: C.129–2003

Figure: *Tom Cribb, bare-knuckle white boxer*, c.1815, Staffordshire moulded lead-glazed earthenware, painted in enamels
V&A: C.130:1–2003

Figure: *Tom Molyneux, black boxer*, c.1815, Staffordshire moulded lead-glazed earthenware, painted in enamels
V&A: C.130:2–2003

Figure group: *Man and woman fighting over pair of breeches*, c.1830, Staffordshire moulded lead-glazed earthenware, painted in enamel colours
V&A: C.131–2003

Figure group: *Group of village musicians*, c.1820, Staffordshire moulded lead-glazed earthenware, painted in enamel colours
V&A: C.136–2003

Figure group: *A couple representing 'Persuasion'*, c.1830, Staffordshire lead-glazed earthenware, painted in enamel colours
V&A: C.137–2003

Figure: *The Death of Munrow*, c.1830, Staffordshire lead-glazed earthenware, painted in enamels
V&A: C.1–2007
Donated by Robert Breckman in memory of his wife Julie

Figure: *Mary Glover as 'Yourawkee'*, c.1837, Staffordshire moulded earthenware
V&A: C.50–2013
Given by Julie and Robert Breckman

Figure: *Mrs Vining as 'Peter Wilkins'*, c.1837, Staffordshire moulded earthenware
V&A: C.51-2013
Given by Julie and Robert Breckman

Figure: *Jules Perrot as 'Albrecht'*, c.1842, Staffordshire moulded earthenware
V&A: C.52-2013
Given by Julie and Robert Breckman

Figure: *Carlotta Grisi as 'Giselle'*, c.1842, Staffordshire moulded earthenware
V&A: C.53-2013
Given by Julie and Robert Breckman

Figure group: *Mr Harwood and Miss Rosa Henry as 'Selim and Zuleika'*, c.1847, Staffordshire moulded earthenware
V&A: C.54-2013
Given by Julie and Robert Breckman

Figure group: *'The Fortune Teller'*, c.1840s, Staffordshire moulded earthenware
V&A: C.55-2013
Given by Julie and Robert Breckman

Jug in the form of Admiral Lord Nelson, c.1840s, Staffordshire moulded earthenware
V&A: C.56-2013
Given by Julie and Robert Breckman

PRINTS

Print: *Cupid's Manufactory*, 1800, by Francesco Bartolozzi, RA, after Francesco Albani, stipple engraving on silk
V&A: E.932-2000
Given by Julie and Robert Breckman

Print: *The Apotheosis of a Beautiful Female*, 1797, by Francesco Bartolozzi, RA, after Rev. Mathew William Peters, colour-printed stipple engraving, partly hand-coloured
V&A: E.933-2000
Given by Julie and Robert Breckman

Print: *Three Nude Children and an Amorino Playing with a Lamb*, 1770, by Francesco Bartolozzi after Simon Cantarini da Paesaro, etching in the crayon manner
V&A: E.934-2000
Given by Julie and Robert Breckman

Print: *Charity* (two impressions, one printed in red, one printed in black), 1787, by Francesco Bartolozzi after John Henry Ramberg, stipple engraving
V&A: E.935:1-2000 and E.935:2-2000
Given by Julie and Robert Breckman

Print: *Tancred and Clorinda*, 1784, by Francesco Bartolozzi after Angelica Kauffman, stipple engraving
V&A: E.936-2000
Given by Julie and Robert Breckman

Wallpaper, c.1780–1800, anonymous, English, unused sheet of wallpaper in the chinoiserie style, hand-coloured etching
V&A: E.937-2000

Print: *Poison Pie*, 2000, by Chris Drury, engraving on black paper
V&A: E.521-2001

Prints: *Stations of the Cross*, 1999, portfolio of 14 prints by Adrian Wiszniewski, linocuts on tenjin paper
V&A: E.522:1 to 14-2001

Print: *Mitki*, 1999, by Vladimir Shinkarev, lithograph
V&A: E.1347-2001

Prints, drawings: Album of prints and drawings (94 items) compiled by Alexander Constantine Ionides
V&A: E.1349:1 to 94-2001
Purchased with the assistance of The Art Fund, the Friends of the V&A, the Julie and Robert Breckman Print Fund and the Marks Trust

Print: *La Salle Labrouste*, 2001, by Erik Desmazières, etching
V&A: E.1400-2001

Print: *Deck Chair*, 1998, by Arturo di Stefano, aquatint
V&A: E.1411-2001

Print: *Julia*, 2001, by Natasha Ramjoorawon, drypoint
V&A: E.1412-2001

Print: *Everything's Fine*, 2001, by Ray Richardson, screen print with woodblock
V&A: E.1413-2001

Print: *Canoe Island*, 2000, by Peter Doig, silkscreen, from the Counter Editions portfolio, 2001
V&A: E.1562-2001

Photograph: Still from *Cross of Iron*, 2001, by Collier Schorr, from the Counter Editions portfolio, 2001
V&A: E.1563-2001

Print: *Dog Brains*, 2000, by Tracey Emin, silkscreen, from the Counter Editions portfolio, 2001
V&A: E.1564-2001

Print: *Flesheater 4*, 2001, by Mat Collishaw, silkscreen, from the Counter Editions portfolio, 2001
V&A: E.1565-2001

Print: *My House I*, 2000, by Christopher Wool, silkscreen, from the Counter Editions portfolio, 2001
V&A: E.1566-2001

Print: *My House II*, 2000, by Christopher Wool, silkscreen, from the Counter Editions portfolio, 2001
V&A: E.1567-2001

Print: *My House III*, 2000, by Christopher Wool, silkscreen, from the Counter Editions portfolio, 2001
V&A: E.1568-2001

Print: *My Man*, 2000, by Gillian Wearing, silkscreen, from the Counter Editions portfolio, 2001
V&A: E.1569-2001

Print: *Regal*, 2000, by Chris Ofili, lithograph, from the Counter Editions portfolio, 2001
V&A: E.1570-2001

Print: *The Cleric*, 2000, by Gary Hume, silkscreen, from the Counter Editions portfolio, 2001
V&A: E.1571-2001

Print: *Thursday (Tony)*, 2000, by Elizabeth Peyton, lithograph, from the Counter Editions portfolio, 2001
V&A: E.1572-2001

Photograph: *Untitled (Swim Trunks)*, 2000, by Jeff Burton, cibachrome print, from the Counter Editions portfolio, 2001
V&A: E.1573-2001

Print: *Untitled (To Nest)*, 2001, by Roni Horn, inkjet print, from the Counter Editions portfolio, 2001
V&A: E.1574-2001

Print: *It's in the Bag*, 2001, by Gavin Turk, lithograph, from the Counter Editions portfolio, 2001
V&A: E.1575-2001

Print: *Atelier René Tazé V*, 1992–3, by Erik Desmazières, etching, aquatint and roulette
V&A: E.1-2002

Prints: *Air Routes of the World (Night)* and *Air Routes of the World (Day)*, 2001, by Langlands & Bell (Ben Langlands and Nikki Bell), screen prints
V&A: E.9-2002 and E.10-2002

Multiple: *Herringbone Floor*, 2001, by Rachel Whiteread, laser-cut birch ply
V&A: E.20-2002

Prints: *Dark Interludes*, 2001, portfolio of prints by Walid Siti, etchings
V&A: E.99 to 115-2002

Poster: *International Times UFO Poster number two*, 1967, by Michael English, silkscreen
V&A: E.121-2002

Handbill: *Uncommon Market*, Roundhouse Jan. 29 1967, probably by Michael English
V&A: E.122-2002

Poster: *Uncommon Market*, Roundhouse, March 19 1967, probably by Michael English
V&A: E.123-2002

Poster: *Uncommon Market*, Roundhouse, March 19 1967, probably by Michael English
V&A: E.124-2002

Poster: *Uncommon Market, IT's Love*, c.1967, by Michael McInnerney, *International Times* poster, silkscreen
V&A: E.125-2002

Poster: *Happy New Life 1968*, 1968, by Michael McInnerney, *International Times* poster
V&A: E.126-2002

Poster: *IT Spontaneous Festival of Underground Movies, Oct. 31–Nov. 5*, 1960s, *International Times* point-of-sale poster
V&A: E.127-2002

Poster: *American Rape of Britain*, 1960s, *International Times* point-of-sale poster
V&A: E.128-2002

Poster: *IT 25*, 1960s, *International Times* point-of-sale poster
V&A: E.129-2002

Flyer: *What does IT All Mean*, 1967, *International Times* flyer
V&A: E.130-2002

Ticket: *Binn Tivy*, ticket for *International Times* First All-Night Rave, Oct. 15 1966
V&A: E.131-2002

Print: Invitation to a happening outside Indica Gallery, Mason's Yard, by Michael English
V&A: E.132-2002

Print: 'Head Shop' business card, 1960s, by Michael English
V&A: E.133-2002

Handbill: Head Shop handbill with sticky back for flyposting, 1960s
V&A: E.134-2002

Postcard: Promotional postcard for 'Flowers in the Rain' depicting Harold Wilson, 1960s
V&A: E.135-2002

Catalogue: Effective Communications Arts Ltd catalogue, 1960s, by Felix Dennis
V&A: E.136-2002

Print: Effective Communications Ltd business card (small version), 1960s, by Peter 'Kipps' Buxton
V&A: E.137-2002

Christmas card: Barry Hall's Christmas card from Goliard Press
V&A: E.138-2002

Handbill: *Don't let the Bastards Grind You Down*, 1968, handbill issued by the occupation committee of Hornsey College of Art
V&A: E.139-2002

Print: JLTY 'O Magic' business card, 1960s
V&A: E.140-2002

Print: Opening announcement for The Sweet Shop, World's End, Chelsea, 1960s
V&A: E.141-2002

Print: Skoob announcement for Betterbooks, 1965, by John Latham
V&A: E.142-2002

Print: New address card, 1966, by Ben Tivy
V&A: E.143-2002

Print: ICA announcement, 1960s, by David Larcher
V&A: E.144-2002

Print: 'Jump Like Alice' business card, 1960s
V&A: E.145-2002

Print: Press reception announcement for The Nice, 1967
V&A: E.146-2002

Greetings card, 1960s, printed in pink and purple
V&A: E.147-2002

Poster: AMM music poster, 1960s
V&A: E.148-2002

Print, sticker: *Oz* trial sticker, 1960s, anonymous
V&A: E.149-2002

Sticker: *Oz* trial sticker, 1960s
V&A: E.150–2002

Sticker: *Oz* trial sticker, 1960s
V&A: E.151–2002

Sticker: *Oz* trial sticker, 1960s
V&A: E.152–2002

Flyer: *International Times 14 Hour Technicolour Dream*,
1960s, by Michael English
V&A: E.153–2002

Handbill: *14 Hour Technicolour Dream*, 1960s, by Michael
McInnerney, International Times handbill
V&A: E.154–2002

Ticket: *14 Hour Technicolour Dream*, 1960s, by Michael
McInnerney, one of two tickets in rainbow printing
V&A: E.155–2002

Ticket: *14 Hour Technicolour Dream*, 1960s, by Michael
McInnerney, one of two tickets in rainbow printing
V&A: E.156–2002

Print: 'Granny Takes A Trip' business card, 1960s, by
Michael English
V&A: E.157–2002

Christmas card from Michael English, 1960s, designed by
Michael English
V&A: E.158–2002

Headed letter paper: Four sheets of Osiris headed paper,
1967, by Michael English / Nigel Weymouth, silver on
white design with typed invoices
V&A: E.159 to 162–2002

Print: Effective Communications Ltd business card (large
version), 1960s, by Peter 'Kipps' Buxton
V&A: E.163–2002

Print: ECAL (Effective Communications Arts Ltd)
compliments slip, 1960s, by Felix Dennis
V&A: E.168–2002

Print: ECAL (Effective Communications Arts Ltd) headed
paper (first version), 1968, by Peter 'Kipps' Buxton
V&A: E.169–2002

Print: ECAL (Effective Communications Arts Ltd) headed
paper (later version), 1968, by Peter 'Kipps' Buxton
V&A: E.170–2002

Print: *The Millennium Ark*, c.2000, a print with contributions
by 26 members of the Society of Wood Engravers, wood
engraving
V&A: E.171–2002

Print: *The Neighbour's Fence*, c.2000, by Hilary Paynter,
wood engraving
V&A: E.172–2002

Print: *Meatballs* from the *Last Supper* series, 1999, by
Damien Hirst, screen print
V&A: E.173–2002

Print: *Cornish Pasty* from the *Last Supper* series, 1999, by
Damien Hirst, screen print
V&A: E.174–2002

Print: *Steak and Kidney* from the *Last Supper* series, 1999,
by Damien Hirst, screen print
V&A: E.175–2002

Pamphlet with print, title page and list of subscribers to
a silver urn by Rundell, Bridge and Co., presented to J.J.
Farquharson for keeping a pack of hounds in Dorset,
1833
V&A: E.216:1–2002

Print: Portrait of James John Farquharson, 1833, etching
and engraving
V&A: E.216:2–2002

Print: *The Royall Oake of Brittayne*, anonymous satire of
Oliver Cromwell ordering the felling of the Royal Oak of
Britain, 1649, engraving
V&A: E.217–2002

Print: *A View from Mr Cosway's Breakfast Room*, 1789, by
William Birch, stipple etching and engraving
V&A: E.218–2002

Print: *Contemplating the Picture*, 1781–4, by John
Raphael Smith after Laneau, stipple etching
V&A: E.219–2002

Print: Portrait of the Late Henry Holland, architect and
builder, 1806, by George Garrard, two proofs and a
lettered impression, etching and stipple etching
V&A: E.220 to E.222–2002

Print: *Sketching from Nature*, 1830, lithograph
V&A: E.223–2002

Poster: *Oz is a New Magazine*, 1960s, by Martin Sharp
V&A: E.275–2002

Poster: *Wonderwall* film poster, 1960s, colour offset
lithograph
V&A: E.276–2002

Poster: *A is for Apple*, 1960s, by The Fool design group,
colour photogravure
V&A: E.277–2002

Poster: *John Lennon*, late 1960s, Beatles poster by
Richard Avedon, colour lithograph
V&A: E.278–2002

Poster: *Paul McCartney*, late 1960s, Beatles poster by
Richard Avedon, colour lithograph
V&A: E.279–2002

Poster: *George Harrison*, late 1960s, Beatles poster by
Richard Avedon, colour lithograph
V&A: E.280–2002

Poster: *Ringo Starr*, late 1960s, Beatles poster by Richard
Avedon, colour lithograph
V&A: E.281–2002

Poster: Group Beatles poster, 1967, by Richard Avedon
V&A: E.282–2002

Badges: A collection of badges (482), c.1960–1980,
various artists and designers
V&A: E.300 to 782–2002

Print: *Tiger*, 1996, by Ken Kiff, colour woodcut
V&A: E.804–2002

Print: *Sun, Woodgrain, Journey*, 1999, by Ken Kiff, colour
woodcut
V&A: E.805–2002

Print: *Robert Macaire Dentiste*, 1837, by Honoré Daumier,
hand-coloured lithograph
V&A: E.831–2002

Print: Transfigurative print comprising two oval stipple
engravings after Angelica Kauffman, 1790s, in a
contemporary frame
V&A: E.832–2002

Print: *The Killing Machines*, 1967, by Ken Sprague, linocut
V&A: E.833–2002

Print: *Return to America* (also known as *The Soldier's
Return*), 1967, by Ken Sprague, linocut and mixed media
V&A: E.834–2002

Print: *My First Lesson in Love*, 1995, by Natasha
Ramjoorawon, set of nine Perspex blocks each
containing an object, including a piece of fabric, print,
rose petal, etc.; the blocks can be interlocked to form a
3D sculpture
V&A: E.836:1 to 11–2002

Print: *Manhattan Tophat*, 2002, by Patrick Caulfield, digital
print for SPACE Cooks project 2002
V&A: E.930–2002

Print: *The Eat (Shit and Die Motherfuckers) Top Ten*, 2002,
by Peter Davies, digital print for SPACE Cooks project 2002
V&A: E.931–2002

Print: *Grit Surprise*, 2002, by Bob and Roberta Smith,
digital print for SPACE Cooks project 2002
V&A: E.932–2002

Print: *Il meglio del meglio All 'Infinito*, 2002, by Gavin Turk,
digital print for SPACE Cooks project 2002
V&A: E.933–2002

Poster advertising *The Economist*, c.2002
V&A: E.936–2002

Poster: *I-D* magazine cover, October 1994, 'The Visionary
Issue'
V&A: E.937–2002

Poster: *I-D* magazine cover, July 1994, 'The Fun Issue'
V&A: E.938–2002

Poster: *Suits © Harvey Nichols*, poster advertising Harvey
Nichols menswear with an image from the film *Reservoir
Dogs*, c.1992
V&A: E.939–2002

Poster for Silk Cut low-tar cigarettes, showing white silk
slashed to reveal purple underneath, c.1990
V&A: E.940–2002

Poster advertising the London Transport Museum shop
V&A: E.941–2002

Poster: *Try Typhoo QT*, poster advertising Typhoo tea,
c.1990
V&A: E.942–2002

Poster advertising Levi's – Indigo
V&A: E.943–2002

Poster: *The tastiest fish aren't always the good looking
ones*, c.1990, poster promoting different varieties of fish
V&A: E.944–2002

Poster for the Design Museum, showing a Lexikon
typewriter
V&A: E.945–2002

Poster for Gilbert and George *For AIDS* exhibition, April to
May 1989 at the Anthony D'Offay Gallery
V&A: E.946–2002

Poster: *Bodies of experience: Stories about living with HIV*,
c.1990, exhibition poster for the Camerawork gallery
V&A: E.947–2002

Poster: *Fight Back*, c.1990, poster for Gay Men Fighting
AIDS (GMFA), showing a boxer
V&A: E.948–2002

Poster: *Semen kit*, c.1990, poster for Gay Men Fighting
AIDS (GMFA), showing two sailors
V&A: E.949–2002

Poster advertising the play *The Birthday Party* by Harold
Pinter at the Royal National Theatre, London
V&A: E.950–2002

Poster: *New Range Sainsbury's Classic Cola*, advertising
poster for Sainsbury's, 1990s
V&A: E.951–2002

Poster: *To and From Los Angeles*, c.1990, poster for Virgin
Atlantic
V&A: E.952–2002

Poster advertising the book *Dr Dog* by Babette Cole,
c.1994
V&A: E.953–2002

Poster advertising *The Penguin Book of Lesbian Short
Stories* edited by Margaret Reynolds, c.1994
V&A: E.954–2002

Poster: *Rainbeau*, 1990s, poster advertising Perrier mineral
water
V&A: E.955–2002

Poster: *The sole eau*, 1990s, poster advertising Perrier
mineral water
V&A: E.956–2002

Poster: *Poetry in meaution*, 1990s, poster advertising
Perrier mineral water
V&A: E.957–2002

Poster: *Better OUT than IN!*, 1994, poster for Campaign for
an Independent Britain
V&A: E.958–2002

Poster: *Honda Come Ride With Us*, 1990s, poster for
Honda CB500
V&A: E.959–2002

Poster: *He gave her flowers, chocolates and multiple bruising*, poster for the Zero Tolerance campaign
V&A: E.960–2002

Poster: *Absolut Athens*, 2005, poster advertising Absolut Vodka
V&A: E.961–2002

Poster: *Royal Opera House Covent Garden Limited presents Royal Ballet in the first performances of Anastasia*, probably 1971
V&A: E.962–2002

Poster: *Royal Opera House, Covent Garden … presents the Covent Garden Opera and Sadler's Wells Ballet*, with details of the programme
V&A: E.963–2002

Poster for the Royal Ballet showing a ballerina
V&A: E.964–2002

Poster advertising the book *Spanky* by Christopher Fowler, 1994
V&A: E.965–2002

Poster: *Dulux Weathershield is good for years*, c.1990, poster for Dulux
V&A: E.966–2002

Poster: *Dulux Varnish with teflon is ten times tougher*, c.1990, poster for Dulux
V&A: E.967–2002

Poster: *Summer. The perfect time to test the Audi Cabriolet*, c.1990, poster for Audi
V&A: E.968–2002

Poster: *My other car's a Porsche, but today I'm in a hurry*, c.1990, poster for Audi
V&A: E.969–2002

Poster: *Brrrrrrr!*, poster advertising Guinness, 1990s
V&A: E.970–2002

Poster: *Temporary colour-blindness*, poster advertising Guinness, 1990s
V&A: E.971–2002

Poster: *It's true, it's all a matter of taste*, poster advertising Guinness, 1990s
V&A: E.972–2002

Poster: *Subliminal advertising? Pure Genius*, poster advertising Guinness, 1990s
V&A: E.973–2002

Poster: *Guinness: Pure Genius*, poster advertising Guinness, 1990s
V&A: E.974–2002

Poster: *Guinness: Pure Genius*, poster advertising Guinness, 1990s
V&A: E.975–2002

Poster: *As far as I'm concerned it's neither public or convenient*, poster for The Spastics Society
V&A: E.976–2002

Poster: *Is this the only time you ever put yourself in our place?*, poster for The Spastics Society
V&A: E.977–2002

Poster for *Tatler*, December 1994 issue, featuring Princess Diana
V&A: E.978–2002

Poster advertising the Winter 91/92 issue of *Arena*, with Elvis on the cover
V&A: E.979–2002

Poster advertising *Esquire* magazine, September 1992, with Madonna on the cover
V&A: E.980–2002

Poster for *The Face* magazine, January 1994, with Naomi Campbell on the cover
V&A: E.981–2002

Poster advertising *Vanity Fair* magazine, August 1993, with Cindy Crawford and K.D. Lang on the cover
V&A: E.982–2002

Poster for *Vanity Fair*, July 1994, with Jacqueline Kennedy on the cover
V&A: E.983–2002

Poster advertising *Vanity Fair*, February 1993, with Princess Diana on the cover
V&A: E.984–2002

Poster advertising *Vogue*, October 1994, colour offset lithograph
V&A: E.985–2002

Print: *Gelam Nguzu Kazi (Dugong My Son)*, 2001, by David Bosun, linocut
V&A: E.1092–2002

Print: *Ap Au Aidal (Cassava and Yam)*, 2000, by Billy Missi, linocut
V&A: E.1093–2002

Print: *The Journeyman*, 2001, by Ellen Bell, mixed media work on paper
V&A: E.1094–2002

Portfolio: *SHOWstudio 01*, 2001, portfolio containing prints, drawings and photographs (49) by various artists and designers
V&A: E.1097:1 to 49–2002

Print: *Evidence 1*, 1996, by Peter Ford, relief print in 6 parts
V&A: E.1098–2002

Print: *Philanderer*, 2001, by Margaret Lanzetta, screen print on birchwood panel
V&A: E.1099–2002

Print: *Northwest D6* from the *Invisible City* series, 2001, by Catherine Yass, inkjet print
V&A: E.1100–2002

Print: *Allegory of Spring*, c.1770, by Francesco Bartolozzi, stipple engraving printed on silk
V&A: E.1105–2002
Given by Julie and Robert Breckman

Prints: Volume of fashion plates from *La Novita* and *Margherita*, 1880s, Italy, hand-coloured engravings
V&A: E.151:1 to 44–2003

Print: *Surveillance*, 2002, by Matthew Radford, etching
V&A: E.152–2003

Print: *TiT*, 2002, by Richard Hamilton, colour screen print
V&A: E.157–2003

Print: *Night Sky* from the *Constellations* series, 2002, by Paul Coldwell, colour inkjet print
V&A: E.164–2003

Print: *Case Studies*, 2002, by Paul Coldwell, photo-etching with relief printing
V&A: E.165–2003

Print: *Carrara*, 2001, Emma Stibbon, woodcut
V&A: E.219–2003

Print: *Tama for a couple*, 2002, by John Davies, etching with hand-drawn additions in pastel
V&A: E.242–2003

Print: *Tama for a Loved One*, 2002, John Davies, etching and aquatint
V&A: E.243–2003

Print: *The Clans and Tartans of Scotland*, 2002, by Georgia Russell, cut paper sculpture from printed book wrapper
V&A: E.333–2003

Print: *Sanctuary*, 2001, by Dan Hays, digital cibachrome print on lenticular plastic
V&A: E.334–2003

Print: *Landscape Idyll*, 1997, by Conrad Atkinson, iris print with hand-colouring
V&A: E.335–2003

Print: *A feast in the house of a rich man*, c.1597–c.1670, by Crispijn de Passe, Junior, engraving
V&A: E.345–2003

Print: *Dear Diary*, 1998, by Sara Fanelli, etching
V&A: E.346–2003

Collage: *Paris – Fluctuat nec mergitur*, 2001, by Sara Fanelli, cut paper and mixed media
V&A: E.347–2003

Poster for the film *Rzeczywistość*, 1961, by Waldemar Świerzy, lithograph, Polish
V&A: E.352–2003

Poster for the film *Wiatr ucichł przed switem*, 1961, by Maria Syska, lithograph, Polish
V&A: E.353–2003

Poster for the film *Woman in a Dressing Gown*, c.1961, by Maurycy T. Stryjecki, lithograph, Polish
V&A: E.354–2003

Poster: Spanish Civil War poster, 1937, by José Bardasano, colour lithograph
V&A: E.359–2003

Poster: Spanish Civil War poster, 1937, by José Bardasano, colour lithograph
V&A: E.360–2003

Poster: Spanish Civil War poster, 1937, by José Bardasano, colour lithograph
V&A: E.361–2003

Poster: *Gronland Eis-Krem*, c.1933, by Fritz Rosen, lithograph
V&A: E.438–2003

Poster: *Starke hand – rettet das Land*, c.1933, by Fritz Rosen, lithograph
V&A: E.439–2003

Poster: *Japanese biscuits*, c.1933, by Fritz Rosen, lithograph
V&A: E.440–2003

Poster: *So wird's nie besser*, c.1933, by Fritz Rosen, lithograph
V&A: E.441–2003

Prints, pattern book: Metalwork pattern book with designs for fire grates, stoves, balconies and fencing, c.1794, produced by M. & G. Skidmore, Founders and Fire Grate Manufacturers, of High Holborn and Clerkenwell, engravings
V&A: E.444:1 to 44–2003

Print: *Two Harlequin Figures*, c.1951, by Ronald Frederick Holmes, colour lithograph
V&A: E.449–2003

Print: *Hartlepool Docks*, early 1950s, by Ronald Frederick Holmes, colour lithograph
V&A: E.450–2003

Print: *Britannia Square*, 1998, by Neil Pittaway, etching
V&A: E.865–2003

Print: *Tiny T.N.T. Tantrum, The Pocket Prince, a Midget Wrestler*, 1973, by Peter Blake, woodcut
V&A: E.866–2003

Print: *Untitled*, 1999, by Maria Magdalena Campos-Pons, colour photogravure
V&A: E.878–2003

Print: *Sunflower Quilting Bee at Arles*, 1996, by Faith Ringgold, colour lithograph
V&A: E.879–2003

Print: *The New Opening to St Martin's Church from Pall Mall East*, c.1827, by Thomas Hosmer Shepherd, etching
V&A: E.909–2003

Print: *The North Front of St Martin's Church*, 1795, by Thomas Malton, aquatint and etching
V&A: E.910–2003

Print: *Trafalgar Square, The National Gallery, St Martin's Church*, 1852, by E. Walker, lithograph
V&A: E.911–2003

Print: *True Likeness of the Beheaded Turkish Officer Ali Bassa (Ali Pasha)*, c.1571, anonymous German broadsheet, woodcut with stencil and hand-colouring
V&A: E.912–2003
Purchased through the Julie and Robert Breckman Print Fund, and supported by the Friends of the V&A

Labels (8) for boxes of Batger's Christmas Crackers,
c.1900–50
V&A: E.1035 to 1042–2003

Print: *Afro Lunar Lovers*, 2003, by Chris Ofili, giclée print
V&A: E.1043–2003

Print: Preface sheet to an edition of eight anti-war posters,
2003, published by the Stop the War Coalition
V&A: E.1044–2003

Poster: Anti-war poster by Peter Kennard, 2003, from the
Stop the War Coalition limited edition of posters
V&A: E.1045–2003

Poster: Anti-war poster by Martin Rowson, 2003, from the
Stop the War Coalition limited edition of posters
V&A: E.1046–2003

Poster: Anti-war poster by David Gentleman, 2003, from
the Stop the War Coalition limited edition of posters
V&A: E.1047–2003

Poster: Anti-war poster by Jamie Reid, 2003, from the Stop
the War Coalition limited edition of posters
V&A: E.1048–2003

Poster: Anti-war poster by Steve Bell, 2003, from the Stop
the War Coalition limited edition of posters
V&A: E.1049–2003

Poster: Anti-war poster by Ralph Steadman, 2003, from
the Stop the War Coalition limited edition of posters
V&A: E.1050–2003

Poster: Anti-war poster by Clifford Harper, 2003, from the
Stop the War Coalition limited edition of posters
V&A: E.1051–2003

Poster: Anti-war poster by Ralph Steadman, 2003, from
the Stop the War Coalition limited edition of posters
V&A: E.1052–2003

Print: *Sushi-Maru II Hira Suzuki*, 1995, by Yosuke Imai,
etching and aquatint
V&A: E.1053–2003

Print: *Fish Soup*, 1996, by Tatiana Kozmina, colour
lithograph
V&A: E.1054–2003

Print: *Iseki Pyxxx II*, 1984, by Kunito Nagaoka, colour
etching and aquatint
V&A: E.1055–2003

Print: *Greek Columns*, c.2000, by Istvan Orosz, etching
V&A: E.1056–2003

Print: *Skarpa III (Slope III)*, 1991, by Jan Szmatloch, etching
V&A: E.1057–2003

Print: *Queue for bread line*, 1956, by Andrei Ushin, linocut
V&A: E.1058–2003

Print: *Leningrad 1942, tram turning point*, 1946, by Andrei
Ushin, linocut
V&A: E.1059–2003

Print: *Spring*, c.1993, by Boris Zabirokhin, etching and
drypoint
V&A: E.1060–2003

Print: *Winter*, c.1993, by Boris Zabirokhin, etching and
drypoint
V&A: E.1061–2003

Print: *After Constable's Elm*, 2003, by Lucian Freud,
etching
V&A: E.1063–2003

Print: *Shepherd's Purse* from the *Nourishment* series, 2002,
by Michael Landy, etching
V&A: E.1064–2003

Print: *Creeping Buttercup* from the *Nourishment* series,
2002, by Michael Landy, etching
V&A: E.1065–2003

Prints: *Dulles (Capital)*, 2001, portfolio of prints by Sarah
Morris, screen prints
V&A: E.1066:1 to 12–2003

Label for box of Batger's Christmas Crackers, c.1900–50
V&A: E.2074–2004

Print: Portrait of Samuel Palmer, 1956, by Leonard Baskin,
wood engraving
V&A: E.2077–2004

Prints: *Kisses and Crosses*, 2000, portfolio of prints by Bob
Law, etchings
V&A: E.2079:1 to 11–2004

Prints: *The History of Plants, according to women, children
and students*, 2002, suite of prints by Christine Borland,
etchings, coloured by hand
V&A: E.2080:1 to 10–2004

Prints: Russian Album, 2001, by Alexander Florensky,
boxed set of 5 screen prints with accompanying CD
V&A: E.2081:1 to 8–2004

Print: *The Deer* from the *Horizons* series, 2000, by Timur
Novikov, screen print
V&A: E.2082–2004

Print: *The Swan*, 1992, by Timur Novikov, screen print
V&A: E.2083–2004

Print: *Lohengrin* from *In the Land of Literature* series, 1996,
by Timur Novikov, gum Arabic print
V&A: E.2084–2004

Prints (5) from the *Lost Ideals of Happy Childhood* series,
2000, by Timur Novikov, lithographs
V&A: E.2085 to 2089–2004

Print: *Red Tower*, 1986–98, by Yuri Avvakumov, screen print
V&A: E.2090–2004

Print: *The Mystery of British Culture*, 2001, by Adam Dant,
hand-coloured lithograph
V&A: E.2091–2004

Print: *La Cubitiere*, 2002, by Raymond Arnold, etching
V&A: E.2093–2004

Print: *L'epauliere gauche*, 2002, by Raymond Arnold, soft-
ground etching and etching
V&A: E.2094–2004

Print: *The Industrial Arts applied to Peace*, 1889, by C.
Roberts after Sir Frederick Leighton, wood engraving
published in The Graphic magazine
V&A: E.2095–2004

Print: *The Industrial Arts applied to War*, 1883, by C.
Roberts after Sir Frederick Leighton, wood engraving
published in The Graphic magazine
V&A: E.2096–2004

Print: *Mickleham Yews III*, 1950, by Paul Drury, etching
V&A: E.3168–2004

Print: *September*, 1928, by Paul Drury, etching
V&A: E.3169–2004

Print: *Evening. Cottages with Pigeon*, 1925, by Paul Drury,
etching
V&A: E.3170–2004

Print: *Forms in a Wood*, 1950–1, by Paul Drury, etching
V&A: E.3171–2004

Print: *Ancient Stones I*, 1960, by Paul Drury, etching
V&A: E.3172–2004

Print: *Lane in Moonlight*, 1928, by Edward Bawden,
engraving
V&A: E.3175–2004

Plate: Copper printing plate engraved with designs for
jewellery, 1747, by Nicholas Mensma
V&A: E.3552–2004

Print: *White Ice*, 2003, by Anya Gallaccio, screen print on
mirror acrylic with glitter; pair with *Black Ice* (E.3554–2004)
V&A: E.3553–2004

Print: *Black Ice*, 2003, by Anya Gallaccio, etching; pair
with *White Ice* (E.3553–2004)
V&A: E.3554–2004

Print: *Loyal and Dependable*, 2002, by Willie Cole, digital
iris print
V&A: E.3580–2004

Print: *Mother Approaching Sixty*, 2003, by Frank Bowling,
etching
V&A: E.3581–2004

Print: *What is an American?*, 2001, by Jaune Quick-to-see
Smith, lithograph
V&A: E.3582–2004

Print: *Archipelago II*, 1998, by Sergei Tsvetkov, open-bite
etching
V&A: E.3583–2004

Print: *Moccasins*, c.2000, by Lynne Allen, etchings with
pulp painting and shellac moulded and stitched to
shape
V&A: E.3584:1, 2–2004

Print: *The Polyphant*, 1960s, designed by Clifford Richards,
gift box from the 'Polypops' series
V&A: E.3676:1, 2–2004

Print: *The Polyowl*, 1960s, designed by Clifford Richards,
gift box from the 'Polypops' series
V&A: E.3677:1 to 3–2004

Print: *The Polybear*, 1960s, designed by Clifford Richards,
gift box from the 'Polypops' series
V&A: E.3678:1 to 3–2004

Print: *The Polytiger*, 1960s, designed by Clifford Richards,
gift box from the 'Polypops' series
V&A: E.3679:1 to 3–2004

Print: *The Polypuffin*, 1960s, designed by Clifford Richards,
gift box from the 'Polypops' series
V&A: E.3680:1 to 3–2004

Print: *The Polypuffin*, 1960s, designed by Clifford Richards,
gift box from the 'Polypops' series
V&A: E.3681:1, 2–2004

Print: *The Polylion*, 1960s, designed by Clifford Richards,
gift box from the 'Polypops' series
V&A: E.3682:1 to 3–2004

Print: *The Polyphant*, 1960s, designed by Clifford Richards,
gift box from the 'Polypops' series
V&A: E.3683:1, 2–2004

Print: *The Polyphant*, 1960s, designed by Clifford Richards,
gift box from the 'Polypops' series
V&A: E.3684–2004

Print: *The Polypuffin*, 1960s, designed by Clifford Richards,
gift box from the 'Polypops' series
V&A: E.3685–2004

Print: *The Polytiger*, 1960s, designed by Clifford Richards,
gift box from the 'Polypops' series
V&A: E.3686–2004

Print: *Polypops Garage*, 1960s, by Clifford Richards, toy
garage designed for the 'Polypops' range
V&A: E.3687–2004

Print: *Polypops Garage*, 1960s, by Clifford Richards, toy
garage designed for the 'Polypops' range
V&A: E.3688–2004

Print: Leaflet introducing the 'Polypops' toy products,
1960s, designed by Clifford Richards
V&A: E.3689–2004

Print: Leaflet introducing the 'Polypops' toy products,
1960s, designed by Clifford Richards
V&A: E.3690–2004

Print: *The Polylion*, 1960s, designed by Clifford Richards for
the 'Polypops' range
V&A: E.3691–2004

Print: Unassembled toy owl, 1960s, designed by Clifford
Richards
V&A: E.3692–2004

Print, toy: *Cathy is a Doll*, 1960s, designed by Cathy
McGowan, ragdoll cutout fabric
V&A: E.3693–2004

Print: Unassembled card box with a heart motif, 1960s,
designed by Clifford Richards
V&A: E.3694–2004

Print: *Rule Britannia*, 1960s, designed by Clifford Richards, unassembled cardboard box
V&A: E.3695–2004

Print: *Passion Flower*, 1960s, designed by Clifford Richards, unassembled cardboard box
V&A: E.3696–2004

Print: *Humbug*, 1960s, designed by Clifford Richards, card gift box
V&A: E.3697–2004

Print: Unassembled card box with flowers and hearts, 1960s, designed by Clifford Richards
V&A: E.3698–2004

Print: *Window Box*, 1960s, designed by Clifford Richards, unassembled cardboard box with a flower motif
V&A: E.3699–2004

Print: *Darling*, 1960s, designed by Clifford Richards, flower-patterned card box
V&A: E.3700:1, 2–2004

Print: *Sentry box*, 1960s, designed by Clifford Richards, unassembled card box
V&A: E.3701–2004

Print: *Sentry box*, 1960s, designed by Clifford Richards, unassembled card box
V&A: E.3702–2004

Print: *Passion Flower*, 1960s, designed by Clifford Richards, unassembled card box with a heart motif
V&A: E.3703–2004

Print: *Slottizoo*, 1960s, designed by Clifford Richards, unassembled toy panda
V&A: E.3704:1 to 8–2004

Print: *Slottizoo*, 1960s, designed by Clifford Richards, unassembled toy dragon
V&A: E.3705:1 to 13–2004

Print: *Slottiwhoswho*, 1960s, designed by Clifford Richards, unassembled toy eagle for the Slotty Range
V&A: E.3706:1 to 7–2004

Print: *Slottizoo*, 1960s, designed by Clifford Richards, unassembled toy cat
V&A: E.3707:1 to 10–2004

Print: *Slottiwhoswho*, 1960s, designed by Clifford Richards, unassembled toy owl for the Slotty Range
V&A: E.3708:1 to 9–2004

Print: *Polypops doll's house*, 1960s, designed by Clifford Richards
V&A: E.3709:1 to 29–2004

Print: Pop-up card, *Carnaby Street*, 1960s, designed by Clifford Richards
V&A: E.3710–2004

Print: *Noah's Ark*, 1960s, designed by Clifford Richards, a 'Polypops' wrapping paper
V&A: E.3711–2004

Print: *Sara gets undressed (lenticular)*, 2004, by Julian Opie, lambda print overlaid with lenticular plastic
V&A: E.3712–2004

Book: *And All Men Kill the Thing They Love*, 2004, by Sara Fanelli, mixed media
V&A: E.3714–2004

Endpaper: Embossed gold brocade paper, 1826–50, by the firm of Renner & Abel, Nuremberg
V&A: E.3716–2004

Endpapers with biblical images, first half of the 19th century, German
V&A: E.3717–2004

Print: *Henley*, 1969, by Julian Trevelyan, etching and aquatint
V&A: E.3718–2004

Print: *Interior of an Amateur Statuary's Workshop* by A.E., 1827, hand-coloured etching
V&A: E.3733–2004

Print: *In Praise of Shadows*, 2003, by Hiroshi Sugimoto, lithograph
V&A: E.3734–2004

Print: *Untitled (Habitation XIII)*, 2002, by Cristina Iglesias, silkscreen on aluminium
V&A: E.3735–2004

Print: *Palingenesis*, 2001, by Kumi Korf, soft-ground etching
V&A: E.3736–2004

Prints: *Palingenesis (B1)* and *Palingenesis (B1)*, 1998, by Kumi Korf, soft-ground etching and aquatint
V&A: E.3737–2004 and E.3738–2004

Prints: *Diamond Dust Volume One*, portfolio published by Paul Stolper Gallery, 2003, containing prints by Peter Liversidge, Linder, Peter Saville, Sir Peter Blake, Gavin Turk and Simon Periton, silkscreen prints with diamond dust
V&A: E.3739:1 to 8–2004

Poster for the film *Sherlock Holmes und das Halsband des Todes*, 1962, designed by Michael Engelmann
V&A: E.3786–2004

Poster for Roth-Händle cigarettes, 1959, designed by Michael Engelmann
V&A: E.3787–2004

Poster for Renault R8, 1963, designed by Michael Engelmann
V&A: E.3788–2004

Poster for Pirelli, 1952, designed by Michael Engelmann
V&A: E.3789–2004

Poster for the *Philadelphia Enquirer*, 1958, designed by Michael Engelmann
V&A: E.3790–2004

Poster: *White Rabbit*, 1967, by Joseph McHugh, published by East Totem West, USA
V&A: E.3792–2004

Poster: *Morning Star*, 1960s, published by East Totem West, USA
V&A: E.3793–2004

Poster: *Be Good To Yourself At Least Once A Day*, 1960s, published by East Totem West, USA
V&A: E.3794–2004

Poster: *Love Space*, 1960s, by Joseph McHugh, published by East Totem West, USA
V&A: E.3795–2004

Poster: *Cheshire cat*, 1967, by Joseph McHugh, published by East Totem West, USA
V&A: E.3796–2004

Poster: *East Totem West*, 1960s, by Joseph McHugh, published by East Totem West, USA
V&A: E.3797–2004

Poster: *White Rabbit In Wonderland*, c.1967, by Joseph McHugh, published by East Totem West, USA
V&A: E.3798–2004

Print: *I dreamt I was driving my car (motorway corner)*, 2004, by Julian Opie, unique C-type print on paper on aluminium
V&A: E.3841–2004

Print: Plate from the suite *Zeno Writing*, 2003, by William Kentridge, photogravure etching and drypoint
V&A: E.133–2005

Greeting card: Artist's Christmas card, 1998, by Euan Uglow, linocut with red felt
V&A: E.134–2005

Print: *Dishrag Diagrammatic*, 1977, by Judith K. Brodsky, colour etching
V&A: E.135–2005

Print: *Women, Love and Philosophy III*, c.1998, by Judith K. Brodsky, lithograph with collage
V&A: E.136–2005

Photograph: View of interior of a portrait cabinet, c.1880, French, albumen print from glass negative
V&A: E.138–2005
Purchased with the support of the Julie and Robert Breckman Print Fund and the Cecil Beaton Fund

Prints (4) from *The Camouflage Suite*, 2004, by Jane Dixon, etchings
V&A: E.144 to 147–2005

Print: Doll (and box) from the *Strategies for Departure* project, 1998, by Cecilia Mandrile, inkjet print on cloth, with thread and plaster moulding
V&A: E.214:1, 2–2005

Prints: I-D Cards (4) from the *Strategies for Departure* project, 1998, by Cecilia Mandrile, digital inkjet print, offset lithography, plastic wallets
V&A: E.215 to 218–2005

Prints: *Award Made During the Invasion and Occupation of Iraq 2003 to Now*, 2004, portfolio by Peter Kennard and Cat Picton Phillips, digital inkjet prints
V&A: E.231:1 to 22–2005

Print: No. 4 (large version) from the suite of 15 plates entitled *Award*, 2004, by Peter Kennard and Cat Picton Phillips, digital inkjet print
V&A: E.232–2005

Print: *Mako Djang (Didgeridoos and Sacred Place)*, 1999, by Peter Nabarlambarl, etching
V&A: E.256–2005

Print: *Kaningarra*, 2003, by Susie Bootja Bootja Napangarti, screen print
V&A: E.257–2005

Print: *The Kingdom Spear*, 2004, by David Thorpe, hand-coloured etching
V&A: E.259–2005

Print: *Untitled*, 2001, by Laura Owens, lithograph with collage
V&A: E.260–2005

Print: *Meteorite Misses Waco Texas* from the suite entitled *Meteorite Lands in the Middle of Nowhere. The Americart Series*, 2001, by Cornelia Parker, printed atlas scorched with meteorite
V&A: E.262–2005

Poster: *Light*, 1937, by Lester Beall, designed for the Rural Electrification Administration, USA, screen print
V&A: E.265–2005

Poster: *Wie Wohnen? Die Wohnung – Werkbund Ausstellung*, 1927, attributed to Willi Baumeister, German, lithograph
V&A: E.266–2005

Poster: *Typenmöbel*, poster advertising an exhibition at the Gewerbermuseum, Basel, 1929, by Ernst Mumenthaler, Swiss, colour lithograph
V&A: E.267–2005

Print: *A Ma Zone*, 2002, by Miss Tic, screen print
V&A: E.274–2005

Print: *Nous sommes tous en situation irrégulière*, 2002, by Miss Tic, stencil print
V&A: E.275–2005

Print: *Goodnight*, 1990, by John Lawrence, wood engraving
V&A: E.276–2005

Print: *Off the Wall*, 2004, by Graeme Nimmo, etching on paper on plasterboard
V&A: E.277–2005

Print: *Nemo*, 2004, by Graeme Nimmo, etching
V&A: E.278–2005

Print: Coat (found object) with screen-printed lining bearing image of Madonna and child with Saints Julian and Lawrence by Gentile da Fabriano, 1998, by Ken McDonald
V&A: E.286–2005

Print: *Red Work 502*, 2004, by Philip Dontsov, screen print
V&A: E.361–2005

Print: *Red Work 501*, 2004, by Philip Dontsov, screen print
V&A: E.362–2005

Print, sculpture: *Self-Portrait*, 2002, by Marilène Oliver, screen prints in bronze ink on acrylic sheets
V&A: E.379–2005
Donated by Robert Breckman in memory of Julie

Print: *Love Supreme*, c.2004, by Sickboy, screen print
V&A: E.382--2005

Print: *The Executioner*, c.2004, by Insect, screen print
V&A: E.383-2005

Print: *In Europe*, c.2004, by 3-D, screen print
V&A: E.384-2005

Playing cards: Uncut sheet of playing cards, *Jeu des Drapeaux*, c.1810, anonymous, French
V&A: E.408-2005

Print: Advertisement for revolutionary playing cards, 1793, probably designed by Jacques Coissieux and published by Jean-Démosthène Dugourc and Urbain Jaume, with grant of patent attached, woodcut with stencil colouring
V&A: E.409-2005

Playing cards: Proof sheet with 7 playing cards from the suite *Nouvelles cartes de la Republique Française*, 1793, designed by Jacques Coissieux, French
V&A: E.410-2005

Print: *Post Office Tower*, 2004, by Celia Paul, soft-ground etching
V&A: E.411-2005

Poster: *Untitled*, from the *O Debates* series, 2004, by Jarbas Lopes, printed on vinyl, layered, cut and woven
V&A: E.487-2005

Poster: *Untitled*, from the *O Debates* series, 2004, by Jarbas Lopes, printed on vinyl, layered, cut and woven
V&A: E.488-2005

Print: *Grown Man*, 2004, by John Kirby, etching with *chine collé*
V&A: E.497-2005

Print: *Little Man*, 2000, by John Kirby, etching
V&A: E.498-2005

Print: *Salisbury – Homage to Constable*, 1976, by Duncan Grant, etching
V&A: E.499-2005

Print: *NCP36*, 2005, by Jennifer Wright, digital print on vinyl
V&A: E.500-2005

Print: *BAKERSROW36*, 2005, by Jennifer Wright, digital print on vinyl
V&A: E.501-2005

Multiple: *Secondhand*, 2004, by Rachel Whiteread, 3D Stereolithograph or Rapid Prototype from laser-sintered white nylon, produced by 3TRPD, Newbury, Berks, and published by Counter Editions
V&A: E.502-2005

Print, frame: *Dawn*, 1912-13, by Theodore Roussel, colour etching, drypoint, aquatint, in frame (gilded and moulded gesso) designed by the artist
V&A: E.503:1, 2-2005

Print: *Canary Construct*, 2003, by Andrew Turnbull, digital inkjet print
V&A: E.516-2005

Print: *Grand Build*, 2003, by Andrew Turnbull, digital inkjet print
V&A: E.517-2005

Photograph: *Shoreline, October 5th 1998*, 1998, by Susan Derges, photogram
V&A: E.528-2005
Donated by Robert Breckman in memory of Julie

Lightbox: *London*, 2004, by Jason Wallis-Johnson, lightbox with Perspex and pierced carbon paper
V&A: E.530-2005

Multiple: *Detective Training*, 2004, by Ellen Gallagher, laser drawing
V&A: E.543-2005

Drawing: Illustration by Rolf Brandt for 'The Black Cat' by Edgar Allen Poe, for the anthology of ghost and mystery stories *Come Not Lucifer*, published 1942, pencil on paper
V&A: E.547-2005

Print: *Richard Braughtigan*, 2004, by Andrew Curtis, lithograph
V&A: E.575-2005

Wallpaper: Panel of wallpaper in the chinoiserie wallpaper style, c.1769, English, hand-coloured etching
V&A: E.597-2005

Wallpaper: Pair of printed overdoor panels by Arthur et Robert, c.1786, colour prints from woodblocks, French
V&A: E.598-2005 and E.599-2005

Poster: *Neues Bauen (New Building)*, 1928, by Theo Ballmer, lithograph
V&A: E.1-2006

Poster advertising the exhibition *Temple und Tee-haus in Japan* at the Gewerbemuseum, Basel, c.1955, by Armin Hofmann, screen print
V&A: E.4-2006

Poster advertising the exhibition *Ausstellung deutsche Gebrauchsgraphik*, 1954, by Armin Hofmann, linocut
V&A: E.5-2006

Poster advertising an exhibition of Henry Moore and Oskar Schlemmer at Basel Arts Centre, 1955, by Armin Hofmann, screen print
V&A: E.6-2006

Poster advertising the exhibition *Geschenk-Abonnemente bringen Freude*, c.1955, by Armin Hofmann, screen print
V&A: E.7-2006

Poster advertising an exhibition of Karl Geiser at Basel Arts Centre, c.1955, by Armin Hofmann, screen print
V&A: E.8-2006

Wallpaper: Portion of wallpaper border, printed with trompe-l'oeil drapery pattern,19th century, by Dufour & Cie, French, colour print from woodblocks
V&A: E.9-2006

Multiple: Umbrella for the exhibition *Portable Fabric Shelters* at London Printworks Trust, 1995, by Sonia Boyce, screen print on rubberized fabric with umbrella frame
V&A: E.21-2006

Multiple: Cushion cover for the exhibition *Portable Fabric Shelters* at London Printworks Trust, 1995, by Bill Woodrow, screen print on cloth
V&A: E.22-2006

Prints (8) from the *Kenyan Insects* series, 2005, by Mandy Bonnell, screen prints
V&A: E.23 to 30-2006

Print: *Untitled*, 2005, by Silver John (Kimani John Mbugua), colour reduction woodcut
V&A: E.33-2006

Print: *Babe Rainbow*, 1968, by Peter Blake, screen print on tinplate
V&A: E.35-2006

Print: *Strange Chambers – Attic*, 2001, by Marlene MacCallum, copper-plate photogravure
V&A: E.209-2006

Print: Artist's stamp, *Passport*, c.2000, by Natalia Lamanova, digital print on perforated paper
V&A: E.210-2006

Print: Artist's stamp, *Official Stamp*, c.2000, by Natalia Lamanova, digital print on perforated paper
V&A: E.211-2006

Print: Artist's stamp, *Bear and Bull*, c.2000, by Natalia Lamanova, digital print on perforated paper
V&A: E.212-2006

Print: Artist's stamp, *War Card*, c.2000, by Natalia Lamanova, digital print on perforated paper
V&A: E.213-2006

Endpaper: Hand-printed endpaper with a weevil pattern, c.2000, by Peter Ford, linocut on Japanese paper
V&A: E.214-2006

Endpaper: Printed endpaper dyed with the Japanese *itajime* dyeing technique, c.2000, by Peter Ford, linocut
V&A: E.215-2006

Print: Artist's stamp, *Plum* from *Fruit Jelly* series, 1990s, by Alexander Kholopov, digital print on perforated paper
V&A: E.216-2006

Print: Sheet of 20 from a set of 80 artist's stamps, *80 Moscow Manhole Covers* from the project *The Best Sewerage For The Best People*, 1996, by Alexander Kholopov, digital print on perforated paper
V&A: E.217:1 to 4-2006

Poster: *Consume*, 1996, banner by Michael Peel, screen print on vinyl
V&A: E.218-2006

Poster: *Control*, 1996, banner by Michael Peel, screen print on vinyl
V&A: E.219-2006

Poster: *Get Rich, Inherit* from the *Modern World* series, 1988, by Michael Peel, screen print
V&A: E.220-2006

Poster: *Don't Explain* from the *Modern World* series, 1988, by Michael Peel, screen print
V&A: E.221-2006

Wallpaper: *Razor Wire*, c.2005, by Matthew Meadows, colour print from woodblocks
V&A: E.257-2006

Print: Advertisement for the Elite Cinema, 1954, by Derrick Harris, wood engraving
V&A: E.290-2006

Print: *Parson Adams and Parson Trulliber*, illustration for the Folio Society edition of *Joseph Andrews* by Henry Fielding, 1953, by Derrick Harris, wood engraving
V&A: E.291-2006

Print: *Handy Spandy, Jack-A-Dandy*, illustration to a children's book, late 1950s, by Derrick Harris, wood engraving
V&A: E.292-2006

Print: Prospectus advertising a forthcoming publication by the Golden Cockerel Press of *Euphormio's Satyricon* by John Barclay, 1954, with wood engravings by Derrick Harris on the front and reverse
V&A: E.293:1-2006

Print: Proof of the frontispiece for *Euphormio's Satyricon* by John Barclay, c.1954, by Derrick Harris, wood engraving
V&A: E.293:2-2006

Print: Portrait of John Barclay for the frontispiece of *Euphormio's Satyricon* by John Barclay, c.1954, by Derrick Harris, line block print
V&A: E 293:3-2006

Print: Portrait of John Barclay for the frontispiece of *Euphormio's Satyricon* by John Barclay, c.1954, by Derrick Harris, wood engraving
V&A: E.293:4-2006

Wallpaper: American Civil War newspaper *The Opelousas Courier*, c.1864, printed on the reverse of a contemporary wallpaper, colour print from woodblocks, newsprint
V&A: E.294-2006

Poster: *Your Britain – Fight for It Now*, 1942, by Abram Games, colour lithograph
V&A: E.295-2006

Poster: *BEA Olympic Games*, 1947, by Abram Games, colour offset lithograph
V&A: E.296-2006

Print: *Winchester College*, 1880, by George Maunoir Heywood Sumner, etching
V&A: E.297-2006

Print: *Love at First Sight*, 2004, by Liz Rideal, monotype on Japanese paper
V&A: E 298:1 to 2-2006

Print: *All London Tracks*, 2005, by Jeremy Wood, archival inkjet print
V&A: E.299-2006

Print: *Self-portrait at the etching table*, 1912, by Hans Meid, etching
V&A: E.300-2006

Wallpaper: 12345, 1999–2000, by Kelly Mark, screen print
V&A: E.323–2006

Print: *My Grandmother's Kitchen*, 2006, by Giulia Zaniol, etching and *chine collé* with metallic pigments
V&A: E.24–2007

Print: *Venice Lagoon*, 2006, by Giulia Zaniol, etching and *chine collé* with metallic pigments
V&A: E.25–2007

Print: *St Mark's Square*, 2006, by Giulia Zaniol, etching and *chine collé* with metallic pigments
V&A: E.26–2007

Poster: *Water for Agriculture*, 1991, Vietnamese Environmental Protection Agency poster by Do Nhu Diem, gouache on paper
V&A: E.29–2007

Poster: *Prevent Destruction of the Forest and its Erosion*, 1991, Vietnamese Environmental Protection Agency poster by Do Nhu Diem, gouache on paper
V&A: E.30–2007

Print: *Similands*, 2006, by Stephen Walter, digital print
V&A: E.55–2007

Print: *Morris/Fruit, Rodchenko/Triple Peaks*, 2006, by David Mabb, block-printed wallpaper with digital print
V&A: E.560–2007

Print: *Morris/Honeysuckle, Rodchenko/Hard Currency*, 2006, by David Mabb, block-printed wallpaper with digital print
V&A: E.561–2007

Print: *Whirlpool*, 2005, by Anne Desmet, wood engraving and collage on seashell
V&A: E.562–2007

Print: *Oxford Storm*, 2005, by Anne Desmet, wood engraving, gold leaf and collage on slate
V&A: E.563–2007

Print: *Birth of a Thought, 1*, 2007, by Susan Aldworth, etching
V&A: E.2547–2007

Print: *Druksland Physical and Social, 15 January 1974, 11.30 am*, 1975, by Michael Druks, offset lithograph
V&A: E.3010–2007

Print: *View of Braziers Park, Ibsden, near Wallingford*, 2002, by Alberto Duman, screen print
V&A: E.3011–2007

Print: *Georgia Russell. Britain: March 2003*, 2003, by Georgia Russell, cut map in acrylic case
V&A: E.3012–2007

Poster: *The Friday Club*, poster advertising an exhibition of paintings and drawings at the Alpine Club Galleries, London, June 30th–July 28th, probably 1920, by Paul Nash, lithograph
V&A: E.3015–2007

Print: *Study of two pears IV*, c.2003, by Judith Rothchild, mezzotint
V&A: E.3133–2007

Print, book: *Which Direction I (You Are Here)*, 2005, by Vito Drago, book, incised and hand-coloured
V&A: E.3178–2007

Print: *Toucans*, 1960s, by Clifford Richards, screen print
V&A: E.3679–2007

Print: *Flamingoes*, 1960s, by Clifford Richards, screen print
V&A: E.3680–2007

Print: *Parrots*, 1960s, by Clifford Richards, screen print
V&A: E.3681–2007

Print: *Swallows*, 1960s, by Clifford Richards, screen print
V&A: E.3682–2007

Print: *Owls*, 1960s, by Clifford Richards, screen print
V&A: E.3683–2007

Print: Surgical gown (green) printed with image of naked male body, made for *Masquerade*, 1998, by Yin Lam, screen print on green cloth
V&A: E.259–2008

Print: Surgical gown printed with image of naked female body, made for *Masquerade*, 1998, by Yin Lam, screen print on white paper
V&A: E.260–2008

Print: *Luc and Ludivine Get Married, No. 7*, 2007, by Julian Opie, laser-cut black paper, in black oval frames
V&A: E.272–2008 and E.273–2008

Multiples: *Zoo Portfolio* published in association with the Zoo Art Fair, London, 2005, mixed media
V&A: E.471–2008

Print: *Le Bon Samaritain*, 1861, by Rodolph Bresdin, lithograph
V&A: E.473–2008

Print: *Epithelium*, 2006, by Paul Morrison, screen print
V&A: E.474–2008

Print: *Mr & Mrs Perry*, 2006, by Grayson Perry, linocuts on patterned paper
V&A: E.475–2008 and E.476–2008

Poster by the Atelier Populaire, *Les Beaux-Arts Sont Fermés, Mais L'Art Revolutionaire Est Né*, 1968, Paris, screen print
V&A: E.762–2008

Print: *Untitled (large text)*, 2011, by Liz Collini, screen print on board
V&A: E.327–2011
Donated by Robert Breckman in memory of Julie

Print: *Untitled (large text)*, 2011, by Liz Collini, screen print on board; proof of E.327–2011
V&A: E.432–2011

Drawing: Preparatory drawing for *Untitled (large text)*, 2011, pen and ink and pencil with correction fluid, on paper; see E.327–2011
V&A: E.433–2011

Print: *Ein Altes Lied*, 1902, by August Brömse, etching
V&A: E.291–2013

ARCHIVE

Archive: Archive material by Cyril Kenneth Bird (Fougasse), including posters featuring Fougasse cartoons (c.1936–c.1955); original annotated designs for Careless Talk Costs Lives (c.1940–c.1945); leaflets, book covers and dinner menus featuring Fougasse cartoons (c.1922–64); certificates awarded to Kenneth Bird (1904–55); press cuttings featuring Fougasse cartoons (1916–64); miscellaneous material relating to Kenneth Bird and his wife (undated)
AAD/2006/1
Purchased with the assistance of the National Art Collections Fund and the Julie and Robert Breckman Print Fund

CERAMICS DEPARTMENT LIBRARY

Hall, John, *Staffordshire Portrait Figures* (London, 1972), CER library 2 b 166
Oliver, Anthony, *The Victorian Staffordshire Figure* (London, 1978), CER library 2 b 162

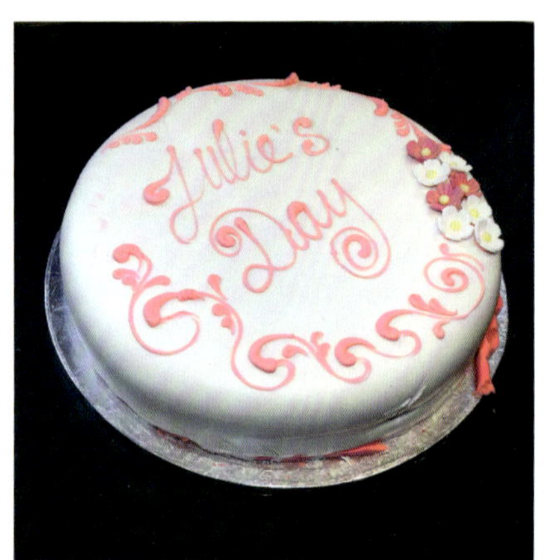

Iced cake for 'Julie's Day'
supplied by Patisserie Valerie
for the tea party at the V&A
on 24 October 2011

away, to corrode.–*v.i.* to take food: –*pr.p.* eat´ing: *pa. t.*
ate (*et or ät*); *pr.p.* eaten (*etn*). – *adj.* **eat'able**, fit to be
eaten.–*n.* anything used as food (chiefly *pl.*).–*n.* **eat´ing-
house**, a place where meals are sold, a restaurant.–**eat
its head off**, used of an animal that costs more for food
than it is worth; **eat one's words**, to take back what one
has said, to recant. [O.E. *etan*; cf. Ger. *essen*, L. *edĕre*,
Gr. *edein*.]
Eau de Cologne, *ŏ dë kö-lŏn´ n.* a perfumed spirit first
made at Cologne in 1709 (often **eau** without *cap.*).– eau de
vie (*ŏ dë vë*)' brandy. [Fr. *eau*, water, *de*, of, *vie*, life.]
eaves, *ëvz, n.pl.* the projecting edge of the roof: anything
similarly projecting.–. **eaves´drop**, the water that falls
from the eaves of a house: the place where the drops fall.–
v.i. to listen in order to overhear private conversation.–*n.*
eaves´dropper, one who tries to overhear private
conversation. [O.E. *efes*, the clipped edge of thatch.]
ebb, *eb, n.* the going back or receding of the tide: a
decline.–*v.i.* to flow back: to sink, to decline.–*n.* **ebb´
tide**, the ebbing tide.[O.E. *ebba*.]
ebony, *eb´ŏn-i,* **ebon**, *eb´ŏn, n.* a kind of wood almost
as heavy and hard as stone, usually black, admitting of
a fine polish.– *adj.* made of ebony: black as ebony.–*n.*
ebónite, vulcanised rubber. [L. *(h)ebenus* –Gr. *ebenos*;
cf. Heb. *hobnïm*, pl. of *hobni, obni–eben*, a stone.]